KU-384-046

Selected Legal Issues
for
Finance Lawyers

Selected Legal Issues
for
Finance Lawyers

Martin Hughes

Members of the LexisNexis Group worldwide

United Kingdom	LexisNexis UK, a Division of Reed Elsevier (UK) Ltd, Halsbury House, 35 Chancery Lane, LONDON, WC2A 1EL, and 4 Hill Street, EDINBURGH EH2 3JZ
Argentina	LexisNexis Argentina, BUENOS AIRES
Australia	LexisNexis Butterworths, CHATSWOOD, New South Wales
Austria	LexisNexis Verlag ARD Orac GmbH & Co KG, VIENNA
Canada	LexisNexis Butterworths, MARKHAM, Ontario
Chile	LexisNexis Chile Ltda, SANTIAGO DE CHILE
Czech Republic	Nakladatelství Orac sro, PRAGUE
France	Editions du Juris-Classeur SA, PARIS
Germany	LexisNexis Deutschland GmbH, FRANKFURT, MUNSTER
Hong Kong	LexisNexis Butterworths, HONG KONG
Hungary	HVG-Orac, BUDAPEST
India	LexisNexis Butterworths, NEW DELHI
Ireland	LexisNexis, DUBLIN
Italy	Giuffrè Editore, MILAN
Malaysia	Malayan Law Journal Sdn Bhd, KUALA LUMPUR
New Zealand	LexisNexis Butterworths, WELLINGTON
Poland	Wydawnictwo Prawnicze LexisNexis, WARSAW
Singapore	LexisNexis Butterworths, SINGAPORE
South Africa	LexisNexis Butterworths, DURBAN
Switzerland	Stämpfli Verlag AG, BERNE
USA	LexisNexis, DAYTON, Ohio

© Reed Elsevier (UK) Ltd 2003

All rights reserved. No part of this publication may be reproduced in any material form (including photocopying or storing it in any medium by electronic means and whether or not transiently or incidentally to some other use of this publication) without the written permission of the copyright owner except in accordance with the provisions of the Copyright, Designs and Patents Act 1988 or under the terms of a licence issued by the Copyright Licensing Agency Ltd, 90 Tottenham Court Road, London, England W1T 4LP. Applications for the copyright owner's written permission to reproduce any part of this publication should be addressed to the publisher.

Warning: The doing of an unauthorised act in relation to a copyright work may result in both a civil claim for damages and criminal prosecution.

Crown copyright material is reproduced with the permission of the Controller of HMSO and the Queen's Printer for Scotland. Any European material in this work which has been reproduced from EUR-lex, the official European Communities legislation website, is European Communities copyright.

A CIP Catalogue record for this book is available from the British Library.

ISBN 0 406 97114 5

Project Management by The Partnership Publishing Solutions Ltd, **www.the-pps.co.uk**
Printed and bound in Great Britain by William Clowes Limited, Beccles and London

Visit LexisNexis UK at www.lexisnexis.co.uk

Foreword

by Hugh Pigott

This is a wide-ranging book which covers with great clarity and a refreshing sense of humour a large number of legal issues and structures found in the practice of domestic and international finance.

Having started with the elements of contract law which apply to every finance transaction, Martin Hughes describes the basic concepts contained in single bank and syndicated loan agreements. After that a chapter on the legal nature of bills of exchange and promissory notes is followed by a fascinating comparison of the different legal structures of bond issues and syndicated loans.

Looking back to my own days in practice, I think I would have found the next three chapters on guarantees of loans and bonds, assignments of choses in action and taking security particularly helpful. It is not every practitioner who can readily call to mind the subtle distinctions between legal and equitable assignments of debt or between legal and equitable choses in action, or for that matter the differences between mortgages and charges or the characteristics which make one legal and the other equitable.

After dealing with these and other issues, Martin explains why it is that, wherever possible, there should be a trust (and a trustee) at the heart of every English law secured or structured financing (starting with the comment that to many, perhaps most, finance lawyers trusts are a bit of a mystery). Other chapters look at drafting and technical issues (such as transferability in syndicated loan agreements and third party rights) and the last two chapters describe how documentary letters of credit work in international trade transactions and address areas of legal risk in sovereign-linked and other credit derivatives.

In his preface, Martin mentions that he sometimes refers to 'black holes', a phrase he uses to refer to difficult or obscure points or areas of law, and goes on to say that 'it is vital to develop an awareness of where the black holes are to be found. No one knows all the answers but every finance lawyer must learn to recognise danger signs'. He subsequently makes the important point, which I remember learning as a young lawyer, that it is always instructive to go back to the textbooks and even more so to read the cases, which often do not say what they are held out as saying.

I believe this book is required reading for all who aspire to be experts in this field of law. It will help them to understand the concepts they work with and to recognise those dangerous 'black holes'.

Hugh Pigott
31 October 2003

Preface

This is not a textbook or a treatise, nor is it a comprehensive guide to any of the topics it covers — so why should you read it? If I have got it right, the answer is that every chapter will be both instructive and enjoyable if you are an aspiring, young or inexperienced finance lawyer; or, perhaps, a seasoned finance lawyer who wants to refresh her memory on a particular topic or a lawyer who practises in a different area but is curious about the concepts and structures employed in banking and capital markets transactions; or a lawyer from another jurisdiction who wants some insight into English law as it affects financial transactions.

The approach I have taken in writing the separate but inter-related chapters that form this book is not to explore very difficult or obscure areas of law, but to try and clarify some (not all) of the core concepts that underly the complex legal structures found in acquisition finance, project finance, trade finance, structured finance and securitisation (to name just some of the modern areas of practice); and in doing so, I sometimesrefer to difficult or obscure points or areas of law as 'black holes'.

It is always important to remember that where, in the course of structuring or documenting a transaction, a black hole threatens to make life difficult, the objective must be to find a way round the black hole or to build a bridge over it. The temptation to explore black holes unnecessarily and at the client's expense should always be resisted. That being said, there are bound to be issues that have to be tackled and a view formed, so the other side of the coin is that it is vital to develop an awareness of where the black holes are to be found. No one knows all the answers, but every finance lawyer must learn to recognise danger signs.

In one of the later chapters I take the liberty of saying that it seems to me that there is a relatively recent tendency among lawyers, certainly in the areas I practice in, to place too much reliance on books which seem to provide all the answers and too little on personal research and analysis. Lawyers these days find themselves obliged to put so much emphasis on what I call processing, 'turning' documents over more frequently and speedily, that there is less and less time for reflection.

I hope this book will be of assistance to lawyers who find themselves in this position. It will not provide all the answers but will, I hope, be a useful source of insight into what the issues are and how they might be addressed.

Each of the chapters has a brief introduction which sets the scene for what is to follow, so I need say nothing more about their contents, save that although it has been my aim to state the law correctly as of 1 September 2003, none of them is intended to provide a full statement of the law on any of the topics it deals with or legal advice with regard to any particular set of facts.

If on a few occasions I mention that I introduced features which are now standard in English law syndicated loan agreements it is because I was fortunate enough to have been involved in their development almost from the start. Insofar as I have made a contribution to the development of the legal aspects of syndicated loans, this was not my doing alone. A substantial part of the credit belongs to Hugh Pigott who was kind enough in 1974 to hire me as a newly qualified solicitor despite my having neither a degree in law – philosophy being a less arduous subject to study – nor any corporate or commercial experience. I am also indebted to Hugh for his support for my efforts to write about the law as it affects finance lawyers and for his help in taking this project forward in the form of this collection of essays.

I have been assisted in the preparation of this book by colleagues too numerous to mention by name – to all of you, many thanks. I wish to express my particular thanks to my secretary, Carol Douglas, to Janet Pugh, Samantha Dickenson and Tegwen Williams in the library at White & Case, London for providing an unending flow of law reports and other materials, to Rachel Hatfield and Etay Katz for keeping me on the straight and narrow in relation to capital markets and regulatory issues respectively and to Marc Chowrimootoo for helping me to think through some of the more puzzling aspects of the law as it affects finance lawyers.

At home, my use of our dining table as a desk, my desk as an enormous pending tray, the floor of a shared study as my filing system – if you have seen my office you will have no difficulty in believing this one – and our kitchen as my study, let alone my having monopolised the computer for weeks, have all been tolerated, if not encouraged!

Thank you, Eda, for your support.

Martin Hughes
Haslemere

1 September 2003

Contents

Table of statutes

References in this table to *Statutes* are to Halsbury's Statutes of England (Fourth Edition) showing the volume and page at which the annotated text of the Act may be found.

Page numbers in bold type indicate where the section is set out in part or in full.

Table of rules and regulations

Table of cases

CHAPTER I

Contracts, consideration and third parties

In a book for finance lawyers, it seems a good idea to start with the common factor in all financing agreements – they are contracts. This is not to say that finance lawyers do not meet many other areas of law, but that at the heart of every financing arrangement there is a contract, usually a number of contracts. So, in this first chapter I will take a brief look at some fundamental principles of English contract law which are of particular relevance to finance lawyers and a preliminary look at the Contracts (Rights of Third Parties) Act 1999, which is dealt with in more detail in Chapter 12.

Freedom of contract

Financing and investment structures utilise basic concepts of the law of contract in a great variety of ways. Whether the transaction is a simple unsecured loan or a complex acquisition financing, the creation of the underlying debt obligations and the roles and relationships of the parties to the arrangements are all matters of contract law. All these activities are regulated to a greater or lesser extent and only infrequently can market practices be safely ignored, but, subject to those restrictions, practitioners and their clients are relatively free to write the contracts they want to write.

There are, of course, many statutes which affect the form, content and enforceability of contracts: the Statute of Frauds 1677 requires guarantees to be in writing; the Unfair Contract Terms Act 1977 restricts contracting parties' rights to exclude liability for negligence; and the Insolvency Act 1986 can invalidate dealings which constitute preferences or transactions at an undervalue. More recently, the Contracts (Rights of Third Parties) Act 1999 has (ironically, given its stated objectives) reduced freedom of contract in certain financial contexts, but, outside the world of consumer finance and investment, parties to financial and investment contracts can contract on more or less whatever terms they choose. Despite this (or is it because of this?) there is a great deal to be said about the law of contract – the 28th edition of *Chitty on Contracts* (Sweet & Maxwell, 2000) runs to 3,020 pages over two volumes. What I will do in this very brief survey of the topic is to highlight a few issues and identify a few black holes.

There is no general requirement under English law for contracts to be in writing, although there are exceptions, such as bills of exchange, certain consumer credit agreements and contracts for the sale or disposition of interests in land, which do need to be in writing, and guarantees which must be evidenced by a written memorandum (although indemnities need not be). If contracts can be made orally, they can be amended orally and this is probably true of contracts which provide otherwise. Even if a court found it difficult to take this view in the face of a provision stipulating that amendments shall only be made in writing – a provision which ought in principle to be capable of oral amendment – it would still be possible for the court to find that, either orally or though a course of conduct, the parties have entered into a collateral contract the substantive effect of which is to vary the underlying contract.

Consideration

Most contracts need not be in writing, but virtually all contracts, other than those made by deed, require consideration to be given by one party (the promisee) to the other(s), letters of credit being an important exception. Anything that is of value 'in the eye of the law' can constitute consideration, such as the payment of a peppercorn – still sometimes found as the consideration in contemporary leases. It is essential that the consideration should 'move from the promisee', but irrelevant whether the recipient of value – and the promisee's suffering a detriment may constitute value – is the promisor (the person who assumes the obligation to the promisee) or someone else. Thus, to take the most common example in a financing context, a lender's agreement to lend to a borrower is consideration for a guarantee given by the borrower's parent. The consideration – a promise to lend – moves from the lender, but moves to the borrower, not to the guarantor.

A number of issues arise in relation to situations where one party to a contract seeks to enforce a later, additional promise by the other party to do more than was originally promised. The basic principle is that performance of an existing contractual obligation is not consideration for a new promise by the other party – this was established by a case (*Stilk v Myrick* (1809) 2 Camp 317 esp 129) where a group of deserting sailors who returned to sail the ship home could not enforce the master's promise to pay them extra wages for doing so. Although the current position would permit recovery if the other party actually benefits and there is no duress (*Williams v Roffey Bros & Nicholls (Contractors) Ltd* [1991] 1 QB 1), this is an area of law best avoided in practice. In other words, ensure that there is fresh consideration for a fresh promise or embody the new arrangements in a deed.

Part performance

If you think that the decision in *Stilk v Myrick* may have been influenced by considerations of social status, you might want to look at *Hirachand Punamchand v Temple* [1911] 2 KB 330, a case decided almost exactly 100 years later, where a legally dubious decision was made in favour of the son of an English baronet who was being sued by an Indian moneylender. The moneylender had lent money to the son and it was held that a part payment by the baronet was consideration for the moneylender's agreement not to sue the son for the balance and that – contrary to the House of Lords' decision in *Foakes v Beer* (1884) 9 App Cas 605 – the son's debt to the moneylender was discharged by the father's part payment, because to decide otherwise would be a fraud on the father. It is a short step from here to the concept of promissory estoppel developed by Denning J (as he then was) in *Central London Property Trust Ltd v High Trees House Ltd* [1947] KB 130 and to his suggestion that a promise to accept a smaller sum in discharge of a larger sum is, if acted on, binding despite the absence of consideration. It ought to follow that performance of part of an existing obligation can be consideration for a new promise (to suffer a detriment by receiving less than the amount due) because receipt of the lesser sum is an actual benefit which, in the absence of duress, allows performance of an existing obligation to support a fresh promise.

Finally, having descended into this intriguing black hole – some people can't resist temptation – I will end the digression by referring to *Pao On v Lau Yiu Long* [1980] AC 614, in which it was decided that a promise to a third party to perform an existing contractual obligation can be consideration for a promise by the third party. In this case, a third party agreed to indemnify the original promisor against any loss suffered by reason of performance of the contractual obligation. This case also confirms the existence of an exception to the past consideration rule where an earlier promise is made at the promisor's request and on the understanding that some future payment would be made.

Past consideration

As it happens, this digression takes us to the classic opportunity for beginners' error in contract law, which arises out of the rule that 'past consideration is no consideration'. In other words, the value to be given for a promise must be given or promised at or after the time the promise is made – 'this is something I made earlier' does not generally work in contract law. Ironically, the problem can arise out of attempts to prevent the problem from arising. If the alleged consideration for a contract is recited and either through poor drafting, or because of the facts, the consideration recited is past consideration, a court might find itself obliged to take the point in circumstances where it would not otherwise have had to do so. Recitals always carry with them an element of risk – they may affect the construction of the contract, where there is some ambiguity, or cause a covenant or warranty to be implied. For this reason, and because there is usually plenty of good consideration to be found in a commercial or financial arrangement, recitals, especially as to consideration, are best omitted.

Offers to the world

Apart from the need for consideration, there needs to be (if a contract is to exist) both a meeting of minds (as to who agrees to do what) and an intention to create legal relations – the absence of such an intention saves many domestic agreements from being enforceable as contracts. The case that we can all remember – *Carlill v Carbolic Smoke Ball Co* [1893] 1 QB 256 – is evidence of both requirements and stands as the archetypal example of both the offer and acceptance analysis of the way in which contracts are formed and of how contracts can be made by a course of conduct. A written 'offer to the world' was accepted by an offeree's putting the smoke ball to the test. The smoke ball didn't provide the promised benefits and the smoke ball company was held to be liable for breach of contract.

This same analysis underlies the concept of 'transferability' in relation to lenders' interests in syndicated loans, a cornerstone of the secondary loan market. A conventionally-structured syndicated loan agreement, such as one of the Loan Market Association's Standard Form Syndicated Loan Agreements, contains provisions whereby buyers (transferees) of all or part of a lender's claims on the borrower can take the place, wholly or partially, of the lender as long as certain procedures are followed. What is happening is that the loan agreement constitutes a standing offer to novate, an offer which is made by all the parties to the loan agreement and which is capable of acceptance by any financial institution which accepts that offer in accordance with its terms. (See Chapters 2 and 9 for more detailed commentary on loan agreements and Chapter 10 for a detailed analysis of the legal basis of 'transferability'.)

Objectivity and intention

Whether or not a contract results from an oral or written exchange is in principle to be determined by an objective test, rather than by reference to the parties' state of mind. Agreement is to be inferred from what has been said, written or done, so a contract will exist if a reasonable person would conclude that the parties intended to be bound by what they said or did, but if one party knows the other has no intention to be bound, there will be no contract. You can find an interesting discussion of these issues in the opening chapters of *Treitel on The Law of Contract*. I mention this to provide an excuse to say two things. First, without works such as Treitel and Chitty, pieces such as this could not be written. Secondly, it is always instructive to go back to the textbooks and even more so to read the cases. It is astonishing how often cases do not say what they are held out as saying.

The presence or absence of an intention to be bound can be of critical importance in practice, for example in relation to the 'heads of terms' which are often agreed between the parties to a financing arrangement before work on the formal documentation begins. The heads of terms as a whole may not constitute a contract – the inability of the court to infer an intention to be bound being critical – but a 'drop dead' fee, payable to the financing institution in the event that the transaction does not proceed, can be enforceable if it is clear that the parties intended this to be a legally binding arrangement. The presence or absence of an intention to be bound can distinguish a guarantee – or an undertaking that is tantamount to a guarantee – from a 'letter of comfort'. In *Kleinwort Benson Ltd v Malaysian Mining Corpn* [1989] 1 WLR 379, a statement by a borrower's parent company to the effect that it was its policy to ensure that its subsidiary could at all times meet its obligations was held to be a statement of policy and not an undertaking to implement that policy – there was no evidence that parties intended to create a binding contract.

The application of the principle of objectivity in other circumstances, for example where two parties exchange their own (preferred) forms of contract, could have unfortunate results – it might be inferred that one party had won the 'battle of the forms' or that there is no contract at all. Such circumstances might prove interesting for a litigation lawyer, but the risk would rarely be one a client could be advised to accept. The advice to the client would be: because it is hard to tell which form of contract will prevail, we should take steps to remove this uncertainty, so you may have to back down.

(Even if all the issues already mentioned have been satisfactorily resolved, it is still easy for an apparently successful contract to fail to achieve what the parties intended – or must be taken to have intended. Contracts can be of no effect – they may be void or capable of being nullified – if the parties are fundamentally mistaken as to a matter of fact, such as the legal or practical possibility of performing the contract. Contracts can also fail, in a legal sense, because of misrepresentation, non-disclosure (fairly easily in the case of insurance contracts, but not often in the case of contracts of suretyship), duress or undue influence or illegality. A good deal more than a single chapter in a book such as this would be required to do justice to the many ways in which contracts can fail.)

Contracts (Rights of Third Parties) Act 1999

The most recent statutory intervention in the law of contract concerns the extent to which contracts can confer rights on third parties – see Chapter 12 for a more detailed review of this topic. Until the Contracts (Rights of Third Parties) Act 1999 came into effect, the general rule (known as the privity rule) was that a third party to a contract could not acquire an enforceable right under that contract. This rule, to which there were numerous complex exceptions, was abrogated by the Act with effect from 11 May 2000. The Act applies to all contracts entered into on or after that date (and to a contract entered into after 11 November 1999 if the contract so provided).

(It is important to note that that application of the Act cannot be excluded – it is a Public Act of Parliament – but it can be made clear in a contract that there is no intention that any third party shall have any right to enforce any term of the contract; a statement in a contract to the effect that the Act does not apply may well have the effect of confirming that this is the intention of the parties but, if taken literally, is incorrect and ineffective.)

The Act is short but fussy, the product of academic and judicial deliberation rather than practical experience and insight. Too much time has been spent on the issue – it was in 1937 that a committee was first asked to report on the topic – and too little input was provided by those at the 'sharp end' of legal practice. Despite this, the Act need not cause too many problems in the financial markets. It does have the capacity to pose some new traps for the unwary, but as its effects are becoming better understood and assimilated into market practice, business carries on very much as usual, at least in the world of finance. A depressing verdict for the last significant development in contract law's first millennium, but perhaps it will take more than three years before real innovations which are based on the Act are introduced. See the concluding section of Chapter 4 – before the postscript – for one suggestion.

An intrusive Act?

The Contracts (Rights of Third Parties) Act 1999 does not simply say that contracting parties may confer enforceable rights on third parties. Instead, it says (s 1) that the parties to a contract may do this by expressly saying so or, if they use language which might be regarded as having this effect –'purports' is the word used in the Act – this is what they will be regarded as having done, unless 'on a proper construction of the contract it appears that the parties did not intend the [relevant provisions of the contract] to be enforceable by the third party'. If this provision is considered in the light of the omission from the Act of a provision allowing the parties to exclude the operation of the Act – and this is where the Act restricts freedom of contract – an important question has to be answered. What is the effect of the Act on contracts, the express purpose of which is to confer rights on third parties – a category of contracts which includes syndicated loans and bond issues? Do the provisions of the Act necessarily apply in such circumstances, even if the parties have worked out – as the markets have – how to achieve their objectives without the assistance (or intrusion) of the Act?

There are two substantive provisions (ss 2 and 5) of the Act to look at here, but first we need to consider s 7(1) which simply says 'section 1 does not affect any right or remedy of a third party that exists or is available apart from this Act'. The Law Commission, who drafted the Act, did not want to override existing statutory and judicial exceptions to the privity rule, but found it impracticable to list them all. As a result, we have an Act which leaves unanswered a key question. Section 7(1) does not say that the provisions of the Act (other than s 1) shall not apply nor that they cannot supplement or overlay the pre-existing law. So do ss 2 and 5 apply, for example, to a syndicated loan agreement which contains structures intended to benefit the lenders' assignees?

Section 2 gives statutory third party beneficiaries the right to block the amendment or rescission of the relevant contract where this would extinguish or alter the beneficiaries' third party rights. However, these 'blocking rights' are subject to any provision of the contract which provides that the contract may be amended or rescinded without the third party's consent. If the contract deals with this issue there need not be a problem, so do not forget to do this. Imagine how awkward it could be for your client if its indemnity in favour of, say, 'the Agent Bank, its directors, employees and agents' could not be amended without the consent of that large, diverse and obstinate group of third-party beneficiaries.

The effect of s 5 is that the courts have a discretion to ensure, for example, that where a contractor's customer has paid over money to the contractor to cover sums due from the contractor to its sub-contractors, those sub-contractors do not get paid twice by exercising third party rights against the customer. (Much of the debate about third party rights related to customer/contractor/sub-contractor issues, in particular problems which have arisen with regard to giving sub-contractors the benefit of exclusion clauses in the main contract.) Section 5, which does not contain a provision allowing for its exclusion, would seem, by its terms, to apply to an assignee on whom a loan agreement confers rights – as loan agreements usually do. However, s 5 is inconsistent with the right of an assignee which has given notice to the debtor to be paid by the debtor even if the debtor has (mistakenly) paid the assignor. In order to ensure that no uncertainty arises, reliance will have to be placed on provisions (which are in any event already in use) which cause assignees to become parties to the loan agreement – and thus cease to be third parties, thereby excluding the application of the Act – once they have agreed to be bound by the terms of the loan agreement.

Time will tell

It is undeniable that the law needed to be reformed – the exceptions to the privity rule, which was established in *Beswick v Beswick* [1966] Ch 538; CA; affd [1968] AC 58; HL were so numerous and difficult to pin down that statutory intervention was inevitable. The process of reform was a lengthy one and, as is often the case, the solution to the problem is not perfect. The Law Commission's proposal not to allow parties to contract out of the Act and the wording of the Act itself, lead to numerous uncertainties, including those I have described.

Time – and judicial decisions – will no doubt remove these uncertainties. For the time being, the message is clear:

• if you intend a third party to acquire an enforceable right under a contract, say so in words which make express reference to the right to enforce the relevant term(s);

- if you do not intend third parties to acquire enforceable rights under a contract, make this intention abundantly clear; and

- if the whole purpose of the contract, or an important part of the contract, is to benefit third parties (such as assignees or subsequent holders of bonds), think carefully about the implications of the Act.

CHAPTER 2

Loan agreements – single bank and syndicated

> **This chapter deals with some of the basic concepts that you will meet in a loan (or loan facility) agreement, an agreement which constitutes a contractual framework under which a debt will arise when a loan is made. Syndicated loan agreements contain provisions of various kinds: some of these deal with the relationship between the lenders and the borrower; some deal with the relationships between the lenders themselves and between the lenders and the agent bank. Other provisions deal with matters such as assignees/transferees, choice of law and dispute resolution.**

Finance lawyers spend a great deal of their time dealing with arrangements under which debt obligations are created through the issue of bonds or other securities, or arise under agreements for the lending of money. Taking these in no particular order, in Chapter 3, I look at bills of exchange, in Chapter 4 at bond issues and in this chapter at loan agreements.

(From time to time, in this chapter and elsewhere, I will refer to the 'LMA Agreements'– by this I mean the syndicated facility agreements first promulgated by the Loan Market Association in October 1999. These agreements, which were most recently updated in January 2003, take forward the process of standardisation in English law syndicated loan agreements which began towards the end of the 1970s. Although less elegant than the individual products of the firms who participated in their creation (having, at least initially, been drafted in committee), these agreements represent the 'state of the art' in syndicated loan agreements.)

A contractual framework

Unlike bonds and other debt instruments, loan agreements do not usually create or evidence debts, which is why a loan agreement does not constitute a debenture. This has always seemed to me to be self-evident – see the definition of 'debenture' in the Financial Services and Markets Act 2000 (Regulated Activities) Order 2001 (SI 2001/544), art 77. In the past, regulatory authorities have been known to take a different view, with the result that lending activities which ought to be regarded as outside regulatory regimes, such as those created by the financial services legislation, have sometimes been regarded as subject to those regimes. However, the FSA's view – which I share – is that a loan or loan facility does not constitute a financial instrument under Art 77 on the basis that a loan or loan facility agreement is not an instrument nor an agreement which itself creates or evidences debt (see notes 13, 14 and 15 in Chapter 10, page 147). As I explain below, such an agreement creates a framework under which loans may be made and it is the making of a loan which gives rise to a debt which will be evidenced by an entry in an account of the borrower with the lender.

A loan agreement creates a contractual framework under which one party (the lender) agrees to lend money to the other party (the borrower), subject to certain conditions being satisfied – one being a request for the money from the borrower – and on specified terms as to repayment of the money borrowed. A debt arises when the money is borrowed, ie when the sum being lent is received by the borrower. (It would not be a good idea when writing a loan agreement to forget to include a provision as to when the loan is to be repaid. Although the loan would, in the absence of a repayment provision, be repayable on demand, this would only be a satisfactory outcome for borrower and lender if the intention was to create an overdraft facility.)

An obligation to repay a loan constitutes a debt, a definite sum of money agreed by the parties as being payable by one party in return for performance of a specified obligation by the other party or upon the occurrence of some specified event or condition. A debt gives to the person to whom it is owed (the creditor) a claim for payment of a liquidated sum and (in contrast to the position where a contracting party seeks compensation for a failure to perform some other type of obligation) no loss or damage need be shown by the creditor when it sues for recovery of the debt. This is why the important case of *Linden Gardens Trust Ltd v Lenesta Sludge Disposals Ltd* [1994] 1 AC 85, HL, does not pose problems for assignees of debts in the way it could for assignees of other contractual claims.

The House of Lords held in that case that if a claim is assigned in the face of the promisor's failure to consent to the assignment (where this is required by the contract), no rights pass to the putative assignee. If the assignee subsequently recovers the price it paid from the assignor on the grounds of total failure of consideration, can the assignor recover its loss from the promisor? The answer is 'Yes' if the claim is a claim for payment of a debt but, so the House of Lords held, could be 'No' in the case of a claim for damages because the loss suffered by the assignor is too remote to be recovered. This principle may, it is true, give rise to difficulties in relation to certain indemnities found in loan agreements, but the assignor's claim to be repaid is unaffected – no loss or damage need be shown in order to succeed in a claim for payment of a debt. This issue is further discussed in Chapter 6, page 80.

Interest and default interest

When money is lent, it will nearly always be lent on terms that the debtor must pay interest on the amount lent. Outside the area of consumer contracts, the parties are free to agree on what rate of interest will apply and how the amounts of interest due will be calculated. However, there have always been concerns about whether a provision increasing the rate of interest on the occurrence of a payment default might be void as a penalty, because it might be regarded as a provision which does not constitute a genuine pre-estimate of loss.

These concerns have been largely dispelled by the decision in *Lordsvale Finance plc v Bank of Zambia* [1996] 3 All ER 156. Although it is only a first instance decision, the judge (Colman J) convincingly held that 'a modest increase' in the rate of interest – 1% was the increase in question – which operates after (but not before) the default is contractually binding as being commercially justified and not *in terrorem* of the borrower. In the course of his judgment, Colman J restated the principle in issue by saying:

> 'The jurisdiction in relation to penalty clauses is concerned not primarily with the enforcement of inoffensive liquidated damages clauses, but rather with protection against the effect of penalty clauses. There would therefore seem to be no reason in principle why a contractual provision, the effect of which was to increase the consideration payable under an executory contract upon the happening of a default, should be struck down as a penalty if the increase could in the circumstances be explained as commercially justifiable, provided always that its dominant purpose was not to deter the other party from breach.'

Interestingly, Colman J concluded his judgment by observing that such provisions are upheld in New York and that:

> 'It would be highly regrettable if the English courts were to refuse to give effect to such prevalent provisions while the courts of New York are prepared to enforce them. For there to be a disparity between the law applicable in London and New York on this point would be of great disservice to international banking.'

The default interest provision which had to be considered in the *Bank of Zambia* case was unusual in one respect. It provided that after a payment default the margin (and the default margin) should be added to each individual bank's cost of funding. This gave rise to the argument that an assignee which buys a loan at a discount has a lower 'cost of funds' than an original lender and should therefore receive less interest than an original lender. Although the argument was rejected, it is not entirely without merit. The 'cost of funds' formulation is often found, not in default interest provisions, but in 'market disruption' provisions (see below) such as those in the LMA Agreements. However clear and unambiguous you think your document is, it can always be improved.

Illegality and unenforceability

It is not difficult to create an obligation to repay a loan. All that is needed is for money to be lent pursuant to a binding agreement to lend – no problems here with consideration. However, it is possible for the repayment of a loan, and the payment of interest on it, to become unlawful where, for example, two countries are at war or United Nations' sanctions prohibit dealings with nationals of a given country. Loan agreements usually deal with this in a provision – the illegality clause – which states that if it is unlawful for the borrower to perform its obligations, the lender may 'accelerate' the loan, ie it may declare the loan to be immediately due and payable – this is wishful thinking, but that is the practice – and provides that the lender shall not thereafter be obliged to make any further loans – this is the realistic (and important) part of this provision.

Illegality of this kind usually arises where relations between countries are in a state of crisis, but it can arise in other circumstances. The Bretton Woods Agreement (which created the IMF), Art VIII, s 2b provides that:

> 'Exchange contracts which involve the currency of any member and which are contrary to the exchange control regulations of that member maintained or imposed consistently with this Agreement shall be unenforceable in the territories of any member.'

The leading case on this section is *UCM v Royal Bank of Canada* [1983] I AC 168, where it was held that the term 'exchange contract' should be construed narrowly as meaning a contract for the exchange (ie sale and purchase) of currencies and not a contract for the provision of goods or services which happens to require an exchange of currencies. In *Mansouri v Singh* [1986] 2 All ER 619 the Court of Appeal held that a negotiable instrument which gave effect to a contract for an exchange of currencies was within the section. Although the section would seem not to cover contracts for the lending of money, it is in any event unlikely that a lender would knowingly lend in breach of a country's exchange control regime, although it might be safe to do so unless the loan was in the borrower's home currency. The English courts will not enforce a contract if it would be illegal to perform the contract in the place where it is to be performed. However, where a loan is in a currency other than the borrower's home currency, this rule would be unlikely to apply just because of local exchange control regulations, because payments of principal and interest are usually required to be made in the country of the loan currency.

A game of two halves

Having identified some issues relating to the debts that arise under a loan agreement, I will look at some of the features of a conventional English law syndicated loan agreement. Even though loan agreements are not drafted in this way, I have always found it useful to regard such an agreement as being divided into two halves, each half being further divisible into three parts. These sub-divisions are intended to shed light on what is going on in a loan agreement (and to avoid a tedious clause by clause approach). The first three sub-divisions, which deal with the lender/borrower relationship, are the following:

- circumstantial provisions − the provisions which describe the circumstances in which the lenders are willing to lend and to continue to lend;

- operational provisions − the provisions which regulate the making of loans, their repayment with interest and the payment flows between the parties; and

- protective provisions − the provisions which are intended to protect the lenders against the adverse effects of such things as taxes, capital adequacy requirements and supervening illegality.

The second set of sub-divisions deals with other aspects of the contractual arrangements, namely:

- transfer provisions − transferability is now one of the corner-stones of a syndicated loan agreement;

- interbank and agency provisions − the provisions which regulate the relationship between the lenders and between the lenders and the agent bank; and

- dispute resolution provisions − the choice of law and jurisdiction provisions.

Circumstantial provisions

A lender, or group of lenders, will take the decision to lend to a borrower on the basis of the circumstances prevailing at the time the loan agreement is entered into, including both the financial condition of the borrower and projections as to the borrower's business activities and financial condition in the future. In effect, lenders lend to the status quo. The circumstantial provisions are the provisions which:

- describe or evidence the status quo (representations and conditions precedent);

- contain undertakings by the borrower with regard to changes in the status quo which are within the borrower's control (covenants); and

- describe changes in the status quo, which, although outside the borrower's control, are regarded as unacceptable by the lenders – events the occurrence of which entitle the lenders to decline to lend any more money and to ask for immediate repayment of any money already lent (events of default).

All the representations the lender wants to be able to rely on should be set out in the agreement. Although it has the usual remedies where a party to a contract has made a misrepresentation, a lender is better protected by the usual provision that an event of default will have occurred if any of the 'representations and warranties' (as they are usually called) prove to have been (materially) incorrect or inaccurate. This contractual mechanism makes it unnecessary, for example, for the lender to prove that it was induced by the misrepresentation to enter into the agreement. (The effect of the Misrepresentation Act 1967, ss 1(a) and 2(2) on a party's right to rescind a contract where a misrepresentation has become incorporated as a term of a contract is uncertain and obscure. Because a lender is unlikely to want to rescind a loan agreement, given its contractual rights, this particular black hole can be ignored in the absence of exceptional circumstances.)

The distinction I have made between covenants and events of default – that covenants cover matters which are within the borrower's control and events of default those which are not – is often ignored, particularly in relation to what are usually called 'financial conditions'. In the late 1970s, a major UK corporate borrower was perceived as being 'in default' when a covenant covering its net worth was 'breached' because its very large minority stake in a quoted company fell sharply in value as a result of problems affecting that company which were not in any way attributable to the borrower. Agreement was in due course reached between the borrower and its lenders, albeit only after the borrower had sought and obtained support from the Bank of England. However, it has always seemed to me that the borrower would have had a good counter-argument to the assertion that, to use the usual language, it had 'failed to perform its obligations under [the financial condition covenant]'– and whether or not I am correct, this is certainly a debate to be avoided. (For a fascinating insight into this and other defining events in the history of the syndicated loan agreement, have a look at Hugh Pigott, 'The Historical Development of Syndicated Eurocurrency Loan Agreements' (1982) *International Business Lawyer*, vol 10(vi), 199 – reproduced in the Appendix.)

Getting 'financial conditions' correctly embedded in a loan agreement is a task of real difficulty, one reason being the application of a principle similar to Heisenberg's famous 'uncertainty principle'– the observer alters the observed. Whenever a lender looks at evidence of a borrower's financial condition, the borrower's actual financial condition will have changed – financial statements are always historic. A related problem is the old chestnut about whether an event of default has to be 'continuing' in order for the lender to exercise its right to 'accelerate' the loan. This is not the place to propose solutions to these problems – and the solutions will depend on who you are advising – but it is important to be aware of them.

I said earlier that an obligation to repay a loan will arise if the loan is made pursuant to a binding agreement to lend. As well as constituting the evidence of the lender's commercial due diligence, the conditions precedent should provide all the evidence (including legal opinions) needed to conclude that the loan agreement is valid, binding and enforceable. Although English law entitles persons dealing with an English company to rely in certain circumstances on the company and its representatives as having the capacity and power to enter into a contract (Companies Act 1985 (CA 1985), ss 35 and 35A), it would not be safe to rely on these provisions where enquiry is made as to these matters – if you ask any questions, you must ask them all.

Operational provisions

As I have said, the way in which I have divided up the contents of a loan agreement does not reflect the way in which loan agreements are usually written. So although the circumstantial provisions will very often, with the exception of the conditions precedent, be grouped together in a loan agreement, this is not likely to be the case with the other sets of provisions. (When asked whether there is a correct order for the provisions of a loan agreement, a former colleague famously remarked that there is no right order, but there is a wrong order.) Thus, the provisions of a syndicated loan agreement dealing with the amount of the loan, the purpose for which the loan is made – my favourite such provision announced that the purpose of the loan was to finance the purchase of 'unarmed helicopters' – the respective commitments of the banks, the conditions to be satisfied before loans are made, rates of interest and repayment terms are likely to be found towards the beginning of the agreement, but not necessarily in precisely that order nor in sequence.

These provisions raise practical issues, rather than legal issues, the most easily overlooked of which – at least, it is one which, many years ago, I overlooked in a first draft – is the need, in relation to a floating rate loan, to match funding periods with 'interest periods' – the periods by reference to which interest payable by the borrower is calculated. This is particularly important where a repayment date falls during an interest period, in which case the loan agreement must provide that the loan is to be 'split' into two parts, one of which must be at least equal to the amount to be repaid and have an interest period ending on the repayment date. This is a specific consequence of the underlying assumption, in a floating rate loan agreement, that the lender will fund the loan by borrowing in the interbank market deposits of amounts and for periods which 'match' the amounts and interest periods of the loan (or loans) outstanding under the loan agreement.

Protective provisions

The 'matched funding' assumption underlies a number of the provisions found in a 'eurocurrency' loan agreement. One such provision is the 'alternative interest rates' (or, as in the LMA Agreements, 'market disruption') provision which would apply if there were a breakdown in the usual interest rate fixing procedures. The purpose of the market disruption clause – so far as I am aware it has never been invoked – is to protect the lenders' yield, ie to ensure that the interest they receive equals the 'margin' over their cost of funds – a requirement which is very clearly explained in Hugh Pigott's article. This is also the purpose of two of the other protective provisions: the 'taxes' provision and the 'increased costs' provision. The first seeks to protect a lender from any reduction in yield attributable to taxes other than those on the net income of the lender in the jurisdiction(s) in which the lender is resident for tax purposes. The second seeks to protect a lender from any reduction in yield suffered by reason of compliance with the requirements of central banks or other regulatory authorities. The borrower's obligations under the taxes provision (at least in part) and under the increased costs provision are expressed as indemnities. Assignments of the benefit of indemnities such as these could be caught by the decision in *Lenesta Sludge* if consents to assignment required by the loan agreement are not obtained – see above (page 13).

Another of the protective provisions is the illegality clause, which I mentioned earlier. The object of this provision is rather more fundamental than the others in that the aim is to ensure that a lender is not contractually obliged to lend where repayment by the borrower would be unlawful. If there were no such provision, the lender might well be liable in damages if it failed to lend, but any loan it made would probably be tainted with the illegality and its repayment unenforceable. The good news, from the lender's perspective, is that the English courts would not compel the lender to make further loans. The courts will not order specific performance of an obligation to lend money on the grounds that damages are an adequate remedy. Indeed, as Lord MacNaghten put it in *South African Territories Ltd v Wallington* [1898] AC 309 at 318, HL:

> 'that specific performance of a contract to lend money cannot be enforced is so well established, and obviously so wholesome a rule, that it would be idle to say a word about it';

and see also Chapter 7, pages 83–84.

Transferability

Although many of the difficulties which can arise in relation to assignment can be circumvented by the use of appropriate clauses and procedures, assignment is inadequate as a means of transfer in the context of loan agreements because obligations cannot (under English law) be assigned. This is inconvenient in relation to loan agreements because the lenders will, as we have seen, always assume an obligation to lend, an obligation which may continue for weeks or months. If a lender wants to divest itself, wholly or partly, of its interest in a loan agreement, it will want to be able to 'transfer' its obligations as well as its rights (and the other parties will want its successor to assume its obligations to them). This led to the concept of 'transfer' procedures which operate, as explained in Chapter 1 (and see also Chapters 9 and 10), through a structure relying on a standing offer to novate. The transfer provisions in a syndicated loan agreement set up procedures under which all the parties to the loan agreement agree (by entering into the loan agreement) that if a lender and a 'transferee' (i) agree upon a transfer of all or part of the lender's interest, (ii) record the agreement – but not the price or other ancillary matters which are to be dealt with separately – in a prescribed form and (iii) deliver this to the agent bank, the transfer will take effect. The effect of a transfer – as expressed in the loan agreement – is that the transferee becomes a party to the agreement with rights and obligations which are the same – the identity of the parties excepted – as those the 'transferor' had before the transfer (to the extent of the interest transferred). The legal principle underlying this structure was well expressed (in a very different context) by Collins MR in *Tolhurst v Associated Portland Cement Manufacturers (1900) Ltd* [1902] 2 KB 660 at 668, where he said:

> 'a debtor cannot relieve himself of his liability to his creditor by assigning the burden of the obligation to somebody else; this can only be brought about by the consent of all three, and involves the release of the original debtor.'

As well as enabling obligations (to lend) to be transferred, the 'transfer certificate' route can be structured so as to give the borrower total or partial control over the type or identity of specific transferees or classes of permitted transferees (there being both credit and tax implications for a borrower). The structure also enables the transferee and transferor (buyer and seller) to document the commercial terms of the transfer separately and, thus, privately. Syndicated loans are a key banking product and structures such as this contribute to their remaining a real alternative to capital markets products.

Interbank and agency provisions

Most of the provisions dealing with the relationships between the lenders and the agent bank will be found in the section of the agreement which deals with the role of the agent bank. Those dealing with lender-to-lender issues tend to be scattered throughout the agreement. For instance, the very important stipulation that the obligations of the lenders are several – one lender is not liable for another's failure to perform its obligations – usually appears very early in the agreement, but the provision which represents the other side of this coin – the 'sharing clause' – is invariably found towards the end of the agreement, as in the LMA Agreements. Perhaps the respective positions of these provisions in a syndicated loan agreement reflects the fact that whereas the concept of several liability is fundamental (as I explain in Chapter 9), the principle embodied in the sharing clause – that a lender which gets more than its rightful share of a sum due from the borrower will share the surplus – is, in practice, more honoured in the breach than in the observance – see Chapter 9, pages 113–114 and 121–122.

(The sharing provision in the LMA Agreements reminds me of a colleague who, had he been asked to draft the rule of golf about who plays first on the green, would probably have explained that the golfers first identify whose ball is whose, then measure the balls' respective distances from the hole and so on. There is a simpler way to do this – see Chapter 11.)

Where international disputes and/or UN sanctions have prevented borrowers from paying all the lenders in a syndicate, those who got paid or otherwise recovered what they were owed did not always share the payments (or only did so after a lengthy delay) and where the problem was that payments could not be made through an agent bank, they were made directly to the affected lenders (thus obviating the need to persuade other lenders to share payments they received through the agent bank).

The content of a modern syndicated loan agreement's agency provisions differs little from agreement to agreement, the LMA Agreements' provisions being typical examples – the basic provisions were identified a long time ago. However, an agent bank is likely to have fewer discretions than it used to have and where it has a mechanical task to perform (for example, making a calculation in relation to amounts due from the borrower), this will be expressly stated rather than being left to be inferred from the circumstances. The agent bank's ability to 'accelerate' the loan at its own discretion usually remains (subject to the views of the borrower as expressed in negotiation) on the basis that an agent bank needs emergency powers where things go wrong. Other than in exceptional circumstances, an agent bank would not 'accelerate' a loan otherwise than on the instructions of the 'majority banks'(or an 'instructing group', as I prefer to call them) – that is a group of banks to whom is owed more than a specified percentage (usually 50 or 66.66%) of the loan (and/ or whose commitments to lend are of the same relative magnitude). The choice of percentage can become a very contentious issue – and different percentages may be needed for different purposes, where, for example, a borrower wants it to be difficult for an agent bank to obtain instructions to accelerate, but relatively easy for it to grant waivers in respect of burdensome covenants – but see Chapter 9, page 118.

A relative latecomer among the agent bank provisions was that giving to the agent bank a right to resign. This provision is certainly necessary from the agent bank's perspective. In the absence of an express term in an agreement creating a principal/agent relationship, the agent can be dismissed but may not resign. A clause will only be implied into a contract of agency if it must necessarily be implied by the nature of the contract and it can hardly be argued that a right to resign is required in order for an agent bank to perform its role. In practice the provision probably achieves less than is thought, particularly where the right to resign is contingent (as it usually is) on the appointment of a successor. (See Chapter 9 for a discussion of a number of the other agent bank provisions.)

Dispute resolution provisions

The great majority of international syndicated loans contain provisions for the resolution of disputes in the courts, although an increasing number of agreements provide for arbitration, especially if the borrower is located in Central and Eastern Europe (where most, if not all, countries are party to the 1958 New York Convention on the recognition and enforcement of arbitration awards). The usual requirement is for the borrower to submit to the jurisdiction of the courts in England and, often, particularly if the borrower is a sovereign or quasi-sovereign entity, New York. (Only rarely does a borrower require lenders to make a similar submission.)

Where the borrower is not an English company, it is also usual to require it to appoint a 'process agent' – an agent for the service of process – in the specified jurisdiction(s). These provisions are rarely contentious, save in the case of sovereign or quasi-sovereign borrowers, where issues of sovereign immunity have to be dealt with – see below.

Until recently, the usual form of jurisdiction clause rather puzzlingly stated that the borrower agrees 'for the benefit of' the lenders to submit to the jurisdiction of the specified courts. This phrase was needed to ensure that where signatories were parties to the 1968 Brussels Convention (incorporated into English law by the Civil Jurisdiction and Judgments Act 1982) the submission would not exclude the jurisdiction of all other signatory states.

The position now is that in relation to a state to which EC Regulation 44/2001 applies, the phrase is not needed because this regulation allows submissions to be non-exclusive. However, the regulation does not apply to Denmark, in relation to which the Brussels Convention continues to apply, nor to the parties to the Lugano Convention (Iceland, Norway, Poland and Switzerland), in relation to which the old 'benefit' wording needs to be used if there is to be a submission to the English jurisdiction by a party against whom the right to commence proceedings in those states is to be retained! (I have explored this particular black hole to a greater extent than I would have wished in order not to mislead you. It remains essential to include jurisdiction provisions in any loan agreement in respect of which any party has a connection to any jurisdiction other than England and Wales and for those provisions to be crafted with the benefit of input from a specialist in this area.)

The presence in loan agreements with a sovereign or quasi-sovereign borrower of two different provisions, each of which – this is the usual approach – seeks to deny to the borrower whatever immunity it might have is also rather puzzling. There is one provision under which (if it agrees to do so) the borrower 'waives' any immunity it may have and another under which it 'consents' to proceedings being brought against it. The first provision is intended to fall within the relevant US legislation, the Foreign Sovereign Immunities Act of 1976, which, oversimplifying somewhat, confers on states (and on majority-owned state agencies) immunity from suit in relation to activities which are not commercial activities carried on, in or having an effect in, the United States, and immunity from attachment and execution, save in relation to property used for a commercial activity on which the claim is based, unless the foreign state (or its agency) has waived its immunity. The second provision is drafted so as to track the relevant provisions of the UK legislation, the State Immunity Act 1978 (enacted so as to keep UK law 'up to speed' with US law), which confers on states (and on separate entities 'acting in the exercise of sovereign authority') similar immunities to the extent the state has not given its consent to the taking of proceedings. The whole area of sovereign immunity is a large but important black hole, which must not be ignored if there is any question of departing from the usual provisions, which are, in effect, market standard provisions.

Legal issues are secondary

The syndicated loan is central to a large part of London's financial markets. Apart from the syndicated loan market itself (and the resulting secondary market), acquisition finance and project finance are important areas where a (complicated) syndicated loan agreement is one of the core documents. Despite this, there are relatively few reported cases which concern syndicated loan agreements, partly, no doubt, because the underlying legal issues are for the most part neither difficult nor obscure – see, however, Chapter 9, page 120 for a brief description of an important, recent case (*Redwood Master Fund Ltd v (1) TD Bank Europe Ltd, (2) UPC Distribution Holdings BV and (3) UPC Financing Partnership*, [2002] EWHC 2703 (Ch) concerning the powers of an Instructing Group and the rights of a disaffected minority under a syndicated loan agreement. It is market practice and the commercial terms of the deal, rather than legal considerations, which dictate the form and content of a loan agreement and, as it happens, the decision in this case supports a position that market practice has developed.

A postscript

A case which is less obviously relevant to a discussion about loan agreements, but in practice sometimes will be, is *Arab Monetary Fund v Hashim (No 3)* [1991] 2 AC 114 in which the House of Lords decided that the English courts would recognize the Arab Monetary Fund as having legal personality and the capacity of a body corporate. This is an important case because it reminds us that we cannot take for granted the existence, as a matter of English law, of a foreign entity (which may be a borrower or a lender) even if it appears to have all the characteristics of a corporate entity.

There are numerous international organisations which have been created by treaty. In many cases the UK is a party to the treaty, in which case there is no problem, and more often than not the International Organisations Act 1968 will have been invoked to confer both personality and immunity on such an organisation. In other cases, however, the UK may not be a party to the treaty and the Act will not apply. In such a case, the entity may not have legal personality as a matter of English law because it falls outside the general rule that a corporate entity's existence as a legal person is determined by reference to the law of the jurisdiction where it was created – a treaty organisation is formed by the treaty, not under the law of a particular jurisdiction.

The House of Lords held that the Arab Monetary Fund, an organisation created by a treaty to which the UK is not a party, would be regarded as a legal person because a decree had been passed in Dubai – which is a party to that treaty – the effect of which was to cause the fund to have legal personality in Dubai. This is still outside the general rule, but the House of Lords needed to find a credible solution and adopted one which is based on comity – the principle that the English courts will respect the view of another court with regard to matters within the jurisdiction of that other court. In doing so, the House of Lords were upholding the first instance decision of Lord Hoffman which, he admitted had as "a logical consequence ... the existence of other emanations of the fund under the laws of other member states" and added "This raises questions of trinitarian subtlety into which I am grateful that I need not enter".

An afterthought

On the day I despatched the final set of proofs of this book for amendment I met, for the first time in 20 years, s 3 of the Partnership Act 1890 which provides that if a lender makes a loan on terms that the rate of interest varies with the borrower's profits, the lender is subordinated to the borrower's other creditors in the event of the borrower's insolvency or its entering into an arrangement with its creditors to pay less than 100p in the pound!

CHAPTER 3

Bills of exchange and promissory notes

> The law relating to bills of exchange is complex, highly
> technical and very difficult to summarise. This chapter
> outlines the basic functions of bills of exchange and seeks
> to describe some of the key concepts in non-technical
> terms. It also identifies some of the types of instrument
> which might be mistaken for bills of exchange.

Bills of exchange – which I will refer to as 'bills' – were developed by
merchants and traders who needed to be able to pay each other without
the need to deliver money – coins are bulky (and easily stolen) and paper
money is a relatively recent invention. In effect, bills were the predecessors
of paper money and are 'to be treated as cash' (Lord Denning MR in
Fielding and Platt Ltd v Najjer [1969] 1 WLR 357). Bills can be payable 'at
sight' or on demand , just as paper money is – 'I promise to pay the
bearer on demand ...' still appears on our banknotes, or at a later date
which is either fixed or determinable (Bills of Exchange Act 1882 (BEA
1882), s 3(1)). (A date is determinable if it occurs after a specified period
of time after a future event which is certain to occur, for example death,
but not if the event may not occur, for example the arrival of a ship at
a particular port.) The ability to make payment by a bill which is payable
in the future enables a buyer to obtain credit and enables the seller to
obtain immediate payment by selling the bill (probably, but not
necessarily) to its bank.

Although in legal terms a bill has the same characteristics as cash, whether it is in fact as good as coins of the realm (or a banknote issued by the Bank of England) depends on the creditworthiness of the persons whose signatures are on the bill. As we shall see, there will normally be at least two signatures on a bill, very often those of the buyer and its bank, unless it is a promissory note (see below) or a cheque, which is a bill of exchange which is drawn on a bank, ie the person who draws the cheque is requesting its bank to pay the payee, and payable on demand (BEA 1882, s 73). Although many of the provisions of the Act apply to cheques – other than a cheque which is crossed 'account payee', which is a non-transferable payment order, not a negotiable instrument (BEA 1882, s 81A(1) added by the Cheques Act 1992, s 1) – I will say nothing more about them in this chapter.

The Act was enacted 'to codify the law relating to bills of exchange, cheques, and promissory notes' and codify here means, as explained by Lord Herschell in an early Court of Appeal decision on the Act (*Vagliano Bros v Governor & Co of Bank of England* (1889) 23 QBD 243 at 260), that the Act sets out the law in full so that its provisions must be construed as they stand and recourse should be had to the old common law rules only where the provisions of the Act are 'of doubtful import' or have a technical or special meaning. The Act puts it the other way round by saying that the old rules continue to apply 'save in so far as they are inconsistent with the express provisions of [this] Act' (BEA 1882, s 97(2)), but either way, the provisions of the Act prevail. Bills are infrequently encountered in the course of an international finance practice, otherwise than in the context of trade finance, but you do need to know one when you see one, because the rules which govern them are so different from those applicable to other contractual promises to pay money, particularly the rules relating to transfers of claims.

There is no point in my attempting to provide anything like a comprehensive treatment of the topic. There is far too much detail and in any event the subject is exhaustively treated in the standard works – *Byles on Bills of Exchange and Cheques* (Sweet & Maxwell, 27th edn, 2002) and *Chalmers and Guest on Bills of Exchange, Cheques and Promissory Notes* (Sweet & Maxwell, 15th edn, 1998). A more practical, but still comprehensive, treatment of the subject is to be found in William Hedley's *Bills of Exchange and Banker's Documentary Credits* (LLP, 3rd edition, 1997) and a shorter but very helpful section is to be found at pp 526–579 in Roy Goode's *Commercial Law* (Penguin Books, 2nd edn, 1995). I could not have written even this short piece without the assistance of those works and anyone who wishes to study the subject in any depth will find them indispensable.

What is a bill of exchange?

Rather than trying to compress a complex area of law into a few pages, I will offer an informal definition of a bill and look at some of the main ways in which bills differ from other promises to pay money. I will also look briefly at instruments which resemble bills or which might seem to be bills and at structures which are intended to achieve objectives similar to those which can be achieved with bills, ie payment mechanisms which provide sellers with immediate payment and buyers with time to pay.

An obvious starting point would be the Act's definition of a bill, which reads as follows:

> 'A bill of exchange is an unconditional order in writing, addressed by one person to another, signed by the person giving it, requiring the person to whom it is addressed to pay on demand or at a fixed or determinable future time a sum certain in money to or to the order of a specified person, or to bearer' (BEA 1882, s 3(1)).

The problem with this approach is that it leads directly to detailed consideration of the highly technical provisions of the Act which, although superbly drafted (as the definition demonstrates), can only be properly understood when the basic concepts are already understood. So, instead of taking this approach I will supply my own highly non-technical (and incomplete) definition and start from there:

> 'A bill is a negotiable instrument which constitutes a means whereby a buyer can give to a seller a right to receive deferred payment from the buyer's bank and the ability to turn the bill into cash by selling it to a third party, probably another bank.'

This attempt at a non-technical definition of a bill of exchange clearly raises a number of questions, three of which I will address (in reverse order):

- what is a negotiable instrument;

- how does the seller acquire rights against the buyer's bank (on the face of it there is no privity of contract between these two parties); and

- how can the seller transfer the bill to its bank?

How are bills transferred?

A bill may be payable 'to the order of a specified person' or 'to bearer'. If the latter, the bill is transferable by delivery (BEA 1882, s 31(2)); if the former, the bill is transferable by its being indorsed (signed) by the person who is the holder of the bill, ie, the payee or a transferee, and delivered to the transferee (s 31(3)). In other words, the basis of the transfer of title to a bill is the transfer of physical possession of the bill. It is here that the enormous difference between a bill of exchange and a simple promise to pay money – such as a promise to repay a loan – starts to emerge. A promise to repay a loan, or to pay any other type of debt, which is not contained in or constituted by a negotiable instrument – not all negotiable instruments are bills – can only be transferred by assignment (a subject I deal with in Chapter 6). It is irrelevant, in this context, whether or not there is an instrument – such as a 'loan note' – which, although not a negotiable instrument, evidences or contains the promise to repay; and if there is such an instrument, title to the instrument cannot be transferred by delivery.

By contrast, even if a bill payable to or to the order of a specified person – such a bill is said to be 'payable to order' – is not indorsed when its holder delivers it to a new holder, the transfer is effective. The transferee acquires whatever rights the transferor had in the bill and the right to require the transferor to indorse the bill (s 31(4)). When a bill is indorsed, the indorser 'engages' that it will be accepted and paid and that the indorser will compensate any holder or later indorser who has to pay (BEA 1882, s 55(2)).

In the case of a bearer bill, delivery alone suffices to transfer title of the bill to a new holder. The transferor of a bearer bill is not under any obligation (on the bill) to the new holder unless it does in fact indorse the bill. If it does, it becomes liable on the bill (*Fairclough v Pavia* (1854) 9 Exch 690).

How is recourse to the drawee acquired?

As I mentioned earlier, the payee of a bill (and each of its and its successors' transferees) acquires recourse to the bank – I am assuming it is a bank, but it need not be – on whom the bill was initially drawn – the buyer's bank in my informal definition of a bill, the drawee in the language of the Act. (This is so unless the bill is 'dishonoured by non-acceptance' – bills have to be presented for acceptance, but I will not be looking at this part of the Act nor at the consequences of non-acceptance.) The drawee is the person who, to use again the language of the Act, is required by the drawer of the bill to pay a certain sum to the order of a specified person or to bearer. Although there would seem to be plenty of consideration to be found – in particular, the payee (or original holder) of the bill will have provided consideration to the drawer (and the Act contains special rules with regard to this, as to which see below) – there is no privity of contract between the buyer's bank and the seller.

The enforceability of claims against the drawee of a bill, despite the absence of privity, constitutes one of the oldest and best established exceptions to the rule that contracts cannot be enforced by third parties, an exception that was well established before the Act created the statutory exception (BEA 1882, s 54). The importance of the principle is borne out by the fact that it is one of the very few exceptions to the privity rule which is expressly carved out of the Contracts (Rights of Third Parties) Act 1999 (as to which see Chapter 1 for a brief introduction and Chapter 12 for a more detailed discussion). It was regarded as impracticable to list in this Act all the old exceptions to the privity rule, but it was essential that no doubts were created with regard to bills.

The obligations of the parties to a bill are contractual, so all (or nearly all) the usual requirements for the creation of a contract – capacity, intention to create legal relations, consideration etc – need to be satisfied. With regard to consideration, however, the position is different because BEA 1882, s 27(1)(b) provides that:

'Valuable consideration for a bill may be constituted by:
(a) any consideration sufficient to support a simple contract;
(b) an antecedent debt or liability. Such a debt or liability is deemed valuable consideration whether the bill is payable on demand or at a future time'.

Paragraph (b) of this section allows a bill to give rise to binding contractual obligations even where the promisee has performed all its obligations before the bill is delivered, ie where there is only 'past consideration', which would not ordinarily support a contract. A straightforward example is a cheque written to pay a supplier of services after those services have been performed. (See *Oliver v Davis* [1949] 2 KB 727, where there was in fact no consideration.)

It sometimes happens that a third party to a transaction will add its name to a bill not for any consideration, but for the purpose of lending its name (and creditworthiness) to a party to the bill. Where this happens, the third party is known as an 'accommodation party' and if it adds its name as acceptor, the bill is known as an 'accommodation bill'. BEA 1882, s 28(2) establishes that an accommodation party is liable to any holder of the bill which is a holder for value, ie a holder which has provided consideration. If the accommodating party (the acceptor) to an accommodation bill pays the holder, it can (although the Act is silent on this issue) recover what it has paid from the accommodated party on the basis that the relationship of the two parties is that of principal and surety – see paras 807 and 812 of Chalmers & Guest.

This result is to be contrasted with the position of a voluntary guarantor who gives a guarantee for valuable consideration, for example a fee from the beneficiary of the guarantee, but not at the request of the principle debtor. Such a 'volunteer' cannot recover from the principal debtor sums it pays to the beneficiary, but would not have been liable to the creditor in the absence of consideration – see *Owen v Tate* [1976] QB 402 (and see also Chapter 5).

The decision in *Owen v Tate* is still the subject of debate, but for the practitioner it establishes an important principle – never let your client give a voluntary guarantee for consideration from the beneficiary. Not only can a voluntary guarantor not recover from the principal debtor, it cannot in these circumstances recover from the beneficiary either – all it has done is to perform its contractual obligations. (The answer is, of course, for the 'guarantor' to agree to buy the debt it wants to 'guarantee' in the event that the debtor fails to pay. This is the contractual equivalent of subrogation.)

What is a negotiable instrument?

A negotiable instrument is one which can be transferred by delivery (and indorsement where appropriate) with the result that the transferee acquires good title despite there being a defect in the transferor's title. To put this another way, and simplifying the position slightly, the purchaser of a negotiable instrument, if it purchases in good faith, for value and without notice of any defect in the transferor's title, takes free of any equities, ie competing rights, that might affect the instrument (unlike the purchaser of an ordinary promise to pay who always takes subject to equities which are sufficiently closely connected to that promise and to other equities arising before notice of the transfer is given to the promisor).

The Act did not introduce the principle of negotiability, which was an established part of the 'law merchant' – the body of law governing trading commercial activities – but it did enhance the principle by introducing the concept of a 'holder in due course' (BEA 1882, s 29(1)). This section states that:

'A holder in due course is a holder who has taken a bill complete and regular on the face of it, under the following conditions; namely,

(a) that he became a holder of it before it was overdue, and without notice that it had been dishonoured, if such was the fact: and

(b) that he took the bill in good faith and for value, and that at the time the bill was negotiated to him he had no notice of any defect in the title of the person who negotiated it.';

and is supplemented by BEA 1882, s 30(2) which creates a presumption, rebuttable by evidence of 'fraud, duress, or force and fear, or illegality', that the holder of a bill is a holder in due course. The picture is completed by BEA 1882, s 38(2) where it is stated that a holder in due course holds a bill 'free from any defect of title of prior parties, as well as from mere personal defences available to prior parties among themselves' and 'may enforce payment against all parties liable on the bill'. The effect of these provisions is that a person who appears to be liable on a bill to a holder in due course has a relatively limited range of defences, such as lack of capacity or authority, forgery or *non est factum* (which in this context means that the person who signed the bill did not realise that it was a bill). Where an elderly man was persuaded to indorse a bill thinking it was a guarantee, the holder, who had taken the bill for value and in good faith, failed in an action to recover the amount of the bill from him (*Foster v Mackinnon* (1869) LR 4 CP 704)).

It is clear that in the 19th century, if not before, bills of exchange were a popular means of obtaining money by deception. Many of the cases cited in the textbooks, and a number of the provisions of the Act, concern circumstances where bills are drawn or endorsed for fraudulent purposes or are procured by fraudulent means. For example, *Vagliano Bros v Governor & Co of Bank of England* (1889) 23 QBD 243, which I have already referred to, dealt with BEA 1882, s 7(3) which provides that where 'the payee is a fictitious or non-existing person the bill may be treated as payable to bearer'. The inclusion of such a provision speaks for itself.

Promissory notes

Most finance lawyers will encounter promissory notes (or, at least, instruments which are referred to as or perceived to be promissory notes) far more often than they encounter bills of exchange, but many such instruments will not be promissory notes within the meaning of that term in the Act. A promissory note is 'an unconditional promise in writing made by one person to another signed by the maker, engaging to pay, on demand or at a fixed or determinable future time, a sum certain in money, to, or to the order of, a specified person or to bearer' (BEA 1882, s 83(1)) and most of the provisions of the Act apply, with appropriate modifications, to promissory notes as so defined. However, a document or instrument will not automatically be regarded as a promissory note just because it contains an unconditional promise to make a payment. Apart from the need for the promise to be one to pay 'on demand or at a fixed or determinable future time', there must be an intention to create a promissory note (see the cases cited in para 2076–2078 and 2112–2114 in Chalmers and Guest). Instruments which contain promises to pay but are not promissory notes will constitute simple contracts to which the ordinary laws of contract, including the usual rules applicable to assignments of choses in action, will apply unless the instrument is a 'negotiable instrument' under the law merchant.

Loan agreements written under English law for borrowers in Latin America very often (at least, they used to) make provision for the issue by the borrower of so-called 'loan notes' which restate or summarise all or a large part of the provisions of the agreement (and this, in my experience, is a practice which is routinely observed in relation to loan agreements written under New York law). It is often said that the reason for this is that the loan notes will give to the lenders access to speedy enforcement procedures in the event that the borrower defaults. I have never had occasion to test this theory and am inclined to think that the use of loan notes in these circumstances is a habit acquired by institutions which have led or participated in many New York law transactions in Latin America, where New York law is more often than not the law of choice. Whatever the reason for the practice, it is clear that such instruments, if governed by English law, are not promissory notes within the Act, but acknowledgments of debt which are to be treated as choses in action.

One of the reasons why such loan notes are not true promissory notes is likely to be that interest on the loan is payable at a floating rate. Other reasons will be the inclusion of provisions for the grossing-up of interest payments if a withholding tax were imposed or for the acceleration of the notes otherwise than for non-payment of a repayment instalment. All of these provisions prevent the note from being a note under which 'a sum certain' is to be paid (BEA 1882, s 83(1)), although BEA 1882, s 9(1) does allow the sum payable by a bill to be 'a sum certain within the meaning of this Act' even though it is to be paid by 'stated instalments, with a provision that upon default in payment of any instalment the whole shall become due'.

Negotiability by custom

Loan notes, such as those I have just described would be treated as acknowledgments of debt, transferable as a choses in action, but there are instruments which, although outside the Act, are regarded as negotiable by custom (and thus as transferable by delivery). 'Custom' in this context is rather a vague concept, but the courts take a robust view with regard to instruments which are actively traded in the markets on the basis that they are negotiable. Thus, as early as 1902, it was said by Bingham J in *Edelstein v Schuler & Co* [1902] 2 KB 144 at 154:

'in these days usage is established much more quickly than it was in days gone by ... therefore the comparatively recent origin of this class of

security in my view creates no difficulty in the way of holding that they
were negotiable by virtue of the law merchant.'

Bingham J was speaking of bearer bonds, but what he said would no
doubt be equally applicable to old-fashioned bearer Eurobonds, FRNs
and certificates of deposit (although the clearing mechanisms now used
in the markets make the issue one of academic interest in most cases –
this is an issue I deal with more thoroughly in the Chapter 4). Nevertheless,
it cannot be supposed that the courts would come to the aid of 'loan
notes' which do not appear to be intended to be negotiable and are not
generally treated as such. Similar instruments are encountered in a variety
of contexts – it is always important not to use instruments whose
negotiablility (or lack of it) cannot be established with certainty.

Avals, indorsements 'without recourse' and forfaiting

A person may indorse a bill otherwise than as a drawer or acceptor and
thereby incur the liabilities of an indorser to a holder in due course (BEA
1882, s 56 whose heading – 'Stranger Signing Bill as Indorser' – tells us
that it does not apply to regular indorsers, ie holders who indorse bills
in the course of transferring title). However, such an indorser would not
be liable to the payee of the bill who cannot be a holder in due course
– see BEA 1882, s 29(1) and see also Goode, pages 551–555. A similar,
but more extensive, concept, that of an 'aval', is found in countries which
are signatories to the 1930 Geneva Convention – the UK is not a
signatory – which provides that payment of a bill of exchange may be
guaranteed by an aval, namely the signing of the bill under the words
'good as aval' or an equivalent formulation (Arts 30, 31 and 32). An
aval benefits not just a holder in due course (or the equivalent) but also
the holder for whose benefit it is given and prior holders (if any).

Another concept, which is found both in English law and in the Geneva
Convention, is that of indorsing a bill or note 'without recourse' (sans
recours). This is expressly contemplated in BEA 1882, s 16(1) and is
permitted by Art 15 of the Geneva Convention. Avals and indorsements
without recourse are vital ingredients in the international financing
structure known as 'forfaiting'. In the basic form of this structure, an
importer will pay the seller by the issue of a note (or series of notes

maturing in sequence) bearing an aval given by a financial institution (based in the importer's country) which the seller will indorse 'without recourse' to a financing institution in the seller's country.

Many years ago, I was involved in a forfaiting transaction under which the sale of a washing machine factory by an Italian exporter was being financed. The commercial contract required all the materials for the factory, the workforce and their equipment and food (and wine, no doubt) to be transported by train from Italy to the buyer in Russia! The complexity of these arrangements exacerbated fears that the buyer might not pay the notes because of default by the exporter. Unlike bills, the notes the subject of a forfaiting transaction may form part of the commercial contract and attract contract risk by association; in other words, if the buyer is dissatisfied it may decline to pay the notes when they mature.

A separate contract

As the courts and the textbooks repeatedly stress, where payment obligations under a commercial contract are effected by means of a bill, the bill creates a new contract which is separate from, and additional to, the commercial contract. A bill of exchange is a means of making payment under another contract and is to be treated as cash. The obligations of the parties to a bill will not, however, always be entirely unaffected by circumstances affecting the commercial contract, although the courts will not regard the enforceability of a bill as contingent on performance of the commercial contract (see *James Lamont & Co Ltd v Hyland Ltd* [1950] 1 KB 585). What will affect the enforceability of a bill, by providing a defence to the drawer of a bill, is a total failure of consideration under the related contract (*Elliott v Crutilley* [1906] AC 7). But, if the bill has been negotiated, the drawer could not set up total failure of consideration as a defence against a claim for payment by a holder who has given value (see, for example, *Banco di Roma v Orru* [1973] 2 Lloyd's Rep 505) and such a holder's knowledge of the circumstances may well be irrelevant (but see Hedley, 3rd edn, pp 86–88). Where there is a partial failure of consideration, the position is more complex, raising issues outside the scope of this chapter.

CHAPTER 4

Bond issues – a banking lawyer's perspective

> **In this chapter, I take a look at bond issues from a banking lawyer's perspective. Banking lawyers (or at least one of them) find some of the features of a bond issue different, if not puzzling. This chapter seeks to identify some of the key structural differences between bond issues and syndicated loans, and ends with a suggestion as to how a new legal structure could be used for bond issues, a structure which would clarify the rights of bondholders and facilitate the creation of security over bonds.**

In Chapter 3 I said that 'there is no point in my attempting to provide anything like a comprehensive treatment of the topic'. The same is, of course, true of this chapter's topic, so what I will do is to look at the structure of an international English law bond issue and identify some of the key structural differences between a bond issue and a syndicated loan, as well as some of the features of a bond issue which strike a banking lawyer – at least, this is how they strike me – as different, if not puzzling. To conclude this introduction, I would add that the subject matter is so complex and changes so rapidly that nothing I say should be taken as a wholly accurate or complete statement of law or practice as at any given date.

Key differences

What I perceive to be the key points of difference between a ('plain vanilla') bond issue and a syndicated loan all flow from the fact that when an issuer seeks to raise money through a bond issue – and I am ignoring private placements, high yield issues, securitisations and all other variants on the base case – the issuer is seeking funds from investors (not lenders) who may or may not be banks or financial institutions. Bonds are debt instruments which constitute investments – as they say in the advertisements, 'the value of bonds and any income from them may fall as well as rise and investors may not get back the amount originally invested' – that can be bought as an investment or simply bought as something to be traded. Despite the increasing convergence of the loan and debt markets, loans (other than 'distressed loans') are not yet generally regarded as investments, although the tide is turning.

Thus, a bond issue will:

* utilise a structure which ensures that bonds are easily tradeable – in contrast to loan agreements, where it has been necessary for transfer procedures to be grafted on to the basic structure;

* as a consequence, contemplate the settlement of trades through a 'clearing system' – here technological change has combined with other factors, primarily the regulatory environment, to transform the way in which bond issues are structured;

* be marketed to a more or less extensive investor base, ranging from professional investors to as large a part of the public as applicable laws and regulations permit – most original participants in syndicated loans are banks and financial institutions;

* be made by an issuer which has sufficient credit standing to attract investors, a characteristic nowadays summed up in the phrase 'investment grade', although the issuers of bonds under variant structures, such as high yield issues or securitisations, may well not be of investment grade – just as borrowers may not be;

* be arranged by one or more investment banks which will 'underwrite' the issue – it or they will commit to place the bonds on behalf of the issuer and to purchase any bonds not sold into the market, but will not generally expect to be left holding any bonds, save for trading

(as opposed to investment) purposes – whereas, historically, the arrangers of a syndicated loan have expected to retain a significant portion of the loan;

- make provision for the issuer's agent – the 'paying agent' – to handle the flow of funds to and from the investors – in a syndicated loan, the agent is invariably the lenders' agent; and

- as a result of all the foregoing points of difference (and others), be documented (very differently from a syndicated loan) under either a 'fiscal agent' structure or a trust structure.

Bonds are traded through clearing systems

It is the essence of a bond issue that the bonds are easy to trade and bearer bonds, which are negotiable by delivery, are the starting point. A bearer bond in traditional form – a promise to pay a specified amount to the holder of the bond – will not be a bill of exchange (because it will contain, for example, 'grossing-up' provisions to cover withholding taxes and 'events of default' permitting the bonds to be accelerated – here bond issues are similar to syndicated loans), but will be negotiable by custom under the law merchant (see Chapter 3, page 33). A registered bond in traditional form, on the other hand, is one in respect of which the 'holder' of the bond is not the person who has physical possession of the bond, but the person whose name appears in a register maintained by a registrar which is the agent of the issuer. Thus, it would seem, title to a registered bond is transferred by means of the making of an entry (pursuant to a request to that effect from the seller) in such a register on the basis that the entries in the register are conclusive as to who owns the bonds, regardless of any notice of competing equitable interests or any notice of any previous loss or theft. In effect, the usual terms of a registered bond issue purport to confer a form of contractual negotiability on the bonds.

One analysis of what is happening is that the holder of a registered bond has, all things being equal, an enforceable claim against the issuer on the basis of the 'offer to the world' principle established by *Carlill v Carbolic Smoke Ball Co* [1893] 1 QB 256 (see Chapter 1, page 5), the issuer's offer to pay the registered holder being accepted by the action of the holder in seeking registration. However, if this analysis were correct, a new debt would arise each time a registered bond is transferred. This would be very unhelpful because it would give rise to concerns about matters as different as the potential need for exchange control consent (or similar requirements) and insolvency issues. An alternative analysis is that the request by the seller to the registrar to enter the name of the buyer in the register operates as an assignment of the seller's claim on the issuer. The difficulty with this analysis is (to simplify the issues somewhat) that even if the entry on the register is regarded as notice of assignment to the issuer, the holder takes subject to equities arising between the issuer and the initial holder of the bond, and perhaps other previous holders – the risk that negotiability removes. This too is an unsatisfactory outcome and there are additional difficulties under either analysis where an entry on the register is the result of fraud. It is not clear that there is a general consensus as to whether one of these analyses or some other analysis is correct.

Under current market practice, however, it is usually the case that bonds which are issued with the intention that they will or can be traded in the international capital markets are represented by a 'global bond' which is held by a depositary institution for account of one or (usually) both of the two European based international clearing systems, Euroclear and Clearstream. Thus, an individual bond which is held in one or both of the clearing systems – in the US, DTC performs a similar function (and bonds may be held in DTC via a nominee for Euroclear and/or Clearstream) – is represented by:

- an instrument (the global bond) which is held neither by the person which in economic terms is the 'holder' of the bond nor by either of the clearing systems, but by a third party – the 'common depositary' – which is a bank acting as nominee for each of the clearing systems; and

- an entry in the bondholder's account (or, more likely, the account of the bondholder's bank or other agent) with the clearing system of its choice.

Global bonds

When an account holder with a clearing system buys a bond, it acquires no proprietary interest in the bond because it neither takes delivery of the (bearer) bond nor has its name entered on the ownership register of the (registered) bond – all that happens is that its (or its agent's) account is credited with ownership of a bond of the amount and type in question. With regard to bearer bonds, this is a long way from the fundamental concept of negotiability – that title to an instrument passes by delivery. The only physical instrument – the global bond – remains in possession of the common depositary and title to an interest in this instrument passes, it would seem, when matching instructions have been given to a clearing system. It is a strange state of affairs in which entitlements in respect of an instrument which is not negotiable – since global bonds never change hands in practice and can only be transferred to another common depositary, they can hardly be negotiable – are actively traded as if they were negotiable instruments, which they are not (if only because there is no instrument which is delivered to effect the transfer).

Ironically, these practices arose in response to extrinsic pressures rather than out of concerns for the intrinsic validity of the procedures themselves. For both regulatory reasons, under the predecessor of Regulation S (see below) and to ensure compliance with TEFRA (see below) – a requirement that still remains – issuers had to ensure that for an initial 'lock up' (or 'distribution compliance') period (originally of 90 days), bonds were represented by temporary global bonds which were not exchangeable for a permanent global bond or for definitives – ie authentic, security printed bonds – until the lock-up period had ended and the persons entitled to the bonds had certified that they were not US persons. The need to use temporary global bonds prompted the investment banks (and their clients) to extend their use so as to reduce (if not obviate) the need to procure expensive and inconvenient security printed bonds which would be left (hopefully not to rot) in the common depositary's vaults. It is the impact and continuing relevance of US securities and tax laws, which here were the catalyst for fundamental changes in market practice and legal structures (as they were with regard to the development of registered bonds – see below), that is one of the most striking differences between the bond market and the syndicated loan market.

(Although it was, of course, United States regulatory policy in the mid-1960s – both the payment of interest on deposits and the availability of credit were restricted – that gave an early boost to the then nascent Eurocurrency market – see the Appendix for a brief description of these events, which was shortly thereafter to be given an even bigger boost by the dramatic increase in the price of oil which occurred in 1973 – see Chapter 9, pages 116–118 for a discussion of the consequences.)

Offers to the public and 'prospectus liability'

As well as the contractual documentation entered into by the issuer, underwriters/arrangers and fiscal agent/trustee in connection with a bond issue, there is another key document – the 'prospectus', 'offering memorandum' or 'offering circular', as it is variously called. This is the document – I will call it the offering circular – the purpose of which is to induce investors to subscribe for the bonds whose terms it describes. As well as describing the terms of the issue, an offering circular will describe, in considerable detail, the issuer and its history, business, management, past and proposed activities, and recent (and projected) financial performance. Where an offer of securities is an 'offer to the public', in the sense that, in general terms, individuals and corporate entities which are not professional investors are being invited to subscribe, the form and content of the offering memorandum will have to comply with detailed regulatory requirements. In the UK, any initial offering of securities to the public will be subject to:

- the provisions of the Public Offers of Securities Regulations 1995 (SI 1995/1537) ('the POS Regulations') unless the issue falls within the list of exemptions provided for in reg 7, the first and most significant of which covers securities which are offered to persons whose businesses involve them in buying or selling securities; or

- if the offer is to be listed by the UK Listing Authority, the applicable listing rules and the duty of disclosure provisions of the Financial Services and Markets Act 2000 (FSMA 2000), section 80.

Both the POS Regulations and the FSMA 2000 regime impose compensation obligations on the authors of offering circulars which mislead those who subscribe for securities and the authors will, in any event, owe a duty of care to subscribers. It is uncertain whether the authors of an offering circular owe a duty of care to holders who acquire shares in the market rather than by subscription.

On the other hand, neither the POS Regulations nor the FSMA 2000 regime apply to loan agreements, so the liability of the authors of an 'Information Memorandum' prepared in connection with a syndicated loan is limited to common law liability under the principle established in *Hedley Byrne v Heller* [1964] AC 465, where it was held that a person who suffers loss as a result of reliance on a negligent misstatement of fact can recover damages from the maker of the statement, provided, of course, that the maker of the statement owes that person a duty of care.

In the US it is section 5(a) of the Securities Act of 1933 which sets out the basic position that, unless a registration statement is in effect – a registration statement being the means whereby more extensive disclosure requirements than those applicable in the UK are imposed in the US – it is unlawful to:

> 'make use of any means or instruments of transportation or communication in interstate commerce [which is defined to include commerce involving any foreign country] or the mails to sell such security through the use or medium of any prospectus or otherwise.'

Those who subscribe for securities have an express right to compensation and subsequent purchasers may have the right to claim damages both under other sections of the 1933 Act and under the infamous rule 10(b)5, made under the US Securities Act of 1934, section 10(b)). Rule 10(b)5 contains prohibitions on the employment of any device, scheme or artifice to defraud, or acts or practices which operate as a fraud or the making of untrue or misleading statements, and is generally regarded as applying to any registered SEC offering and any offering pursuant to rule 144A. Where it does apply, the practice is for counsel to both the issuer and the underwriters to issue letters to the underwriters which effectively constitute assurances that counsel, having reviewed the offering circular and other relevant materials, is not aware of any non-compliance with rule 10(b)5. The rule does not, however, apply to an issue which falls within the 'safe harbor' provisions of Regulation S – offshore transactions which are not marketed in the United States.

There is no short and simple way to describe the effects of US securities legislation and the foregoing summary does not even scratch the surface of a complex regime which, in the eyes of the US authorities, is of worldwide application. US securities laws can never be ignored in the context of bond issues and, to make matters worse, it is not just US securities legislation which has an impact on English law bond issues. As I mentioned earlier, the US tax legislation known as TEFRA (the Tax Equality and Fiscal Responsibility Act of 1982) had, and continues to have, an impact on how transactions are structured because, if its requirements are not complied with, sanctions are imposed on an issuer of bearer bonds and a tax advantage otherwise available to a non-resident bondholder may become unavailable.

Issuers and underwriters

The issue of bonds is one of the three principal ways in which a corporate or sovereign entity can obtain medium or long term finance from the international capital markets, the other ways to do this being the borrowing of money from a bank or syndicate of banks or the issue of shares. This oversimplifies the position – companies borrow money from shareholders and countries raise money in their domestic markets but, to make the point another way, bond issues are one of the core products in international finance. Generally speaking, only borrowers/issuers whose debt instruments are (or will be) rated Baa or better by one of the established rating agencies – usually Standard and Poor's or Moody's – have access to both the loan and bond markets. Entities whose debt instruments have or would have a lower rating can usually only raise funds through borrowing or through the issue of equity or convertible debt issues. Again, there is plenty of oversimplification here – an issuer will have separate ratings for its short-term and its medium-/long-term debt – and there are many ways in which funds can be raised in specialised markets. Currently important examples are:

- 'high yield' bonds, which are used in specific contexts, such as acquisition finance; and

- securitisation, where revenue streams as diverse as mortgage repayments, credit card receivables and natural gas sales proceeds are used to collateralise issues of debt instruments.

Until relatively recently, the role of the underwriters of a bond issue was quite different to that of the arrangers of a syndicated loan. A group of banks arranging a syndicated loan would expect to make and retain, on a more or less permanent basis, all or a significant part of the loan and, in the case of a revolving facility, the commitment to lend of the banks who participated in the facility would continue throughout the life of the facility (subject to the terms of the facility). A group of underwriters, however, will generally arrange or participate in a bond issue with the intention of not ending up as holders of the bonds – an underwriter's role is that of a backstop who takes bonds only if the market proves unwilling to do so. In this context, nothing has changed for the arrangers of bond issues but for the arrangers of loan facilities, the position is now rather different.

Revolving facility or medium-term notes

The transfer procedures in a contemporary syndicated loan agreement – whether it is a term loan or a revolving facility – are designed to ensure both that the arrangers can easily 'sell down' their initial exposure to the borrower and that their obligations to lend can also be transferred. The arranging banks may well start out with the intention of selling the whole of their exposure as soon as practicable, perhaps even before the loans are made. The difficulty of 'pricing' the sale of obligations, and the natural reluctance of borrowers to relinquish control over who it is that has promised to make the loans, inhibit the creation of an active secondary market in 'undrawn commitments', and this reflects another key difference between bond issues and loan agreements. A bond issue is a once-only affair – bonds do not carry with them a further or continuing obligation to subscribe, whereas loan agreements often do. Even here, however, the loan and bond markets are converging, so that a borrower/issuer of sufficiently high credit standing can choose between a revolving loan facility and a medium-term note programme, which is, in effect, a framework under which a series of bond issues can be made. Once an initial offering circular has been produced, further drawdowns can be made on the basis of a brief pricing supplement describing the terms of the drawdown, together with a supplemental offering circular, if this is required to update the original.

Fiscal agents and trustees

There are two different ways in which a bond issue may be structured – the fiscal agent structure and the trust structure. Under both structures there will be a 'principal paying agent' which is the agent of the issuer through whom payments to the bondholders will be made. This is to be contrasted with the position under a syndicated loan, where the 'agent' will invariably be the agent of the banks. Under the fiscal agency structure, the bondholders as a group have no representative – the fiscal agent is the issuer's agent; under the trust structure the bondholders can, in a non-technical sense, be said to be represented by the trustee because the trustee is the route whereby the bondholders can communicate with the issuer and there will be a provision that states that the trustee will hold the benefit of a promise by the issuer to pay the principal of and interest on the bonds on trust for the bondholders. This provision operates as a declaration of trust, one of the two ways in which a trust (your last will and testament aside) can be created – see Chapter 13, pages 184–190 and 196–200 for a discussion of how trusts can be created and how agency structures differ from trust structures.

The trustee's discretions

The trustee will have fairly wide discretions, such as whether to call for early payment where events of default have occurred, but will, in practice, convene a bondholders' meeting and seek instructions from the bondholders as to how such discretions should be exercised – there are similarities here between the trustee's role and the role of the agent bank in a syndicated loan. There is also a very significant difference in that in an English law bond issue a meeting of bondholders – and this is also the case under the fiscal agency structure – has very wide powers to modify the terms of the bonds, powers which extend to the reduction or cancellation of the issuer's payment obligations. I am not aware of any syndicated loan agreements having contained such provisions. It is only relatively recently, as a result of banks' experiences in sovereign and corporate restructurings, that syndicated loan agreements have come to include provisions permitting certain amendments of the agreement to be made otherwise than with the concurrence of all the banks – see Chapter 9, pages 118–121 for a discussion of this and related issues.

The bondholders' rights

Although the powers of the bondholders as a group are the same whether the fiscal agency or trust structure is used, the rights of individual bondholders under the two structures are quite different. Where there is a trustee, it will have the right to sue for payment of the bonds in the event of default and the trust deed will contain a provision – the no action provision – to the effect that an individual bondholder can itself enforce its claim against the issuer only if the trustee, having become entitled (after a default in payment) to enforce its claim against the issuer, fails to do so within a reasonable period of time after being requested to enforce that claim. As before, it is not immediately clear how the bondholders have acquired their claims – is it by assignment (of a beneficial interest under a trust) or through an offer to the world (becoming a beneficiary by procuring the making of an entry on a register)? – nor what sort of claim they have (under a global bond structure).

Where there is a fiscal agent, the bond will provide that an individual bondholder may call for early repayment of the bonds it holds in the event of default. Under traditional structures, bondholders would have had or been able to obtain 'definitive' bonds, and an individual bondholder would have been able to exercise this right. However, the global bond structure which is now often used leaves the bondholders with no evidence of their claims against the issuer other than their (or their agents') accounts with the clearing system. For this reason, it is now customary for an issuer's obligation to be supported by a deed poll, under which the issuer assumes a direct obligation to pay the bondholders if a default has occurred. The rights this provides to the bondholders are clearly not acquired by assignment, but are acquired when default occurs. It would seem, therefore, that under the fiscal agency structure, new debts arise just when the issuer defaults. This is a very unsatisfactory state of affairs; the default may occur shortly after the issuer has entered into bankruptcy proceedings – not a time for fresh obligations to be assumed!

An alternative analysis

The most striking feature of a registered bond issue, from the perspective of contract law, is that registered bonds do not usually contain a promise to pay – holders are entitled to receive certificates that evidence their entitlement to receive payment. As we have seen, a holder's entitlement to receive payment arises either as the beneficiary of a trust (where the trust structure is used) or under a deed poll made by the issuer (where the fiscal agency structure is used) and in both cases the transfer of title issues arise. (Once again, it was US law that led to the use of registered bonds which developed in the context of private placements into the US in response to certain TEFRA requirements.)

It seems to me that correct analysis – but it is not an appealing one – is that the purchaser of a registered bond is not purchasing a debt but is, in effect, acquiring an entitlement to participate in a process whereby money which was paid to the issuer – by the subscribers – is repaid. Looked at in this light, registered bonds are more like registered shares than bonds, a conclusion reached by Dr Joanna Benjamin in her contribution – 'Recharacterisation Risk and Conflict of Laws' (p 37) – to The Oxford Colloquium on Collateral and Conflict of Laws, *JIBFL Special Supplement*, September 1998. A contractual framework is established under which bundles of rights – labelled 'bonds' – can be 'transferred' from one person to another in the sense that a purchaser – a new 'holder' – acquires a bundle of rights identical to that held by the seller, the fundamental rights being the entitlement to receive interest and the principal amount of the bond (at maturity) through the paying agent process. The nearest thing to a debt in this process is the issuer's promise to put the principal paying agent in funds so that the bondholders can receive their entitlements. Moreover, although bearer bonds undoubtedly constitute debts, the payee is the Common Depositary and, like the holder of a registered bond, the holder of a bearer bond has, it seems to me, acquired an entitlement to participate in a process rather than an interest in a bond – a rather fragile process in relation to which a trustee or a deed poll is the glue.

A new legal structure

By way of a conclusion I will put forward three propositions (which may, to some extent, run counter to the received wisdom on these matters):

- in a conventional bond issue there are no negotiable instruments;

- as a result, the Contracts (Rights of Third Parties) Act 1999 (C(RTP)A 1999) can be used to cause global bonds (which are governed by English law) to confer on bondholders direct rights against the issuer – the Act does not apply (s 6) to a contract on a bill of exchange, promissory note or other negotiable instrument (see Chapter 12); and

- the areas of legal risk which should concern bondholders have nothing to do with negotiability and everything to do with transfer, delivery and settlement risk.

In an issue of registered bonds, the question of negotiability does not arise (irrespective of which analysis of the legal structure is correct) and, as I have mentioned, a bearer global bond cannot be negotiable because it will, in practice, never change hands and because its transferability is restricted. There is, of course, no case law directly on the point, but the basic position under the law merchant is that instruments come to be regarded as negotiable not just because the market regards them as negotiable but where the instruments are used in a large volume of transactions (see the judgment of Bingham J in *Edelstein v Schuler & Co* [1902] 2 KB 144 where (just over 100 years ago) he said (at 154):

'... in these days usage is established much more quickly than it was in days gone by; more depends on the number of the transactions which help to create it than on the time over which the transactions are spread.'

In any event, if it is helpful for a global bond not to be negotiable, so that the Act's provisions can be relied on, an express provision to this effect can be written into the bond.

The Contracts (Rights of Third Parties) Act 1999, s 1, provides that a third party may enforce a term of a contract if the contract expressly provides that it may. If a global bond is written as a contract, between the issuer and the common depositary, which is expressed to benefit the bondholders as a class:

- the bondholders will have enforceable rights against the issuer;
- the clearing systems can function as they do now; and
- there will be no need for deed polls to be used.

Three ancillary issues need to be considered, the first two of which arise out of provisions of the Act. Firstly, in order to acquire a right to enforce the terms of the bond, a bondholder will need to have 'communicated [its] assent to the [issuer]' – C(RTP)A 1999, s 2(1)(*a*) – and, secondly, a contractual regime will have to be substituted (as the Act permits) for the statutory provisions, which would require the consent of all bondholders for any amendment (to the terms of the bond) which would extinguish or alter the bondholders' rights – for a review of s 2(1) and other provisions of the Act, see Chapter 12. The first of these issues can be addressed through a communication given by a subscriber or purchaser to the issuer through the clearing system and the usual provisions dealing with power of a meeting of bondholders to modify the terms of the bond can constitute the contractual regime for amendments. Finally, a consequence of this analysis is that a bond issue made under a trust structure could confer on the bondholders direct rights which might conflict with the usual 'no action' provisions. The solution to this will be to write the bond so that the rights it confers on the bondholders are only those they are intended to have.

In practical terms, these proposals are not as radical as they might seem in that the market's existing practices would remain virtually unchanged – only the communication of assent required by the C(RTP)A 1999 will require a small adjustment to existing practices. What they might do, if implemented, is clear the decks – get negotiability off the agenda – and remove the need for the very complex analysis (see below) that is currently required in order to establish and characterise bondholders' claims.

A postscript

The conventional analysis – which I have to confess to having studied only after developing my own analysis – is that the holders of bonds have co-ownership interests in the related interest owned by their custodian/account holder/broker. This is because the needs of the market require that a holder's rights should be treated as proprietary, but at the same time the holder's relationship should be confined to its immediate intermediary and the:

> 'only way in which both market needs can be met is by characterising [the holder's] interest as a derivative interest of the same character as the interest from which it is derived' (see The Nature and Transfer of Rights in Dematerialised and Immobilised Securities, Roy Goode, (1996) 4 JIBFL 167).

I find this market-driven analysis, which leads to a chain of trust relationships, unconvincing, but it is one which has found favour with legislators in Belgium and Luxembourg (for the benefit of the clearing systems) and in the US (in the UCC). I do, however, agree with Professor Goode's conclusion that, in the context of a conventional, permanent global bond structure, bondholders:

> 'have no claims against the issuer or a higher-tier intermediary but are entitled to the fruits of the securities entitlement coming into the hands of their custodian.' ((1996) 4 JIBFL 167 at 173).

Whatever the correct analysis, there remains a third party rights issue to be dealt with. If a permanent global bond is not a negotiable instrument, the Act will apply and, by virtue of C(RTP)A 1999, s 1(1)(b), the bond will confer enforceable third party rights on the bondholders if its language is apt to do so – as in 'the issuer shall pay to the bondholders ... ' – unless on a proper construction of the bond it appears that this was not intended. It would be better to use the Act and be done with it.

CHAPTER 5

Guarantees of loans and bonds

The law relating to guarantees is another topic which is complex, technical and difficult to summarise, although less so than the law relating to bills of exchange. In this chapter, I first identify the key objectives which, from a creditor's perspective, are to be achieved in a guarantee, then look briefly at some contracts which have features in common with guarantees and finally alert you to a trap for the unwary.

A guarantee is a document which makes lawyers hope that the precedent they are starting with is a good one and that not too many questions are asked – by their client or by the opposition – about what this, or that, provision means or why it is there. In order to give a full answer to such questions, most of us – and this certainly includes me – would need to check the position in one of the leading works of reference on the subject. The task of remembering the purpose of a particular provision or why it is worded as it is, is probably easier if you have in your mind a clear picture of the key objectives which, from the creditor's perspective, are to be achieved in a guarantee. As well as knowing which provisions should be in a guarantee (and why), a finance lawyer needs to be aware of the ways in which a creditor's intention to obtain third party protection by way of guarantee may be thwarted. I will consider some contracts which are not guarantees (although they have some similar characteristics) and will end by alerting you to a major trap for the unwary that exists in relation to guarantees, a trap which arises not out of the provisions of the guarantee, but out of the circumstances in which it is given. First, however, I will describe and discuss what I perceive to be the key objectives of a guarantee which, I will assume, is given in respect of indebtedness incurred by way of loan or through the issue of bonds.

The key objectives

The creditor's key objectives can be summarised in four brief propositions:

- a guarantee is a contract under which the guarantor is to assume contractually binding obligations;

- the guarantor promises to the other party to the contract (the creditor) that a third party (the debtor) will pay debts it owes to the creditor;

- the guarantor is to remain liable until the creditor has been paid in full; and

- the guarantor should waive the various defences otherwise available to it as a 'surety' (that is as someone who is answerable for the performance of an obligation by another).

A guarantee is a contract

A guarantee is a special form of contract and all the usual rules regarding the formation of contracts apply to guarantees; for a brief review of these rules, see Chapter 1. In particular, the creditor must provide consideration if the guarantor's promise is to be enforceable (unless the guarantee is contained in a deed, which for reasons I will mention later, it often will be). The nature of the consideration provided by the creditor can determine one of the more important characteristics of a guarantee, namely whether or not it can be terminated by the guarantor; this is something else I will look at later. As well as the usual rules, there is a requirement that a guarantee (but not an indemnity) must be in writing. The Statute of Frauds 1677, s 4 provides that no proceedings may be taken to enforce a 'promise to answer for the debt default or miscarriages of another person' unless 'the agreement ... or some memorandum or note thereof' is in writing and signed by or on behalf of the promisor.

It is easy to remember that an indemnity need not be in writing, but it would be foolish, for two reasons, ever to rely on this well-known principle. First, it is not as easy as it might seem to decide whether a particular contract is a contract 'in the nature of an original obligation' and thus outside s 4 – see *Harburg India Rubber Comb Co v Martin* [1902] 1 KB 778, CA, at 784. For instance, a promise to put someone in funds to pay a bill of exchange at maturity given in consideration of that person's agreement to accept the bills, has been held to be outside s 4 – see *Guild & Co v Conrad* [1894] 2 QB 885, CA, but in the *Harburg* case, a promise to provide a bill of exchange for a debt due from a company to a third party was held to be within s 4.

Another illustration – in fact, a number of illustrations – of the difficulty in deciding whether an obligation is or is not within s 4 – can be found in the Court of Appeal's decision in *Actionstrength Ltd v International Glass Engineering IN. GL. EN SpA* [2001] EWCA Civ 1477, [2002] 1 WLR 566. One of the tests is, it appears, whether the promisor's payment is to be made out of its own funds, which will bring the obligation within section 4, or out of funds of the debtor (the other person), which will take the obligation out of s 4. In the course of his judgment, Simon Brown LJ remarked 'a relatively recent authority which provides a convenient starting point for the determination of this issue is this court's decision in ...' and cited an unreported case. I will share my views with you on the subject of unreported cases at the end of this chapter.

Determination of whether an oral commitment is or is not within s 4 requires investigation of a black hole your client will never want you to have to investigate, unless you have been called on to sort out someone else's mistake. The second reason for not relying on the fact that indemnities need not be in writing is that it will always be an uphill struggle to demonstrate the existence of an oral contract. Lawyers should place reliance on the existence of an oral contract only as a last resort.

Although consideration is necessary to make a guarantor's promise enforceable, it is not necessary for the consideration to be described in the guarantee. There was once a rule to this effect, but this was abolished nearly 150 years ago by the Mercantile Law Amendment Act 1856, s 3. In fact, it can be harmful to describe the consideration in a guarantee because it may prove impossible, under the rules of evidence, to use oral evidence to cure a defect in the description. For example, perfectly good consideration might accidentally be described as if it were past consideration and this might lead to the failure of proceedings taken to enforce the guarantee. One way to address these issues is to have a guarantee executed as a deed; consideration is then unnecessary and there is no risk of producing a defective description of whatever consideration there is.

The third party will pay

The distinction between guarantees and indemnities is of no real importance where the primary purpose of the agreement which the promisor enters into is to provide to the creditor recourse to the promisor in relation to debts owing or to be owed to the creditor by a third party. Even if the language used is that of an indemnity, the Statute of Frauds 1677, s 4 will apply and, whether or not the contract is described as a guarantee or an indemnity, the promisor will be a surety.

Any person who is secondarily liable to put a creditor in the position it would have been in had the principal debtor performed its obligations is a surety. Such secondary liability may be expressly assumed, as in a guarantee or in a mortgage, or inferred from the circumstances, as where a lender knows that, as between two co-debtors, it is intended that one shall be primarily liable and the other only secondarily - see *Rouse v Bradford Banking Co* [1894] AC 586, a case which it is better to cite than to read. This has a very important, practical consequence. Where two or more borrowers of a loan, or issuers of bonds, are jointly liable in respect of the loan, or the bonds, the contract regulating or creating their indebtedness must, for safety's sake, treat each of them as a surety *vis-à-vis* the other(s).

Sureties have a variety of rights which, if not properly dealt with, can operate to the detriment of the creditor – as we shall see. So, if you are not sure who is the principal debtor and who is the surety, you should treat them both as sureties. (Although it has been held by the House of Lords – in *Duncan, Fox & Co v North and South Wales Bank* (1880) 6 App Cas 1 – that, so far as the creditor is concerned, there is no contract of suretyship if the creditor is not on notice of any actual or implied suretyship, it would seem likely that the existence of joint debtors would constitute constructive notice of a contract of suretyship.)

Rights of appropriation

Where a surety is a guarantor, its liability is in principle no less and no greater with regard to the guaranteed obligations than that of the person whose performance it has guaranteed. Among other things, this 'co-extensiveness principle', as it is sometimes called, makes it important that the terms of a guarantee should recognise that debtors and creditors, including guarantors and the beneficiaries of guarantees, always have rights of appropriation. In other words, where a debtor pays an amount to a creditor, the debtor may specify which of several debts it is discharging (in whole or in part) and, if it fails to specify how the payment is to be applied, the creditor may choose − a position (which can be varied by contract) sometimes summed up as 'first right to debtor, second right to creditor'. This is important to a surety, and thus to the beneficiary of a guarantee, because of the so-called rule in *Clayton's case* (*Devaynes v Noble, Clayton's case* [1814-23] All ER Rep 1), which holds that where no debtor or creditor election has been made, whether by contract or at the time of payment or receipt, payments to a creditor discharge the debtor's debts to the creditor in the order in which they were incurred − 'first in, first out'.

As a result, a guarantee will usually give to the guarantor the right to open a new account with the debtor − or to be treated as if it had done so even if it fails to do so − if the guarantor's obligations terminate or if demand for payment is made of the guarantor. In the absence of such provision, a subsequent payment to the creditor might, because of the rule in *Clayton's case*, reduce the amount the creditor could claim from the guarantor - the 'frozen' amount owed by the guarantor at the time of termination or demand would be reduced by the subsequent payment. Opening a new account defeats the rule − strictly speaking a presumption − because the rule only applies to debits and credits made to a 'running account', that is, a single account which is used to record a debtor-creditor relationship in the way that a current account does.

If a guarantee does not contain the 'new account' provision, the rule in *Clayton's case* could operate to the benefit of a guarantor who has guaranteed a specific debt which is evidenced by an entry on a running account or a guarantor whose 'continuing' guarantee is determined by revocation or otherwise (so that the guarantee has come to an end and has ceased to cover new debits to the guaranteed account − see Andrews

& Millett, *Law of Guarantees* (Sweet & Maxwell, 3rd edn, 2000, p 279). However limited the application of *Clayton's case*, do not (if you are representing the proposed beneficiary of a guarantee) be persuaded to omit the 'new account' provision; if properly drafted, it should do no harm even where it is not needed.

Continuing obligations

Guarantees usually contain another provision which is generally regarded as addressing issues raised by *Clayton's case*, this being the provision to the effect that the guarantor's obligations shall be continuing obligations which shall not be satisfied or discharged by any intermediate payment or settlement of the guaranteed obligations and which shall continue in effect until the discharge in full of the guaranteed obligations. The aim of this provision is to make it clear that the guarantor is to be liable for the ultimate balance owed by the debtor to the creditor, so that the guarantee covers whatever is owing irrespective of any presumed appropriation to the contrary. Again, there is no reason for a creditor to agree to omit this provision even if it and the 'new account' provision both address the same issue.

Payment in full

It would seem to be stating the obvious to say that the beneficiary of a guarantee wants to be paid in full, but this apparently simple objective is threatened by a number of obstacles. In particular, the parties have to establish what it is that is being guaranteed and the guarantee has to be worded so as to achieve the desired objective.

Specific debts

The simplest form of guarantee would be one under which the guarantor guarantees to the creditor the payment by the debtor of a specific debt. Not a very likely circumstance, perhaps, but one which could occur in practice, particularly in a trade context; for example, a parent company may guarantee its subsidiary's obligations to pay the purchase price under a contract for the sale of goods. In this context, two issues immediately spring to mind. The first issue is that it would not be difficult for such a guarantee to be given in return for 'past consideration' – the seller of the goods might well have entered into the sale contract before seeking the guarantee of the parent company (although a fresh promise by the seller to the parent company would be good consideration for the guarantee – see the sections on Consideration and Part performance in Chapter 1). The second issue is the relevance in such circumstances of the rule in *Clayton's case* which would apply if the sale contract were one of many entered into between the same parties and in relation to which the seller maintains a running account to determine the amounts from time to time owed to it by the buyer.

The lesson to be learned from this example is that in apparently straightforward circumstances – a parent company guarantee is sought because a trade credit limit is exceeded – serious problems could result from a failure to take the issues as seriously as if the transaction were large, complex and high profile.

Continuing guarantees

At the other end of the scale is an arrangement under which a parent company guarantees to a bank the performance by its subsidiary of all the subsidiary's obligations to the bank, the sort of guarantee that is sometimes referred to as an 'all moneys' guarantee. Such a guarantee is technically a 'continuing' guarantee and here things become more complicated because some continuing guarantees are revocable, ie they can be terminated by the guarantor, and some are not. A continuing guarantee is revocable by the guarantor unless the consideration provided for it is 'entire' rather than 'divisible'. (I need to explain these obscure and unfamiliar terms, but first want to mention that a continuing guarantee may apparently be revocable even if the guarantee is contained in a deed – see Andrews & Millett, para 8.03, note 7, (although an offer to give a guarantee made in a deed is not revocable – see para 2.06). This is puzzling. The distinction between the two types of guarantee is based on the nature of the consideration, but it is not clear to me how an analysis based on consideration can determine the position in relation to a guarantee contained in a deed where consideration is not required.)

The test (with regard to termination) is whether the guarantee is given in return for the beneficiary's doing or agreeing to do something which is, subject to its own terms, irrevocable or whether the beneficiary can choose to do whatever it is that it is expected to do. In the first case, the consideration is entire, in the second, it is divisible. Thus, if a bank enters into a loan facility agreement under which it is obliged (if requested and subject to the terms of the agreement) to make advances to the borrower, a guarantee of the borrower's obligation will not be revocable at the instance of the guarantor any more than the bank can unilaterally revoke its commitment. On the other hand, if a bank extends an uncommitted facility to a borrower – which includes an overdraft facility which can be called in on demand – a guarantee of the borrower's obligations will be revocable. As it was nicely put by Bowen J in *Coulthart v Clementson* (1879) 5 QBD 42:

> 'Various explanations have been offered of this reasonable, though implied, limitation. The guarantee, it has been said, is divisible as to each advance and ripens as to each advance into an irrevocable promise or guarantee only when the advance is made . . . Whether the explanation be the true one or not, it is now established by authority that such continuing guarantees can be withdrawn on notice . . .'

The practical consequence of all this is that unless it is clear that the consideration is entire, a guarantee should be contained in a deed (which may offer the beneficiary some protection) and should contain a clause providing for its termination by notice from the guarantor. It is essential to make express provisions for the termination of a guarantee which is revocable in order to provide certainty as to what obligations are covered by the guarantee. This topic is a little black hole all on its own, but the important practical point is that in the case of a revocable guarantee which is payable on demand – and most guarantees are payable on demand (so that no limitation period begins until demand is made) – the guarantor will be under no liability if a valid demand is not made before the guarantee is terminated. One way of avoiding this is to use a termination provision which provides that the guarantor shall be entitled to terminate the guarantee by, say, one month's notice and shall be liable for all sums validly demanded before expiry of that period. An alternative approach is to use a provision which, by saying that termination shall not affect the liability of the guarantor with regard to guaranteed obligations in existence at the time of termination, seeks to provide to the beneficiary the ability to demand at a later date payment of amounts which were contingent at the time the guarantee was terminated.

Subrogation

Guarantees may be limited in time or in amount. I do not recall having met a guarantee which was limited in time, but it is not unusual to meet guarantees which are limited in amount, either because this is the commercial deal or because, under the law of the guarantor's place of incorporation (or, perhaps, that of its principal place of business), the guarantee must be limited in amount if it is to be enforceable in that jurisdiction – this is not an uncommon requirement.

Where a guarantee is limited in amount, the guarantee may be written in two ways: the guarantor may guarantee a part of the debt, ie that part which is equal to the stated limit, or it may guarantee the whole debt subject to a limit on the guarantor's liability. From the beneficiary's perspective, it is important that the second route is taken. If it is, then unless the whole debt has been paid, the beneficiary may prove for the whole debt in the insolvency of the debtor – even if the guarantor has paid the amount it is obliged to pay – but the guarantor may not even prove for what it has paid. See, by way of contrast, *Re Sass* [1896] 2 QB 12 where Vaughan Williams said that a surety for part of a debt 'has the right, having paid part of the debt . . . to stand in the shoes of the principal creditor'.

This right of subrogation, which gives to a guarantor which has paid the obligations the subject of its guarantee the right to stand in the shoes of the person it has paid, arises not out of contract but out of the relationship between the surety and the creditor. It was confirmed and extended by the Mercantile Law Amendment Act 1856, s 5, a section which gave statutory effect to the equitable principle that a debtor must indemnify a surety who pays its debts and extended the surety's rights to benefit from any security held by the creditor in respect of those debts. Where only part of a debt is guaranteed, a guarantor which has paid that part can then exercise its rights of subrogation and has the right to share in security held by the creditor even where that security was held for both the guaranteed debt and for other debts. A creditor would not want to share its security in such circumstances.

Because of the threat posed by a guarantor's rights of subrogation, which can be waived by the guarantor, a guarantee will often contain a provision under which the guarantor agrees not to exercise its rights of subrogation and, in particular, not to prove in a liquidation of the debtor in competition with the beneficiary. Another, perhaps better, approach is to give to the beneficiary the right to decide when the guarantor should exercise such rights and to require the guarantor to hold any sums received as a result of its doing so on trust for (or for the account of) the beneficiary.

Suspense accounts

Another provision usually found in a guarantee is one which says that the beneficiary may credit any sums it receives or recovers pursuant to the guarantee to a suspense account. The result of a beneficiary's putting a sum received on a suspense account is that the sum received does not reduce the amount of the beneficiary's claim, in a liquidation or otherwise, because the beneficiary has not appropriated the sum to the outstanding debt. As a result, the guarantor acquires no right to be indemnified by the debtor and, thus, no provable claim in the liquidation of the debtor. A suspense account provision does not, however, operate so as to permit a creditor to revive a debt which has been extinguished through a statutory set-off on insolvency – see *MS Fashions Ltd v Bank of Credit and Commerce International SA (in liquidation) (No 2)* [1993] 3 All ER 769.

Marshalling

As well as the right of subrogation, a guarantor has another, less frequently mentioned right – the right of marshalling – which is the right to require a beneficiary which has made demand of the guarantor to have recourse to other security the beneficiary holds before taking proceedings against the guarantor. This right applies where the guarantee and the other security relate to the same debt. As with rights of subrogation, the right of marshalling is subject to the terms of the guarantee, which may entitle the beneficiary to release or not to enforce other security it holds for the guaranteed debt.

Defences are waived

This brief discussion of equitable rights that can be waived, modified or excluded leads naturally to the fourth of the key objectives set out at the beginning of this chapter – that the guarantor should waive the various defences otherwise available to a surety. The way this objective is usually achieved is by including a provision which says that the beneficiary may, without affecting or impairing its rights against the guarantor, do certain things which, in the absence of such a provision, would have this effect. I will state what things these are and then look in a little more detail at just two of them. The activities in question are: varying the arrangements with the debtor; taking, giving up, perfecting or enforcing – or not doing so – other security held for the guaranteed obligations; utilising – or not utilising – other sources of payment and taking – or not taking – steps or proceedings against the debtor.

Freedom of action for the beneficiary is the keynote; freedom to handle its relationship with its customer in whatever (honest) way it thinks fit and freedom to take (or not take) and manage whatever security it wants (and can obtain) to secure payment of the guaranteed obligations. The specific freedom I will look at is the ability to vary the arrangements with the debtor, ie in the classic phrase, the ability to give 'time or indulgence' to the debtor and the ability to agree with the debtor a variation of the underlying agreement pursuant to which the debtor will or may become indebted to the beneficiary.

Time or indulgence

The basic rule is that if the creditor gives to the debtor more time to pay, the guarantor is discharged – see *Swire v Redman* (1876) 1 QBD 536. The reason for the rule has always been explained as being the guarantor's right – probably not often exercised – of paying off the guaranteed debt and suing the debtor in the name of the creditor (subrogation again). It does not matter how the extension is documented, how short it is or how little harm it causes the guarantor, but it must, it seems, be an extension which is enforceable by the debtor. It is the usual practice, however, to assume that any waiver, however informal (such as one giving rise to a promissory estoppel), would discharge the guarantor.

Variation of the principal contract

Any material variation of the underlying contract without the guarantor's consent will discharge the guarantor – the rule in *Holme v Brunskill* (1877) 3 QBD 495 (and see also *Rees v Berrington* (1795) 2 Ves 540, in which Lord Loughborough LC described the rule neatly when he said (of a surety): 'You cannot keep him bound and transact his affairs (for they are as much his as your own) without consulting him'). The rule applies even where the variation would seem commercially beneficial to the guarantor unless 'it is without enquiry evident that the alteration is unsubstantial or that it cannot be otherwise than beneficial to the surety' – per Colton LJ in *Holme v Brunskill* at 505. In practice, no guarantee should omit the provision which says the creditor may vary the underlying agreement without consent, although it would in any event be usual to obtain a guarantor's consent to any such variation, however slight (and it always has to be borne in mind that agreements can be varied by conduct). Consent will not be implied simply because a guarantor knows about a variation of the underlying arrangements nor is a guarantor obliged to point out to a creditor that it may lose its rights against the guarantor through a particular course of action (*Polak v Everett* (1876) 1 QBD 669). If the guarantor does consent, it is bound by the new arrangements. As explained by Colman J in the course of his lengthy judgment in *Credit Suisse v Borough Council of Allerdale* [1995] 1 Lloyd's Rep 315 at 371, 372, a guarantor who consents to a variation is giving up an equitable right rather than creating a new guarantee (which is why a consenting guarantor will continue to be bound by its guarantee irrespective of whether or not any fresh consideration is provided by the beneficiary).

Contracts which are not guarantees

Having reviewed the contents of a guarantee, I will now look at some contracts which are not guarantees, but which have some features in common with them.

Contracts of insurance

A guarantee is a contract under which the guarantor agrees to ensure that where a third party – the debtor – fails, for example, to repay a loan, the lender will nevertheless get paid in full. How are we to distinguish this from a contract under which an insurer agrees with a company which extends credit to purchasers of its products that if a purchaser fails to pay, the insurer will pay? The answer is – with difficulty. It is surprisingly hard to find a satisfactory test with which to decide this question, which can be critical because of the differing levels of disclosure applicable to the two types of contract and the ease with which a surety (but not an insurer) can be released by alterations to the terms of the obligation which are being underwritten. Before describing the issues in a more detail, I will share with you a wonderfully self-serving observation made by Lord Atkin in the course of his judgment in the leading case of *Trade Indemnity Co Ltd v Workington Harbour and Dock Board* [1937] AC 1:

> 'I may be allowed to remark that it is difficult to understand why businessmen persist in entering upon considerable obligations in old fashioned forms of contract which do not adequately express the true transaction. The traditional form of marine policy is perhaps past praying for, but why insurance of credits or contracts, if insurance is intended, or guarantees of the same, if guarantees are intended, should not be expressed in appropriate language, passes comprehension. It is certainly not the fault of lawyers'.

The truth is that it is the law and the lawyers who sit in judgment over their peers who, over the years, have made this a difficult issue.

As we have seen, any material variation of a guarantee made without the guarantor's consent will discharge the guarantor. No such rule applies to contracts of insurance because, it is sometimes said, an insurer has a primary and not a secondary liability, so an insurer is not a surety. If this can be regarded as an advantage that policies of insurance have over guarantees, the duty of disclosure which the law imposes on a would-be insured puts things into perspective. A contract of insurance is one of 'the utmost good faith', at least so far as the insured is concerned. A guarantee, by contrast, will not be vitiated by 'the mere non-communication to the surety by the creditor of facts known to him affecting the risks to be undertaken by the surety' (Romer LJ in *Seaton v*

Heath [1899] 1 QB 782 at 792), although fraud and misrepresentation will have the same effect in relation to a guarantee as in relation to any other ordinary contract.

It will usually be clear whether a contract is a guarantee or a contract of insurance, but none of the simple tests that can be proposed is conclusive. An insurer will require payment of a premium, but guarantors often require fees. A guarantor must do its own diligence, but if the circumstances are sufficiently unusual – itself a question of fact – there may be a burden of disclosure on the beneficiary. To make matters worse, what is presented as a guarantee may in fact be a contract of insurance or, which has the same practical effect, be a guarantee which is at the same time a contract of the utmost good faith. To quote Romer LJ again:

> 'Many contracts . . . may with equal propriety be called contracts of insurance or contracts of guarantee. Whether the contract be one requiring *uberrima fides* or not must depend on its substantial character and how it came to be effected'.

This tautological muddle is best avoided by calling a spade a spade – if it is insurance, be wary of dressing it up as a guarantee (and vice versa). Or, as was done when 'risk participations' entered the secondary loan market, if you think your contract may be a hybrid – or you are not sure – you may want to treat it as being both a guarantee and a contract of insurance. The first standard form of English law risk participation agreement, for which I was responsible, contained both suretyship provisions and expressly contemplated the need for the 'seller' to make full disclosure (but this is no longer the practice).

Comfort letters

A 'comfort letter' is one which a lender may take from a third party to a transaction, for example, the parent company of the borrower, in order to be able to demonstrate – to itself – that the third party approves of or supports (in business terms) the proposed transaction between lender and borrower. For example, a comfort letter will often confirm that the parent will (or intends to) continue to own the borrower. Such letters can accidentally subject the third party to legally binding obligations, but from the recipient's perspective are best treated as if they could never do so; and, from the issuer's perspective, best not written. The fine distinctions which the courts have been forced to make when considering comfort letters send the clear message that if a third party is to underwrite a debtor's obligation, a proper guarantee should be used; the uncertainty which comfort letters engender is not helpful. The leading English case is *Kleinwort Benson Ltd v Malaysian Mining Corpn* [1989] 1 WLR 379. It contains an inordinately long discussion of the issues – prompted by an indefensible first instance decision – and ends with the resounding observation that the 'consequences of the decision of the defendants to repudiate their moral responsibilities are not matters for this court'. This case is important, however, with regard to the role of intention in the formation of contract. See the section headed 'Objectivity and intention' in Chapter 1.

Performance bonds

A performance bond is, if properly written, a promise to pay, which the courts will treat as having the same effect as a promissory note – see *Edward Owen Engineering Ltd v Barclays Bank International Ltd* [1978] QB 159. Performance bonds are given by banks to third parties who want some effective sanction if the banks' customers fail to perform their obligations, usually under construction, engineering or similar contracts. From a bank's perspective, the 'cleaner' the bond – the closer it is to a promissory note – the better, so that the bank does not get caught up in the dispute between the contracting parties.

Voluntary guarantees

I have now reached the point where I can discuss my favourite case, which is a sad thing to possess. *Owen v Tate* [1976] QB 402 concerned, I think I am correct in saying, an old lady, a generous friend and a bank, but is nevertheless a case with serious, practical implications for finance lawyers and their clients. Suggestions have been made that it was wrongly decided – indeed it has been severely criticised – but until the House of Lords decides otherwise, it provides a clear statement of the rights – or lack of them – of someone who gives a guarantee without being asked to do so by the debtor. To explain why this matters, I will describe a transaction in respect of which it was very fortunate that I had read about the case a few weeks earlier – sometime in 1977 or thereabouts.

My (new) Swiss client had a subsidiary (in Latin America) which wanted to borrow money which would be repaid over eight years. Unfortunately, no bankers were willing to lend eight-year money into Latin America at that time. (The Latin American debt crises of the late 1970s and early 1980s were not helped by the fact that as the risk of lending grew perceptibly worse, bankers lent for shorter periods. The resulting 'bunching' of maturities made a significant contribution to the debtor countries' problems – see Chapter 9 for a more detailed treatment of this topic.) My client told me that it had agreed to guarantee the last two years' maturities of the proposed eight-year loan. Stop, I said, you must not do that; what you must do is agree to buy those maturities from the lender if default occurs – in effect, enter into a risk participation arrangement with the lender (although that was not a term which was then in use).

There is a fine, but critical, set of distinctions here. A risk participation arrangement may have some of the characteristics of a contract of suretyship – as I mentioned earlier – and these can be dealt with by contract. But, more importantly, if a guarantor enters into a valid and binding guarantee without having been asked to do so by the debtor, it will have no recourse, by way of subrogation or otherwise, to the debtor. This is what *Owen v Tate* decided.

It is important to be clear on this. If a risk participation were written as an obligation to indemnify the beneficiary – rather than as a commitment to purchase or fund the underlying claim – *Owen v Tate* would have the effect of denying to a risk participant who has paid recourse to the debtor by way of subrogation.

Conclusion

Once again, it is not possible to do more than identify some key issues in the course of a few thousand words. The law relating to guarantees is complex, often ancient and full of areas for debate and development – and the same can be said of many standard form guarantees. If you find yourself having to attack or defend a guarantee in contentious circumstances, you may need to investigate some of the many black holes which are to be found in this area of the law. If, however, your job is to negotiate the terms of a guarantee for the beneficiary, what you need is a good feel for what your client can safely amend or omit – as long as your standard form is good enough. If you are advising the guarantor, you need to know what your client can realistically expect the beneficiary to agree to amend or omit and the better the starting point – your adversary's standard form – the easier your task will be.

Three postscripts

1   I have made no mention of the various reasons why a guarantee may fail because of fraud, duress or other circumstances nor of any issues as to corporate capacity or benefit which may need to be considered in practice. These are issues which would require separate and extensive treatment.

2   While writing this chapter, I began to wonder whether there should be a law against unreported cases being used as precedents or cited in textbooks. I have not been able to get hold of a copy of the case – *National Westminster Bank Ltd v French* (20 October 1977, unreported) – that is cited in support of the proposition that even a guarantee contained in a deed can be revocable. This is very frustrating – I cannot tell you what the case said nor express an informed opinion on it. If decisions are privately held and recorded, the judicial process will lack the transparency that it should have.

3   It is puzzling, given the complexities surrounding guarantees and the need for the beneficiary of a guarantee to prove loss, why creditors who want protection from a third party against a debtor's default do not seek to obtain a performance bond, or another variety of 'demand guarantee', as these instruments tend to be called, rather than an old fashioned guarantee. This is something we lawyers should address – see for example *Trafalgar House Construction (Regions) Ltd v General Surety & Guarantee Co Ltd* [1996] AC 199, in which the need for the beneficiary of an old fashioned 'surety bond' to prove loss was as easily demonstrated as was the form a genuine 'on-demand' guarantee should take.

CHAPTER 6

Assignments of choses in action

> **'Chose in action' is not a term which can be easily defined, if it can be defined at all. The term takes its meaning from judicial usage and the law is correspondingly labyrinthine. In this chapter, I take a brief look at the ways in which choses in action are categorised and how, when and with what effects they can be assigned.**

It is troubling to read in *Halsbury's Laws* (4th edition (reissue)) 1991, vol 6, Choses in Action, para 1, note 2 (which volume I will refer to as *Halsbury*) that the phrase has been used to describe such a variety of things that:

> '... it is impossible to give an accurate and complete definition of what it means and may include at the present day.'

On reflection, however, we should not be too worried, for it is just as impossible to define what a chair is – the important thing is that we know one when we see one. I was once asked by a philosophy lecturer at university to define a chair. As I think was foreseen, I soon gave up. Whatever test you think may work – four legs, it is for sitting on, or whatever – proves to cover various items of furniture, a stool, a table, a bench, but not to pin down what we mean by a 'chair'. What is happening is that both 'chose' and 'chair' have the meanings we allow them to have through the way in which we use them.

What is a chose in action?

The closest you can get to a definition of 'chose in action' is to say that it means an item of property which has no physical existence, but which can be enforced by action, literally a 'thing in action'. (Modern statutes tend to say 'thing in action', which is a shame, because this is an inelegant phrase which contravenes the first rule of drafting, namely, that if it is not elegant, it is wrong. The corollary, that if it is elegant, it is correct is, of course, not true – see Chapter 11.)

Since the term 'chose in action' takes its meaning from judicial usage, the only way to be sure that something is a chose in action is to find a case which says that it is – at this point, the philosophical approach greets the real world. The range of things which have been held to be choses in action is remarkably wide and reinforces the view that the term is incapable of exhaustive definition. Amongst many others, the following claims or rights have been held to be choses in action: a mooring right; a right of action arising out of a tort; a share in a racehorse; a right of proof in liquidation; and the right of a person entitled on an intestacy to have the estate duly administered.

Debts are choses in action

Fortunately, it is clear that debts and the benefit of contracts, which are the types of claims I will be considering in this article, are choses in action. Examples of this type of chose in action are debts arising under contracts for the sale of goods or for the supply of power, debts evidenced by bank accounts or debts constituted by loans or bills of exchange. The main reason why these are the types of chose in action most frequently encountered by finance lawyers is that contracts or instruments which generate a flow of funds can be used by lenders or bondholders as security for obligations of the borrower or issuer. The proper way to take security of this kind is to take an assignment of the chose in action (except, as we shall see, in circumstances where a lender wants to use as security money which the debtor has deposited in (or will pay into) an account with the lender). I will end this chapter with a brief look at this special case; the main task is to consider how choses in action are to be assigned and what risks and difficulties an assignee of a chose in action will have to contend with. Given the context, I will refer to the person against whom a chose in action can be enforced as the 'debtor'.

Terms of art

In order to keep things (relatively) simple, it is helpful to talk first about the terminology and then to deal with the meaning of numerous 'terms of art' which are found in this area. There are 'legal choses in action' and 'equitable choses in action' and there are 'legal assignments' and 'equitable assignments'. Only an assignment of a legal chose in action can be a legal assignment and then only if certain statutory requirements are satisfied. Any other assignment is an equitable assignment, so there can be equitable assignments of legal choses in action (as well as legal ones), but an assignment of an equitable chose in action will always be an equitable assignment. To put this another way, most assignments of choses in action are equitable assignments, but if certain conditions are satisfied, such an assignment may be a legal assignment.

Legal assignments

What are the conditions which are to be satisfied if an assignment of a chose in action is to be a legal assignment? The conditions are set out in (or derived from) the Law of Property Act 1925 (LPA 1925), s 136(1):

'Any absolute assignment by writing under the hand of the assignor (not purporting to be by way of charge only) of any debt or other legal thing in action, of which express notice in writing has been given to the debtor, trustee or other person from whom the assignor would have been entitled to claim such debt or thing in action, is effectual in law (subject to equities having priority over the right of the assignee) to pass and transfer from the date of such notice:

(a) the legal right to such debt or thing in action;

(b) all legal and other remedies for the same; and

(c) the power to give a good discharge for the same without the concurrence of the assignor:

provided that, if the debtor, trustee or other person liable in respect of such debt or thing in action has notice:

(*a*) that the assignment is disputed by the assignor or any person claiming under him; or

(*b*) of any other opposing or conflicting claims to such debt or thing in action;

he may, if he thinks fit, either call upon the persons making claim thereto to interplead concerning the same, or pay the debt or other thing in action into court under the provisions of the Trustee Act 1867.'

The first point to note is that LPA 1925, s 136(1) deals with the assignment of 'any debt or other legal thing in action'.

'Any debt or other legal thing in action'

Historically, a legal chose in action had been one which, before the coming into effect of the Supreme Court of Judicature Act 1873, could be enforced by an action at law (as opposed to an equitable chose which would have been enforceable only by a suit in equity) but which, ironically, would have been regarded as assignable in equity but not at common law. This rather pleasing asymmetry is neatly reflected in the classic definition (for statutory purposes) of a 'legal thing in action' provided by Channell J in *Torkington v Magee* [1902] 2 KB 427 at 430–431:

'the words "debt or other legal chose in action" mean "debt or right which the common law looks on as not assignable by reason of its being a chose in action, but which a Court of Equity deals with as being assignable".'

It is sometimes said that if a debt is to fall within LPA 1925, s 136(1), it must be for a definite sum. This is probably because in the headnote of *Jones v Humphreys* [1902] 1 KB 10, the case cited in support of this proposition, the case is wrongly described as having decided that 'the assignment, not being of a definite and ascertained amount, was not such an assignment as is contemplated by section 25 of the Judicature Act 1873' [which was subsequently re-enacted as LPA 1925, s 136]. In fact, what Lord Alverstone CJ said in his brief, leading speech was that 'there is no doubt that an absolute assignment of future debts may be a good assignment for the purposes of the section ... [but] an assignment of an undefined portion of future debts will not come within it' – the assignment in question was of 'so much and such part [of the assignor's earnings as a schoolmaster or otherwise] as shall be necessary and requisite for payment' of the debt he owed to the assignee.

Why does this apparently minor issue matter to finance lawyers? The answer is that if only a debt for a specific sum can be the subject of a legal assignment, a loan which carries the benefit of floating rate interest provisions and indemnities from the borrower could not be the subject of a legal assignment nor could many other revenue generating contracts. The decision in *Jones v Humphreys* – and the helpful part is, strictly speaking, an obiter dictum, but one which I am sure correctly states the law – deals with this issue, but does not solve all the problems which are encountered in the context of assignments of loan agreements. Contracts may impose restrictions on assignment and, more fundamentally, there is the question of whether a given contractual right is or is not capable of assignment. As can be seen from the case where a mooring right was held to be a chose in action which was capable of assignment (*J Miller Ltd v Laurence and Barnsley* [1966] I Lloyd's Rep 90), the English courts take a very robust view on this issue. In that case, the judge concluded that the mooring right was assignable because there was 'nothing in the contract itself or in the surrounding circumstances to suggest that the benefit of the contract was not intended to be assignable'. In a similar vein, the Earl of Halsbury LC said in one of the leading cases on the topic (*Tolhurst v Associated Portland Cement Manufacturers Ltd and Imperial Portland Cement Co Ltd* [1903] AC 414, HL):

> 'I quite agree that the fact of the word "assigns" not being in the contract is immaterial if it is ascertained that the intention of the contract is that it should be assigned.'

However, not all contractual rights are capable of assignment. I will return to this topic later.

The statutory requirements

LPA 1925, s 136 specifies three requirements which need to be satisfied if an assignment of a debt or other legal thing in action is to be a legal assignment:

- the assignment must be in writing 'under the hand of' – in other words, duly signed by – the assignor;

- the assignment must be 'absolute' and not purport to be by way of charge; and

- written notice must be given to the debtor or obligor on whom the assignor has the claim which is the subject of the assignment.

A fourth and very important requirement is that for an assignment to be within s 136 it must be an assignment of the whole of the debt or chose in action (*Williams v Atlantic Assurance Co Ltd* [1933] 1 KB 81, CA). An assignment of part of a debt will be an equitable assignment even if the express requirements of s 136 are satisfied.

There are two things to be said about the first requirement. First, it is one of the relatively rare instances in English law of a contract which must be in writing if the parties' objectives are to be achieved (another being a contract of guarantee, as mentioned under the heading 'The key objectives' in Chapter 5). Secondly, there is authority – see *Wilson v Wallani* (1880) 5 Ex D 155 – for the view that signature by an agent is not sufficient. This was a first instance decision on a similarly worded reference in the Bankruptcy Act 1869, s 23 to a disclaimer by a trustee being made 'by writing under his hand'. If this decision is correctly to be regarded as applying to s 136, care needs to be taken with regard to the way in which assignments of choses in action are executed. However, with regard to a UK company, the provisions of the Companies Act 1985, section 36 will prevail and, in the case of a foreign corporation, it ought at least to be the case that the signature of a duly authorised officer of the corporation will suffice, subject to compliance with other applicable laws.

Absolute assignments

The second requirement is of particular interest to finance lawyers. This is because 'absolute' does not mean quite what you might take it to mean, with the result that an assignment taken by way of security *can* be an absolute assignment, and thus a legal assignment, as long as it is drafted properly.

The distinction which the Act is making is that between an assignment whereby the whole of the debt is transferred to the assignee and an assignment under which the assignee is given a security interest in the debt. To quote from Halsbury (para 16), 'the fact that the assignment is expressed to be by way of security is not by itself sufficient to make it purport to be by way of charge only' so a mortgage *'in ordinary form which transfers the property with a proviso for redemption and reconveyance'* (emphasis added) is an absolute assignment within the Act and 'the "proviso" will be implied if an assignment, which is absolute in form, is in fact made by way of security'. It follows that the correct way (given the opportunity) to take security over a debt (or a revenue generating contract) is to take an outright assignment with a provision stating that after the 'secured obligations' have been paid, the assigned property will be reassigned to the assignor (at its request and cost).

Notice to the debtor

The third requirement which has to be satisfied in order for an assignment to be a legal assignment is that written notice of the assignment is given to the debtor. If such notice is not given (and you should note – although I have 'mislaid' the authority for this proposition – that a notice given before the assignment has been made may well not be effective), the assignment will be an equitable assignment, valid as between the assignor and the assignee, but leaving the assignee without protection against equities (see below) subsequently arising between the debtor and the assignee and the claims of later assignees who do give notice.

The effect of a legal assignment is that the assignee becomes the owner of the debt in place of the assignor which no longer has any right to sue for the debt and cannot give a good discharge for it. If the debtor were to pay the assignor after having received notice of the assignment, it could be required to pay again by the assignee – see Section C in Chapter 8. Thus, a lender who takes a legal mortgage of a chose in action becomes the owner of the chose; in many instances, this is the position the lender will want to be in, but not always. For example, a lender may well not want to be the owner of shares it takes as security because there may be adverse tax, accounting and other implications, especially if the lender does not agree to exercise its voting rights in respect of the shares only as directed by the mortgagor (see CA 1985, Sch 10A, para 8, and note also that LPA 1925, s 136 is not regarded as applying to shares because they are not transferred by assignment (*Torkington v Magee*)).

Equities and priorities

An assignee of a chose in action always takes the chose subject to 'equities' – claims the debtor has against the assignor or its predecessors in title, which exist at the time notice is given and are sufficiently closely connected to the contract which is the subject of the assignment (*Torkington v Magee*). In other words, if at the time notice is given the debtor has a claim against the assignor, for example, in respect of a defect in goods supplied or a wrongful failure to make further advances, the assignee will take subject to that claim irrespective of whether the assignment is legal or equitable.

There is nothing to be done about such prior equities, other than to seek warranties from the assignor to the effect that there are none, but the giving of notice freezes the position, so it is in an assignee's interest to give notice as soon as the assignment is effected. This also applies to equitable assignments, in relation to which an assignee's title is only effective as against the debtor when notice has been given (*Dearle v Hall, Loveridge v Cooper* (1828) 3 Russ 1). It is not generally necessary for the notice to be in writing nor is it necessary that it be the assignee who gives notice. What matters is that the debtor is made aware of the fact of the assignment. *Dearle v Hall* also established the rule that, as between competing equitable assignees, priority is determined by the order in which notice was given to the debtor unless either the later assignee knew of the earlier assignment when it took the assignment or it had constructive notice of the prior assignment.

Just as notice of an equitable assignment need not generally be in writing, so too the equitable assignment itself will not always need to be in writing. This provides a means of avoiding stamp duty in certain circumstances (which I will describe below), but there are circumstances where a notice of an equitable assignment or the assignment itself does need to be in writing. A notice of an equitable assignment need only be in writing where it concerns an assignment of an equitable interest in trust property (because otherwise the notice cannot affect the priorities of completing claims – LPA 1925, s 137(3)), whereas an equitable assignment must be in writing if the interest being assigned is an equitable interest of any kind (whether or not arising under a trust) (LPA 1925, s 53(1)(c)). This latter point needs to be remembered and has an important practical consequence in relation to the following stamp duty saving structure which makes use of assignments made otherwise than in writing.

The offer and acceptance route

This structure uses the offer and acceptance by conduct route to effect an assignment – see the section headed 'Offers to the world' in the Chapter 1, page 5. A chose in action, such as receivables under a sales contract, is offered for sale pursuant to a master agreement and the offer is accepted by the purchaser by means of the making of a payment calculated by reference to a formula or procedure set out in the master agreement. The effect of LPA 1925, s 53(1)(c) is that the same structure could not be used if the purchaser wanted to sell on its claims to a third party. The other issue which needs to be borne in mind when this structure is used is that a liability to pay UK stamp duty (which only applies where there is a stampable document which relates to something to be done in the UK) can be incurred if the sales are confirmed or evidenced by ancillary documents. Thus, it is important that the sales are effected by, and only by, the offer and acceptance by conduct route.

Enforcement by assignees

The position of the assignee under a legal assignment is clearly spelt out by LPA 1925, s 136 – the assignee has the legal right to the debt or thing in action and 'all legal and other remedies for the same'. The assignee can, therefore, sue the debtor to the exclusion of the assignor, but only where the circumstances are such that before the Act – strictly, its predecessor – the assignee could have sued in the name of the assignor (*Torkington v Magee* (again)). This is another area where the apparently straightforward provisions of s 136 lead to complexities that flow from the law as it was before the statutory provisions were enacted. Similar complexities exist in relation to equitable assignments. Here, the assignee cannot usually sue in its own name, but can if the chose in action is equitable and the assignment is absolute. These are black holes which I will not venture into any further, save to mention the generally applicable requirement that all necessary parties must participate in proceedings, so in cases where an assignee needs the participation of its assignor, it can join the assignor as defendant if the assignor will not join in bringing the action.

Assignability

As I said earlier, not all contractual rights are capable of assignment. There are some special cases of non-assignable contractual rights, such as the salary of a judge or a military person, but the three classes of non-assignable choses in action which are of relevance in the context of this article are 'bare causes of action', contracts containing restrictions on assignment and contracts involving personal skill or confidence. The first is a public policy requirement, one which has become less rigid than it used to be, so that if the assignee has a commercial reason for taking the assignment or if the right of action is incidental to property acquired by the assignee, the assignment may be valid. For example, an insurer can take an assignment of the insured's rights against a defaulting contract party (*Compania Columbiana de Seguros v Pacific Steam Navigation Co* [1965] 1 QB 101) and as long ago as 1868 the courts upheld the right of an individual to purchase shares in a railway company in order to challenge certain acts of its directors (*Bloxam v Metropolitan Rly Co* (1868) 3 Ch App 337 at 353).

Of more relevance to finance lawyers are choses in action which are not assignable by reason of the terms on which they are created. In particular, contractual rights – such as a lender's rights to be repaid – are often expressed to be assignable only with the consent of the debtor. The effect of such a prohibition was considered in detail by Lord Browne-Wilkinson in the House of Lords' decision in *Linden Gardens Trust v Lenesta Sludge Disposals Ltd* [1994] 1 AC 85 where he concluded (at 109) that:

> 'an assignment of contractual rights in breach of a prohibition against such assignment is ineffective to vest the contractual rights in the assignee.'

It is increasingly common for banks to 'securitise' their loan portfolios – just as it is very common for lenders to require the consent of their borrowers in order to assign the benefit of loans – and in this context the nature and effect of restrictions on assignment of loans is a key issue.

The somewhat surprising (at the time) decision in *Don King Productions Inc v Warren* [1998] 2 Lloyd's Rep 176 (affd, [2000] Ch 291, [1999] 2 All ER 218, CA) – see Chapter 13 page 189 – to the effect that a prohibition on assignment does not necessarily preclude a declaration of trust, threw a lifeline to banks seeking to securitise their loan portfolios. Prior to that decision, it was difficult to find any authority for this view.

The black hole discussion

In the wake of the *Lenesta Sludge* decision, concerns were expressed (see the article on this topic at 1994 *JIBL* 431–434) that a failed assignment of a debt might operate to extinguish the debt. A brief debate on this issue – a colleague and I responded to this suggestion (see 1995 *JIBL* 153–154) – focused on the differences between actions to recover debts and actions for damages. The proponents of this very troubling view asserted that an assignor which has purported to assign the benefit of a debt in contravention of a contractual prohibition could only sue the debtor for loss (suffered by reason of it having to return the consideration for the sale to the assignee) and that this loss would be too remote to be recoverable from the debtor. They further asserted that the attempted assignment in breach of the prohibition constitutes a repudiation which makes the creditor's right to an action in debt unavailable. This truly is a black hole, but one of some importance – the 'weakest link' in the pessimists' argument being the view that an assignment in breach of a prohibition constitutes repudiation because it is an attempt by the assignor to put the performance of the contract out of its power. A lender which seeks to assign all or part of its interest in a loan will not purport or seek to do any such thing – it has performed its primary obligation, which was to lend the money in the first place.

Whatever the merits of the views expressed at the time, it is clear there could be difficulties with regard to some of the claims which a lender has under a loan agreement and may wish to assign, eg claims under 'increased costs' provisions (although careful drafting can address these problems). This is just one of the reasons why the use of transfer procedures remains the preferred route for sales of loans in the secondary markets – see Chapters 2, 9 and 10.

Bank accounts

Finally, or nearly so, a brief word about bank accounts and the issues raised by the infamous decision of Millett J in the *Charge Card* case (*Re Charge Card Services Ltd* [1987] Ch 150) where he held that it is conceptually impossible for a bank to take a charge over (let alone an assignment of) a customer's account with the bank, a so-called 'chargeback'. Whatever the differing opinions of judges, academics and practitioners may be with regard to chargebacks, it is likely that all are united in the view that an attempt by a bank to take an assignment over an account held with it – not being an assignment taken in some different capacity, as a trustee, for example – would fail because the 'assigned claim' would merge with the obligation of the bank evidenced by the account. The *Charge Card* decision was effectively reversed by Lord Hoffmann's judgment in the case usually referred to as *BCCI (No 8)* – *Re Bank of Credit and Commerce International SA (No 8)* [1998] AC 214, although the view he expressed was 'strictly an obiter dictum, though obviously ... of the highest persuasive value' as Sir Roy Goode said in a fiercely critical article in (1998) 114 LQR 178. These are matters I will revert to in Chapter 7 – see pages 97–98. For present purposes, the important element in Lord Hoffmann's judgment was the emphasis he placed on the fact that an equitable charge (or assignment) can be overreached by a bona fide purchaser for value of the legal interest in a (legal) chose in action who takes without notice of the prior equitable charge.

A quotation

To conclude this Chapter, I will leave you with a brief quotation from the report of the proceedings in *Bloxam v Metropolitan Rly Co* (see above, page 79), during which counsel for the defendants, a railway company building an extension from Moorgate to Tower Hill and 'cooking the books' in order to do so, said to the Court of Appeal in Chancery:

'The company may manage its affairs foolishly, but the Court of Chancery will certainly do it worse.'

Brave words – and he lost his appeal.

CHAPTER 7

Taking security: some dilemmas and dichotomies

> This chapter is an essay in sonata form, the first subject being the idea that there are a number of common dilemmas and dichotomies which are encountered when security is taken and the second being the somewhat arbitrary way in which English law develops through judicial decisions. By way of a coda the article ends with a further look at security over bank accounts.

This collection of essays arose out of a series of articles in Butterworths Journal on basic legal concepts for finance lawyers, particularly those with relatively little experience of banking and capital markets activities. The articles were not, and nor are these essays, intended to be 'how to …' manuals nor – a curse on the name – 'bluffer's guides'. It did, however, prove difficult to prevent a piece entitled 'Taking security' from becoming either a bland (albeit brief) description of the different ways in which security can be created or a tedious summary of what steps have to be taken in order to obtain security.

The solution I eventually found to this problem, which prevented me from writing the original article for many weeks, is based on the identification of the following dilemmas and dichotomies which regularly confront finance lawyers:

- is it a mortgage or is it a charge;

- is it a legal charge or an equitable charge;

- is it a fixed charge or a floating charge;

- is the charge (or mortgage) registrable under the Companies Act 1985 (CA 1985), s 395; and

- is it a mortgage or a sale and purchase agreement?

By addressing these questions I will not provide anything like a guide to taking security, but will, I hope, clarify some puzzling issues and help you not to make some of the easier (and easier to avoid) errors that are frequently seen or made in practice.

Mortgage or charge?

From the way in which the terms 'mortgage' and 'charge' are usually used, it would not be clear whether this is a substantive or linguistic distinction or, indeed, whether the two words are not in fact synonymous. Historically, however, the words do have distinct meanings even if, as we shall see, they are now more or less interchangeable. A good starting point for an enquiry into what the words used to mean and how they are now used is the original meaning of 'mortgage' as a security arrangement under which the owner of property (the 'mortgagor') transferred title to that property to another person (the 'mortgagee') on terms that the mortgagor would get back the title to the property upon its discharging its obligations to the mortgagee. This was the way – the only way (apart from a pledge) – in which security could be created at common law. An agreement to transfer title to property – as opposed to an actual transfer – was, however, recognised by the courts of equity on the principle, to quote Lord Macnaghten in *Tailby v The Official Receiver* (1888) 13 App Cas 523 at 546 – a case in which the efficacy of an agreement to assign all future book debts was upheld – that 'equity considers as done that which ought to be done' – see Chapter 13, page 187.

Thus far, so good – a mortgage is a simple common law concept and equity will come to the aid of someone who has the benefit of an agreement to grant a mortgage. Equity will not, however, come to the aid of someone who has the benefit of an agreement to make a loan nor will it force a prospective borrower to borrow. As Challis J put it in *Western Wagon and Property Co v West* [1892] 1 Ch 271 at 275: 'A court of equity will not decree specific performance of a contract to make or take a loan of moneys, whether the loan is to be on security or not' – for a rather blunter judicial statement to the same effect, see Chapter 2, page 20.

A perpetuities digression

Reading *Tailby* reminded me of another dilemma which, although not strictly relevant to the issues I am addressing in this article, is encountered in practice sufficiently often – and this is a recent development – to justify a digression. Where security is to be given for the benefit of a group of creditors it is usual (and correct) for the security to be given to a trustee. In this context, the practice has arisen of making provision for a perpetuity period in the security trust deed which sets out the terms on which the security is held. (A point to note here is that the trust should be created either by transferring or charging the relevant property to the trustee or, rarely appropriate, by having the trustee declare itself trustee of property it already holds. It is not correct to create the trust by means of a purported 'appointment' of the trustee by the creditors. See Chapter 13 for a more detailed discussion of how trusts are created.)

But I digress again. The question I want to consider is why it is thought that there is a need for a perpetuity period in a security trust deed. The rule against perpetuities applies (to oversimplify) to the vesting of contingent interests in property, but, on the face of it, no contingent interests arise under a security trust deed and, in any event, the House of Lords confirmed in *Knightsbridge Estates Trust Ltd v Byrne* [1940] AC 613, that the rule against perpetuities does not apply to mortgages.

The only concern that I can identify is that the trustee might be thought to have a contingent interest in property acquired by the mortgagor after the date of the mortgage. But this is a misconception. A mortgagee has no interest, contingent or otherwise, in after-acquired property until the mortgagor acquires that property. What it has is an immediate right of future enjoyment of the interest created when the security attaches to the property.

To quote again from *Tailby*, this time from the speech by Lord Watson, who (at 533) observed that where a future chose has been assigned (and there is no uncertainty as to its identification) 'the beneficial interest will immediately vest in the assignee'. Perhaps the use of the word 'vest' has misled someone into thinking there are some potentially dangerous contingent interests floating around.

After-acquired property

As I was saying before these digressions, a mortgage is a common law concept, but a charge is a creature of equity. In equity, all that is required to provide security to a creditor is for the 'chargor' to make it clear that this is its intention, subject to the requirement that the property the subject of the security be adequately defined. An important advantage of a charge (as opposed to a mortgage) was that in equity the security created by a charge would extend to property acquired by the chargor after the charge was given (*Holroyd v Marshall* (1862) 10 HL Cas 191). At common law this could not happen without a transfer to the mortgagee of the new property. Although *Holroyd v Marshall* concerned a fixed charge, the decision paved the way for judicial recognition (or creation) of the concept of a floating charge in *Re Panama, New Zealand and Australian Royal Mail Co* (1870) 5 Ch App 318. It was held in this case – by Giffard LJ at 322 – that a charge over:

> '"the said undertaking" was a charge "over all the property of the company, not only [property] which existed at the date of the debenture, but [property] which might afterwards become the property of the company".'

Mortgage, charge or pledge?

The old, common law form of mortgage is no longer of general application because of LPA 1925, s 85(1) which provides that a mortgage of freehold land:

> 'shall only be capable of being effected at law by either a demise for a term of years absolute, subject to a provision for cesser on redemption, or by a charge by deed expressed to be way of legal mortgage';

and in relation to leasehold property a mortgage is created by way of demise for a term one day less than the term of the lease.

By contrast, the only way to create a legal mortgage of a chose in action is by an outright transfer of title, usually by an assignment which satisfies the requirements of LPA 1925, s 136 – see the section headed 'Legal assignments' in Chapter 6 – with a provision for a retransfer on redemption. Shares are an exception to this, as (in a different way) are negotiable instruments; and chattels are a different story altogether. Although a registered share is a chose in action, title to a registered share will be transferred not by assignment but by registration in the name of the transferee/mortgagee – see Chapter 6, page 77.

(Registered shares also constitute an exception to the general rule that in relation to choses in action priority as between competing mortgagees is determined by who first gave notice to the 'debtor'. In the case of shares the House of Lords decided – in *Société Générale de Paris v Walker* (1885) 11 App Cas 20, HL – that priority is determined by the usual rule that the first in time prevails, subject to the claims of a bona fide purchaser for value of the legal title to the shares – as to which see my comments on pages 95–96 under the heading 'Bona fide purchasers'.)

Where security is taken by means of the delivery of a negotiable instrument, whether a bearer share or a bill of exchange payable to bearer, what the recipient obtains is a pledge, not a charge or a mortgage. As a result, as stated by Cozens-Hardy in his delightfully short, single paragraph judgment (is this a record?) in *Harrold v Plenty* [1901] 2 Ch 314, the holder of the security is 'in a very different position from an ordinary mortgagee. He has only a special property in the thing pledged. He may obtain a sale, but he cannot obtain a foreclosure', foreclosure being the right of a mortgagee to extinguish, with the leave of the court, the mortgagor's equity of redemption. Since leave is discretionary and will not be given unless the secured obligations exceed the value of the security, the distinction will not often make much difference in practice.

A pledge is created 'by a delivery of possession of the thing pledged, either actual or constructive' (see *Official Assignee of Madras v Mercantile Bank of India* [1935] AC 53, PC, at 58, in which Wright LJ provided a thorough review of the law relating to pledges). The 'thing pledged' can be anything to which title can be transferred by delivery. As with many of the topics covered in this chapter, a good practical guide to the subject can be found in *Lingard's Bank Security Documents* (Butterworths, 1993), a new edition of which continues to be eagerly awaited.

Legal or equitable?

The term 'legal charge' is often regarded as being synonymous with the term 'legal mortgage' and the term 'equitable mortgage' as being synonymous with 'charge' or 'equitable charge'. I find these habits confusing and unhelpful and prefer to use the terms more precisely. A 'mortgage' is a security arrangement under which title is transferred to the mortgagee and a 'charge' is a security arrangement under which an equitable interest is created without a transfer of property. Thus, an equitable mortgage is a security arrangement created by an agreement to transfer property to the mortgagee, an agreement which – *Tailby* again – equity will regard as having been performed. One of the differences between a mortgage and a charge is that (as with a mortgage and a pledge) a mortgagee has the right to foreclose, but a chargee does not. A charge is always equitable unless, as I have already mentioned, it is a 'charge by way of legal mortgage'.

However, the practice of using these terms interchangeably is too well established for anything to be done about it. See, for example, CA 1985, s 396(4) which says that 'in this Chapter "charge" includes "mortgage"' and LPA 1925, s 205(1)(ii) which takes the opposite approach and provides that a mortgage 'is defined to include any charge or lien on any property for security money or money's worth'. Perhaps the rather odd use of 'is defined to include' tells us that whoever drafted the provision was also uncomfortable with the practice. But perhaps not – in *Evans v Rival Granite Quarries Ltd* [1910] 2 KB 979, Buckley J tells us that 'a floating security is not a specific mortgage of the assets, plus a licence to the mortgagor to dispose of them in the course of his business, but it is a *floating mortgage* ...' (emphasis added).

Before I leave this subject, I will briefly illustrate the concept of an equitable mortgage by reference to shares (necessarily registered, not bearer) in an English limited company. As I said, an equitable mortgage is a security arrangement under which the mortgagor agrees to transfer property. So, in an equitable mortgage over shares, the mortgagor will usually be required to deposit with the mortgagee both the share certificate and a completed, signed but undated share transfer form. Charges over shares – as I have mentioned, CA 1985 permits me to call a mortgage a charge – are interesting because they are not included in the list of charges which are registrable under CA 1985, s 395 but they are in practice usually registered. This is because almost invariably the property the subject of the charge will include rights to receive dividends; such rights could well be 'book debts' and charges over book debts are registrable under s 395.

Fixed or floating?

This is a distinction which has given rise to a great deal of debate and you would be justified in asking to be spared any further comment on the topic. However, now that we have – in *Brumark Investments Ltd* (*Agnew v IRC* [2001] BCC 259, on appeal from the Court of Appeal in New Zealand in *Re Brumark Investments Ltd*) – a decision which ought to be a watershed in the debate, the task of writing about this topic is easier than it used to be. Although *Brumark*, being a Privy Council decision, is, strictly speaking, of persuasive (albeit very persuasive) authority only, it is a decision which may well stand the test of time.

The second subject

Before we explore (or, rather, learn from others who have explored) the metaphysics of book debts – are they divisible or indivisible, is a debt a different thing from its proceeds? – it is worth pausing to consider how it is that English law develops as it does: in fits and starts, taking the wrong road from time to time, getting lost, turning round and even, sometimes, ending up where it began. This is an exaggerated but not wholly inappropriate description of the progress of English law as it applies to security over book debts. What happens – and because I only infrequently get involved with litigious matters, I realised this relatively recently – is that any argument is worth running (and is run) in English litigation. If there is a chance – not necessarily a reasonable chance – that the court will accept a particular argument, it does not matter if the argument is, in business or common sense terms, wholly without merit as long as the client's interests are served.

Viewed from the perspective of a disinterested party, English litigation is based on the premise that ultimately it does not matter who wins or loses, it is how you play the game – run your arguments and if you win, good for you. This is a perception which is succinctly confirmed by the observation of Cummings-Bruce LJ which is quoted in Chapter 14, page 205. Thus it is, that for more than ten years, as stated by Hubert Picarda QC in his comprehensive (but pre-*Brumark*) review of the topic in 'Labels: A Voyage Round Fixed and Floating Charges' ((2001) 3 *JIBFL* 114) there have been 'two strands of authority vying for supremacy' in the cases concerned with security over book debts. And thus it is, that in the penultimate paragraph of the judgment in *Brumark* we find Lord Millett characterising a key assertion of the receivers (the appellants) as 'simply playing with words'. So fundamental is this approach – that opposing counsel run the arguments that support their respective causes on a 'who dares, wins' basis – that the plaintiff's counsel in *Harrold v Plenty* [1901] 2 Ch 314 put the case for the defendant who did not bother to turn up. As the judge put it, 'Mr Pollock has put before me all the authorities which might help the defendant'. Mr Pollock no doubt also knew how to behave himself on the sports field.

Where does *Brumark* take us on the vexed question of when and whether a charge over book debts and/or their proceeds will be a fixed or floating charge? The historical importance of the question was, of course, that fixed charges rank ahead of preferential creditors in a liquidation, but floating charges do not. The coming into force of the Enterprise Act 2002 on 15 September 2003 alters our perspective on this issue, but I am pleased to say that this vindicates my decision to accept 1 September 2003 as the cut off date for this book.

In simple terms (and subject to *Brumark*) a floating charge is a charge which permits the chargor (which can only be a company) to deal with the charged assets in the ordinary course of its business, but which acquires the characteristics of a fixed charge, ie the chargee's consent is required for disposals, upon the happening of specified events, such as a payment default or the presentation of a winding-up petition – this process being usually referred to as 'crystallisation'. The point at issue in *Brumark* was 'whether a charge over the uncollected book debts of a company which leaves the company free to collect them and use proceeds in the ordinary course of business is a fixed or floating charge' (per Lord Millett).

The charge in question was expressed to create:

> 'a fixed charge on the book debts of the company which arise in the ordinary course of business and their proceeds, but not those proceeds which are received by the company before ... the charge ... crystallises or is enforced ...'.

Although there are some apparent inconsistencies in the case law, which was thoroughly reviewed in *Brumark*, it is clear that the key issues are whether the chargor is free to deal with its book debts in the ordinary course of its business – the usual test – and what this means in the context of book debts.

In the case of book debts the usual test had, in the eyes of some practitioners, been seen as being satisfied where the chargor had the right to dispose of the proceeds – the money received from the debtors, but not the debts themselves – without the consent of the chargee (usually a bank). The perception that this was the case led to *Re New Bullas Trading Ltd* [1994] I BCLC 485, CA, a case in which the Court of Appeal had to consider a document which provided that two charges were to be created: one over the chargor's book debts – purportedly a fixed charge; and another over the proceeds of the book debts – which was stated to be a floating charge. In his judgment Nourse LJ expressed the view that book debts could be the subject of fixed charges and that whether or not they were in any particular case was a matter of construction.

The Privy Council disagreed, stating that there is a two-stage process:

- first, ascertain the rights and obligations of the parties (and this is a matter of construction); and

- secondly, determine whether, as a matter of law, these rights and obligations are or are not consistent with the existence of a fixed charge.

Having disposed of one or two other issues, the Privy Council concluded (at para 48) that in order 'to constitute a charge on book debts as a fixed charge, it is sufficient to prohibit the company from realising the debts itself, whether by assignment or collection'. The Privy Council also stated (para 48) that 'it is not inconsistent with the fixed nature of a charge on book debts for the [chargee] to appoint the company its agent to collect the debts [on behalf of the chargee]' as long as the account into which the proceeds are paid both is, and is operated as, a blocked account.

Confused or confusing?

In passing, their Lordships poured scorn on the idea that a book debt can be separated from its proceeds and were of the opinion that an attempt 'in the present context' to separate the ownership of the debts from the ownership of their proceeds (even if conceptually possible) 'makes no commercial sense' (para 46).

This is confusing, if not confused. The issue is not who owns a debt and its proceeds but the fact, as their Lordships admit, that 'a debt and its proceeds are two separate assets' (also para 46). The two assets are wholly distinct: one is a claim on the company's customer, the other a claim on the company's bank. All of this is, it seems to me, much ado about nothing. What stands in the way of taking one fixed charge over the book debts (and their proceeds, for good measure) and (subject to *Charge Card* issues – as to which see below) another fixed charge over a designated bank account into which the proceeds must be paid (as in *Re Keenan Bros Ltd* [1979] 2 Lloyd's Rep 142)? This, I would suggest, is a structure which is both supported by *Brumark* – the real issue being the level of control the chargee has over the bank account – and avoids the ontological debate about whether a debt and its proceeds have separate existence.

Registrable or not?

Under CA 1985, s 395, certain charges created by English companies are void against a liquidator of the chargor unless the instrument creating the charge and certain prescribed particulars are delivered to the registrar of companies within 21 days of the charge's creation. There are a number of circumstances in which there can be doubts about whether a mortgage or charge is registrable under CA 1985, s 395 – a mortgage or charge which should be, but is not, registered within the specified period of 21 days will be void as against a liquidator of the mortgagor/chargor.

One problem area relates to the creation of security by what CA 1985 refers to as an 'oversea company' which has no registered place of business in England but which may or may not in fact have an established place of business in England.

(I still recall my embarrassment some years ago at the huge merriment caused by my use of the term 'oversea company' at a meeting in Frankfurt attended by representatives of about a dozen continental European banks – the phrase was instantly seized on as confirming the 'little Englander' nature of our culture. Unfair, but the use of the term in our legislation is a reflection of a certain perspective, as was that famous headline 'Fog in Channel – Europe Cut Off'.)

As many readers of this book will know, the law on this point was considered – and made – in *Slavenburg's Bank v Intercontinental Natural Resources Ltd* [1980] 1 All ER 955. This first instance decision established that if an oversea company has an established but unregistered place of business in England – references to England in a context such as this are, of course, to be construed as references to England and Wales – a charge that would be registrable if the company did have a registered place of business in England is itself registrable.

Because it is difficult – if not impossible – to be certain that a given chargor does or does not have an established place of business in England, the usual practice is to seek to register all 'registrable' charges given by non-UK companies; and in this context a charge over property which could be brought into England and Wales is registrable. Any such attempted registration will be rejected by a polite letter from Companies House which will nevertheless record the particulars of the '*Slavenburg* registration' in a special register!

A further, surreal twist to this already bizarre state of affairs is added by the decision by the Registrar of Companies that CA 1985, s 398(2), which allows extensions of time with regard to charges created out of the United Kingdom over property situated outside the United Kingdom, does not apply to so-called *Slavenburg* registrations.

(It is always rewarding to read the cases – and equally unrewarding to read the headnotes, which are wrong as often as they are right. In *Slavenburg* the high spot occurs when Lloyd J observes that counsel for the bank 'has submitted that, though I am entitled to read the Bermuda

Companies Act 1923, I am not entitled to draw any conclusion as to its meaning', adding 'I need not deal with that submission although it is hardly a submission which commends itself to me'.)

Charges on book debts

Other difficulties arise from the fact that only those types of charge which are listed in CA 1985, s 396(1) are registrable. One of the types of charge which has to be registered is a charge on book debts of the company creating the charge. There are those who say that a credit balance in a bank account is a book debt and those who say it is not. The better view is that for the purposes of s 395 such a credit balance is a book debt, being a debt (owed to the account holder) which arises in the course of a business and which 'would or could be entered in well-kept books relating to that business' (see *Independent Automatic Sales Ltd v Knowles and Foster* [1962] 3 All ER 27 at 34). (The decision of Hoffman J (as he then was) in *Re Brightlife Ltd* [1986] 3 All ER 673 – to the effect that the phrase 'book or other debts' did not include a credit balance at the bank – was a decision about the meaning of a provision in a debenture and not a decision on the meaning of s 396 (1).)

Other issues arising out of the list of registrable charges contained in s 396(1) include:

- the meaning of the phrase 'any issue of debentures'; and

- the scope of s 396(1)(c) which makes registrable a charge created or evidenced by an instrument which, if executed by an individual, would require registration as a bill of sale.

These are not difficult issues, but it is important to be aware of them.

A conspicuous absentee from the list of registrable charges is a charge over shares, but as I have already mentioned, a charge over shares will in practice be registrable because part of the charged property will consist of rights to receive dividends and other rights which are registrable as book debts. Thus, the rule in practice is: if in doubt seek to register a charge by delivery of the charge and the particulars called for by CA 1985, s 395(1). The registrar of companies may decline to register a particular charge, but *Slavenburg* suggests that a chargee is protected if it has done everything it can to secure registration of a charge which is subsequently found to be registrable. We should also remember that *Brumark* tells us – or reminds us – that any charge which is not a fixed charge will be a floating charge. As a result, these grey areas are only of relevance where we are dealing with what we know to be fixed charges, all floating charges being registrable under s 396(1)(f).

Sale or security?

For a variety of reasons (some now historic) contracting parties have sometimes sought to characterise secured loan transactions as something different; for instance, as a sale and lease-back or as a sale and repurchase agreement. This may be done with a view, for example, to avoiding the registration requirements of CA 1985, s 395, but (as Sir Roy Goode points out in *Commercial Law*, Penguin, 2nd edn, 1995, p 652) the 'question to be decided is not whether the transaction would have the effect of avoiding the application of the relevant statute – for parties are free to organise their affairs in such a way that they escape legislation they consider burdensome – but what is its legal nature'. This is an important point which needs to be absorbed if concerns about 're-characterisation' – a fashionable concept with significant emotional overtones – are not to get out of hand.

The courts will re-characterise a transaction if the documentation is a sham – not something many of us would wish to be party to – or if the true effect of the document is different to what the parties thought it was. In this context it should be noted that *Brumark* 're-characterised' a fixed charge as a floating charge. Re-characterisation is not confined to the 'sale or security' question.

The law relating to re-characterisation was discussed at length in *Welsh Development Agency v Export Finance Co Ltd* [1992] BCC 270, in which can be found numerous statements which could come straight from *Brumark*. Compare, for instance, the observation of Staughton LJ that 'the correct process ... is to look at the operative parts of the document in order to discover what legal transaction they provide for' or Dillon LJ's statement that 'the question [of what the parties agreed] can arise ... where there is some objective criterion in law by which the court can test whether the agreement ... does or does not fall into the legal category in which the parties have sought to place their agreement' with Lord Hoffmann's assertion in *Brumark* that if the parties' intention is to grant rights 'which are inconsistent with the nature of a fixed charge, then the charge cannot be a fixed charge however they may have chosen to describe it'.

Unfortunately, Dillon LJ also expressed the view that:

> 'there is no one clear touchstone by which it can ... be said that a document ... which is expressed as an agreement for sale must necessarily, as a matter of law, amount to no more than the creation of a mortgage or charge on the property expressed to be sold.'

This reminds me of the remark of Lord Atkin, which I quoted in Chapter 5, to the effect that it is not the lawyers but the businessmen who cause these problems. On the contrary, it is the courts who are not able to provide business people (and their advisers) with the means to distinguish between, for example, contracts of guarantee and contracts of insurance or between contracts for the sale of goods and contracts which create security over goods. As I point out in the next and final section of this Chapter, the landmark decision – for it is surely that – in the case known as *BCCI (No 8)* [1998] AC 214 has signally failed to give practitioners comfort in yet another area. Despite that decision, documentary techniques devised to overcome the uncertainties engendered by the *Charge Card* [1987] Ch 150 decision look set to remain in use in the face of an apparently 'commercial' decision made on slightly dubious legal grounds – but more of that in a moment.

Bona fide purchasers

I am going to end this article on the topic – security over bank accounts – with which I ended Chapter 6. Someone said to me shortly after the original version of this Chapter was published 'oh, you're the one who's obsessed with choses in action'. Not quite – but since loans, bonds, and most of the other contracts that finance lawyers deal with are or generate choses in action, it is a topic that does crop up from time to time. What I have to say concerns another dilemma – does it matter whether equitable security over a bank account is taken by way of a charge or by way of assignment? Before answering this question, I want to confess that this question recently caused me (to my great surprise) to encounter what the person who taught me double entry accounting called a 'confusion barrier'. Confusion barrier is the name this lecturer gave to that period of incomprehension that often occurs between being introduced to (and seemingly understanding) a novel concept or set of concepts – such as debits and credits, assets and liabilities – and getting to the position where you can apply them more or less intuitively and with confidence (not that everyone gets there with double entry accounting).

The confusion barrier I encountered arose out of Lord Hoffman's remarks – in *BCCI (No 8)* – about the equitable doctrine of the purchaser for value of the legal estate in the context of charges over bank accounts. I started to think that there was some conflict between this doctrine and the rule in *Dearle v Hall*, which deals with priorities as between equitable assignees – see Chapter 6 under the heading 'Equities and priorities'. The answer, I now think, is that there are two different regimes and you can choose the one you want to apply. As between themselves equitable charges rank in order of their creation (the first in time ranking ahead of any other) but equitable assignments rank in order of notice to the debtor, which can confirm (or not) that it has received no prior notice of assignment (save that an equitable assignee cannot get ahead of an earlier equitable assignment of which it has actual or constructive knowledge) (see Chapter 6, page 77).

An equitable charge is also, as I mentioned earlier, subject to the claims of a bona fide purchaser for value who without notice of the charge purchases the legal title to the property the subject of the charge. Thus, the assignment route will usually be the one to use, but in some circumstances, for example where it is impracticable for notice of assignment to be given or where the chargor must, perhaps for tax reasons, retain the legal title, it may be appropriate to use a charge.

A further reason for using the assignment route is that as between a legal assignee and an equitable assignee of a chose in action 'priorities fall to be determined *as if* [emphasis added] the legal assignment had been effected in equity, not in law' (Phillips J in *E Pfeiffer Weinkellerei-Weinenkauf GmbH v Arbuthnot Factors Ltd* [1988] 1 WLR 150 at 162). Two questions arise: why is this so, and why was it only in 1987 – when the case was decided – that the point was established?

The answer to the first question is that in LPA 1925, s 136 it is stated that an assignment which satisfies the requirements of the section is 'effectual in law (subject to equities having priority over the right of the assignee)'. And the parenthetical qualification is to be construed in the light of the position when s 136 was enacted, which was that such an assignment was effectual (to use the language of the Supreme Court of Judicature Act 1873) 'subject to all equities which would have been entitled to priority over the right of the assignee if this Act had not passed' (s 25(6) of that Act). The effect of this provision is to refer us back to a time when legal (or statutory) assignments of choses in action did not exist – the 1873 Act invented them. So in this sense, in this context, legal assignments are to be treated as if they were equitable assignments!

The answer to the second question is simply that in challenging the defendant's counsel's view that his client was a bona fide purchaser for value of the legal estate, with priority, as such, over an equitable assignee, the plaintiff's counsel opened the door to a conclusion which is as correct as, at first sight, it is surprising. In order for the point to be so clearly established we had to wait for the right facts to present themselves and for the right arguments to be run.

Chargebacks

There is, of course, one particular circumstance in which it is important whether equitable security is taken by way of charge or by means of an assignment – this is where the property the subject of the security is a debt owed by the putative chargee. No one thinks that an assignment will work in this situation – the assignee's claim would merge with its obligations. But, as I indicated at the end of Chapter 6, where I said I would revert to the topic in this chapter, there are radically different views as to whether a charge – a 'chargeback' – can be taken in such circumstances. Sir Roy Goode's position is that Buckley LJ got it right in the Court of Appeal in *Halesowen Presswork and Assemblies Ltd v National Westminster Bank Ltd* [1971] 1 QB 1 at 46, [1972] AC 785, when he said 'no man can have a lien on his own property'. Lord Hoffman's view is that such observations do not address the real issue, which is that a chargeback is like any other charge save that 'instead of the beneficiary of the charge having to claim payment from the debtor, the realisation would take the form of a book entry' (*Re Bank of Credit and Commerce International (No 8)* [1998] AC 214 at 226–227).

This is no need for me to attempt to adjudicate between these two positions, although I have a preference for the view that a chargeback is effective, as did Dillon LJ in the *Welsh Development Agency* case where he cited *Re Jeavons, ex p Mackay, ex p Brown* (1873) 42 LJ Bcy 68 – better reported, he said, in (1873) 8 Ch App 643 – as authority for this view (which it is, although, as so often, the headnote gets it wrong, incorrectly stating that the court upheld the existence of a lien rather than a charge). Unfortunately, although the point was put in issue by counsel for the trustee in bankruptcy – a man, he said 'cannot have a charge on a debt which is due from himself' – the point was not argued: 'I entertain no doubt that there is a good charge [on the royalties] because they are part of the property and effects of the bankrupt' was the response from Sir W M James LJ.

The practical effect of the chargeback debate, which was started by Millett J in *Re Charge Card Services Ltd* [1989] Ch 497, is that practitioners still use the 'triple cocktail' of set-off, 'flawed asset' and charge which is perceived to provide a safe route through – or round – this most visible of contemporary black holes. Under that structure the creditor obtains from the person providing security:

- money which is paid to the creditor on terms that no obligation to repay that sum to the payer arises unless certain events have occurred (for example, certain debts are paid);

- an express right to set off its (eventual) obligation to repay that sum against the secured obligations; and

- (for good measure) a charge over the payer's claims on the creditor for payment of that sum.

If this seems convoluted, it is; and if it seems a shame that resort has to be had to such devices, it is. In Hong Kong, for example, an ordinance was swiftly passed to remove the doubts engendered by the *Charge Card* decision and to permit 'chargebacks'. However, given the quality – or lack of it – of recent legislation (such as the Contracts (Rights of Third Parties) Act 1999 and the Trustee Act 2000), we are probably better off with the judicial decision-making process, random as it is, than we would be if Parliament woke up to the need for English law, as the law of choice for a large part of the world's commercial and financial activities, to develop in an orderly fashion.

CHAPTER 8

Let's keep it simple

This chapter contains the text of my response to the Law Commission's Consultation Paper (No 164) – 'Registration of Security Interests: Company Charges and Property other than Land' – which was published in June 2002. The processes whereby law reforms are developed in the UK are less than satisfactory and the way in which the creation of security under English law is being addressed bears this out.

The consultation paper was completed in June 2002 and circulated in early July for 'comment and criticism only' rather than as the final view of the Law Commission. Not only does the consultation paper not represent the Law Commission's final view, the approach it takes, which is to 'formulate proposals that could be introduced in respect of companies' on the basis that reforms applying to non-corporate debtors will be made at a later stage, is not even the Commission's preferred approach, which would be to follow the practice adopted in other jurisdictions of introducing a system which applies regardless of the legal personality of the debtor (1.18 – *this and other similar references are to the numbered paragraphs of the consultation paper*).

History of the lack of progress

Why is it that such a comprehensive and, because it has a tendency to convince the reader by reason of its style rather than its substance, an almost too well written consultation paper of some 308 pages does not reflect its authors' preferred approach? Surely, something is wrong here. Why are we being invited to comment on a solution in which the Law Commission has little or no confidence? The answer, of course, and this is clearly not the responsibility of the consultation paper's authors, is a lack of political will. (There is a second critical issue, which is whether the Law Commission's preference is the best approach. As will become clear, I think not, but first things first.)

Lack of parliamentary time

There is, it seems, no intention on the part of the government to make parliamentary time available for the primary legislation which would be required to implement a single system for all types of debtor, so it is proposed to take a piecemeal approach and to use secondary legislation under a Companies Bill in order, initially, to reform only the law relating to security given by companies – a process which may, in any event, lead nowhere, as was the case with the Companies Act 1989, Pt IV.

The Law Commission cannot be blamed for this lamentable state of affairs, but, given the political imperatives, have they taken the right approach (even if it is not their preferred approach)? There are good reasons for concluding that they have not although, to be fair, they do stress that the steps they propose are not ideal and that lack of legislative time is the culprit.

Other jurisdictions

The consultation paper quite rightly puts a lot of emphasis on the experience of other jurisdictions. Given that the main thrust of the consultation paper is that we should move to a notice-filing system for company charges similar to that constituted by Article 9 of the United States' Uniform Commercial Code, it is right that we should look for guidance to that system and to the similar systems adopted in Australia,

New Zealand and most Canadian jurisdictions. However, there is a need to learn from our own experience as well, not only with regard to substance, but also with regard to the degree of success we have had in implementing any new or improved system. If we look at our own experience from that perspective, what do we find? The answer is nothing, no progress, no legislative improvements over a 30-year period during which we had:

- the Crowther Report (1971), whose consumer credit recommendations were implemented but whose security and notice-filing recommendations were not;

- the Diamond Report (1989), whose recommendations on those two topics suffered the same fate; and

- the Companies Act 1989, whose provisions with regard to the registration of company charges have not been brought into force.

Anyone who is interested in these topics owes a debt of gratitude to Professor Hugh Beale QC and his colleagues, the authors of the consultation paper, for providing us with very compact and helpful descriptions of the current state of the law and of the history of this lack of progress. One of the lessons to be learned from this history is that although the lack of political will is a serious impediment – 30 years of deliberation without progress – so too is the inability to 'keep it simple'.

A need for effective reform

What is needed, if all that can be done in the near future is to alter the law relating to security given by companies, is the introduction of an effective and efficient system for the registration of corporate security as presently capable of being created. There is no need to address quasi-security – that is, the effects of hire purchase, finance leases and title-retention as viewed through the eyes of another creditor – or consumer issues in a hurry. The first task is difficult and important enough on its own to constitute a suitable case for treatment; and if time is short, as it seems to be, success on this front would be a major achievement, particularly if what is done addresses the 'chargeback' and *Slavenburg* issues (each of which, despite the best efforts of the courts, is an embarrassing stain on English law's reputation).

As well as there being a need to fit the ambition to reform to the time available for deliberation and debate, it is also important that any proposed reform be kept as simple and uncomplicated as possible – something lawyers tend to be not very good at! The proposals regarding the introduction of a notice-filing system are made more complicated than they should be by reason of a reluctance to be sufficiently radical. There is a desire to be rid of outworn concepts, but the old learning has a tendency to creep back in, the most striking example being the proposed reliance on estoppel to resolve issues arising out of the difficulty that can exist in deciding whether a charge is fixed or floating charge. Estoppel is a venerable concept but should not be an important part of a new legal regime in (to be optimistic) the year 2003.

Five proposals

With a view to identifying ways of simplifying the proposed new regime, I will put forward and seek to justify just five proposals (on the basis that by 'security' I mean security as presently understood under English law).

(a) Registrable security should only be effective (with regard to both the contracting parties and third parties) when the documents have been signed and dated and a statement to that effect has been filed, rather than being effective as between the contracting parties when the documents have been signed and dated and effective against third parties when such a statement is filed. I will call this the 'one-stop security' approach.

(b) With regard to floating charges, the position should be that any restriction on the chargor's freedom to deal with the property the subject of the charge should be filed in order to be effective and filing should be the only way of putting a third party on notice of such a restriction.

(c) Since notice to the debtor is a practical necessity in the case of security which is taken by way of assignment of a chose in action – something which the consultation paper ignores – such a notice should be given, and the fact of its having been given filed, in order for the security to be effective.

(d) Bank accounts – strictly speaking, the rights evidenced by entries in a bank account – should be treated like any other chose in action, so that no issues relating to what the consultation paper refers to as 'control' would be relevant.

(e) The law relating to security should, so far as it affects consumers, remain based on the existing law (subject to the repeal of the Bills of Sale Acts); what works for companies should not necessarily be expected to work for consumers.

The Law Commission's proposals

Before setting out these five proposals, I should provide you with a very brief summary – no more than a thumb-nail sketch – of what it is that the Law Commission is proposing, in case you have not had the time or the inclination to read all 308 pages of the consultation paper and to consider the 130 or so provisional proposals and consultation questions – helpfully summarised in Part XII of the consultation paper.

A notice-filing system

The basic proposal is that we should replace the existing registration scheme for company charges with an electronic system under which statements describing a security arrangement and/or the fact of its having been entered into are filed in a central registry. Numerous related issues are discussed, in particular: priorities as between competing interests – the first to file will usually have priority; the consequences of failing to file; erroneous filings; the rights of purchasers; and the question of whether some kinds of security should be exempt from the requirement that a statement be filed.

Quasi-security

In addition, it is proposed that 'quasi-security' arrangements, such as hire-purchase and conditional sale arrangements should be included, initially 'as if' they were security arrangements and subsequently on the basis that, under a suggested re-statement of the law of security, they be re-characterised as security arrangements and made subject to substantially the same substantive law as applies to security as that term is currently understood.

Other reforms

The consultation paper deals also with a number of other topics: providing to non-corporate business debtors the same ability to create security as that possessed by corporate debtors; widening the consumer's ability to create security over personal property; developing a re-statement of the law of security so as to cause security and quasi-security to be subject to the same regime. In the spirit of keeping this article as simple and straightforward as possible, I will not attempt to say any more about these topics, save for my observations with regard to consumer security, as to which see section E below.

The devil is in the detail

It is always the case with any complex set of proposals for law reform that much of the difficult issues are to be found in the detail and the Law Commission's proposals are no exception. To take just three examples, it is proposed that:

- 'turnover trusts' used to effect subordination would be registrable (6.55) [see Chapter 13, pages 191–193];

- outright sales of receivables (unless effected as part of a larger transaction such as the sale of a business) would be registrable – although not treated as security arrangements – so that potential purchasers can establish whether the receivables have already been sold (7.43/7.44));

- by the same token and for similar reasons, outright transfers of receivables to an SPV (special purpose vehicle) in a securitisation would be registrable (7.42–7.43), despite their not even resembling security arrangements – an unexpected proposal in a consultation paper on the registration of security interests.

I would be very surprised if many practitioners active in acquisition finance, receivables financing and securitisation have noticed these proposals which, from their perspectives, may well be seen as highly undesirable. If nothing else, the consultation paper provides a significant challenge to professional support lawyers who work in these areas!

A   Filing required for contractual efficacy

The policy underlying a system for the registration of security is that impressions of 'false wealth' are to be avoided (1.9) so as to enable purchasers and security takers to know what they are getting and who has priority.

A digression

In this context the suggestion that – save where a debtor has attorned to a secured creditor – possessory security should not be registrable, on the grounds that prospective purchasers and security takers can discover the existence of such security for themselves, is an odd one.

This approach would create an area of risk where there need not be one – the risk of failing to discover the possessory security; would cause the register to be less complete than it would otherwise be; would mean that the priority of a pledgee with respect to another secured creditor may fall to be determined by the existing law – hereinafter referred to as 'the old law'; and, because advance filing will be permitted in respect of registrable security (but, obviously, not of exempt security), would cause a pledgee to rank behind a non-possessory security holder who pre-registered even though the pledgee itself could not pre-register. What a lot of anomalies result from a wish to preserve an old principle!

One-stop security

The policy objectives could, I suggest, be achieved, and some difficulties avoided, if the simple (albeit somewhat radical) approach of providing for 'one-stop security' were to be taken. In other words, it could be provided that a security arrangement would take effect only when the parties have signed the relevant documents and the related notice – or 'filing statement' – has been filed. As long as there is in place a simple and effective electronic filing system – a necessity for any notice-filing system – it will be just as easy to complete a transaction in this novel way as it is to complete a transaction by means of the conventional two stage process of creating security and then registering it.

It is easy to demonstrate that this approach would not render unachievable the many improvements notice filing can achieve, but what problems would it solve, what issues would it address?

1 No issues could arise between purchasers and holders of unregistered security – it is convenient to use 'filed' and 'registered' (and related expressions) as synonyms – because if there is no relevant entry on the register, there is no security – and that is that. No questions can arise, for instance, as to whether or not a purchaser is a subsequent purchaser who did or did not give value (see 4.174–4.177).

2 It has been suggested that proposals such as those made in the consultation paper may create a 'human rights' problem (3.41–3.43) because to deny a person rights by reason of a failure to file a notice could be a disproportionate deprivation of property. This view would clearly be untenable under the one stop security approach, where the filing is required to be made in order to acquire the property in the first place.

3 If a company could only create security through the filing (by the company or the security taker) of a notice, the maintenance by the company of its own register of security it has given – as is required under the current regime – would have no purpose save with regard to security which is exempt from registration. The tenuous case for such registers (3.18) would effectively disappear.

4 Under existing notice-filing systems in other jurisdictions, a failure on the part of a creditor to file a financing statement can affect both the efficacy of the security as against unsecured creditors and a liquidator and the creditor's priority in a liquidation (4.55–4.56). The effect of the one-stop security approach would be that a creditor which fails to file will at best be an unsecured creditor. A considerable incentive for debtors and creditors to use the system as intended.

5 A further benefit would be the irrelevance of the old law to all non-exempt security arrangements. There would be no possibility of there being a dispute between two or more holders of unregistered security because there would be no such thing as unregistered security – security would be registered or exempt. There is an incentive here to minimise the types of security which are exempt.

Are there disadvantages?

If there are advantages to the one stop security approach, what are the disadvantages? An obvious point to consider is the impact of erroneous entries on the register. It would clearly be unhelpful to all the parties to a transaction if a security arrangement (or a wider arrangement) were to be of no effect (or could not be implemented) simply because of a filing error, but then it is just as unhelpful if a person who signs a document turns out not to have been authorised to do so! Some mistakes are simply best not made.

The Law Commission's solution to filing errors seems to me to be just as workable in relation to filing errors under the one stop security approach as it is to conventional filing errors. What it proposes is that a filing would be ineffective if a properly conducted search against the name and company number of the giver of security does not reveal the filing (4.41). Other errors would not invalidate the filing but the security taker would not be able to claim a greater right than that stated in the filing or, if less, provided for in the documents.

It is not obvious to me that there are significant drawbacks to the one stop security approach. On the contrary, there is more than a mere incentive to file, it becomes a necessity, just as due execution is essential. Electronic completion involving electronic filing can be seen as the contemporary analogue of the hallowed 'do not date' approach which would be replaced by a statement to the effect that 'this [charge] shall take effect on the day the fact of its execution is duly filed'.

B   Floating charge restrictions to be filed

The Law Commission expresses the view that both a floating charge and its negative pledge, if there is one – and there invariably is – should be filed (4.130). However, it swiftly recants (4.136) by observing that reliance on the registration of negative pledges would 're-import the doctrine of notice just at the moment that we are trying to move away from that doctrine to a simpler system'. This is another puzzling view given that the whole object of notice filing is to put third parties on notice of a company's dealings. So too is the observation which follows to the effect that 'it would be better to provide simply that a floating charge does not give the company authority to create subsequent security having priority to the floating charge'. Such authority does not derive from the floating charge, it is a power which the company has – under the current law – and which the charge document may restrict.

Estoppel again

This 'strongly held view' of the Law Commission (4.136) leads also to the need for estoppel to operate for the protection of a later chargee if a fixed charge is mis-described as a floating charge. Apart from the oddity, again, of reliance on estoppel, the Law Commission's preferred approach makes it necessary for undue reliance to be placed on the filing party's view – or, perhaps, the contracting parties' view – as to whether the charge is fixed or floating, something both practitioners and the courts have found difficult to get right in the years leading up to the decision in *Brumark Investments Ltd* (*Agnew v IRC* [2001] BCC 259).

A different approach

There is a different approach, which is to require that any restrictions which are imposed with regard to the creation of prior ranking fixed security should be filed. If this approach is combined with the one stop security approach, a relatively simple position can be reached in which a floating charge can be allowed to say one of two things: (*a*) the chargor can create prior ranking fixed security or (*b*) it cannot; and the person effecting the one stop security filing would be required to specify – perhaps by 'checking' the appropriate box on an electronic form – whether (*a*) or (*b*) applies. This would remove the role of estoppel in such matters: the charge would be what it was filed as; any contrary provision in the contractual document would be invalid (a position contemplated in 4.136, note 214); and no other form of notice – or lack of it – would have any effect.

C   Notices of assignment to be filed

One of the cornerstones of a notice filing system is that 'neither the distinction between legal and equitable interests nor notice (whether actual or constructive) has any role to play' (4.119). This statement is not only puzzling for reasons I have already mentioned; it is also strikingly at odds with the practicalities of taking security over a debt obligation. Where a debt is assigned, the debtor will not know that it should pay the assignee unless and until – and this is so whether the assignment is outright or secures obligations of the creditor or a third party – it has received a notice of assignment giving it both formal notice of the assignment and revised payment instructions. The rule in *Dearle v Hall (Dearle v Hall, Loveridge v Cooper* (1828) 3 Russ 1) – that priority is determined by notice – is well grounded in the practicalities: priority goes to the person who first informs the debtor that there is a new 'owner' of the debt and, if it is well advised, that payment should be made to the new owner rather than to the original creditor.

The Law Commission's proposals would have the peculiar result that a notified, unfiled assignment (to X) will rank after a subsequent filed but un-notified assignment (to Y) – but the debtor will pay X rather than Y. If the one-stop security approach were to be adopted and the filing requirement were that the statement to be filed must (correctly) state that an assignment has been entered into and that a notice of assignment has been given, the anomaly I have just described would fall away. (And anyone wishing to achieve what can now be achieved by an un-notified assignment would simply take a charge rather than an assignment.)

D 'Control' should not be relevant to security over a bank account

A related area where the Law Commission's proposals would appear to make life more complicated, rather than simpler, is the taking of security over a bank account. Their proposal (5.51–5.52) is that both 'chargebacks' – where a bank takes a charge over a customer's account with the bank – and charges over bank accounts in favour of third parties should only be possible if the taker of security takes 'control' over the account and that such charges should be exempt from registration.

Taking the second point first, it is not obvious that exemption from registration would be helpful. The main consequence of exemption would be that security over bank accounts would remain subject to the old law. If there is an opportunity to get rid of the potential for confusion under the old law with regard not only to chargebacks but also with regard to the tension between the assignment and equitable charge routes for security over money obligations, the opportunity should be seized. [For further commentary on this topic see the passage under the heading Bona fide purchasers in Chapter 7.] The perceived lack of a need for third parties to be notified of chargebacks and third party account charges (5.51–5.52) is not a reason to deprive those who take security in this way of the benefit of the new system – and this is what exemption does.

Control over a bank account

The use of the concept of control, a concept imported from the US – where it has not proved helpful – into an area which can function perfectly well without it is a cause for concern. 'Control', as envisaged by the Law Commission (and described at 5.51, note 94), signifies that where a third party takes an assignment of a bank account 'an agreement is entered into between the debtor, secured party and the bank providing that the bank will comply with the instructions originated by the secured party directing disposition of the funds in the deposit account without further consent of the debtor'. This almost fanciful description – fanciful because an acknowledged notice of assignment usually suffices, whether or not a contract arises – is based on the mistaken premise that a secured party will not in practice lend against the security of a bank account without that level of control.

Bank accounts are used as part of the transaction mechanics in diverse areas of banking, capital markets and project finance activities, usually without a specific focus on 'control', which may be or may not be obtained. 'Control' is not the right test and there is no reason why filed and notified assignments and un-notified charges should not continue to be available as valid and registrable security arrangements with regard to bank accounts.

E   Keep the old law for consumers

I mentioned earlier that there may be a strong argument in favour of retaining the old law for consumer security rather than applying a new company security law just for the sake of homogeneity. If consumer security is not to be registrable the old law will be the obvious choice as the basis for consumer security, if only because it addresses a number of the issues which need to be addressed in a satisfactory manner. There are no registration issues, no problems with floating charges and even quasi-security in the guise of hire-purchase is addressed in a manner which seems to work well for both the consumer and the provider of credit.

As to whether consumer security should be registrable, the Law Commission is equivocal. It envisages that consumers should be able 'to create security over individually-specified items of existing personal property' (10.33), but then goes on to worry about how to protect innocent purchasers of consumer goods (10.37–10.47). Leaving aside cars and boats, as the Law Commission does, it is not clear who, apart from loan sharks, would benefit from the enhancement of the consumer's ability to create security over personal property.

This is a topic which should be dealt with entirely separately. The last thing a new company security law needs is the sort of subliminal or half thought-through consumerism that is to be found in the Contracts (Rights of Third Parties) Act 1999, an Act which would have been greatly improved if it had contained a provision allowing it to be excluded otherwise than in the context of consumer contracts.

The Law Commission also easily reaches the conclusion that the Bills of Sale Acts should be repealed. It is astonishing to read that consumers and others are still entering into contracts within those Acts – there were, it seems, as many as 2,840 bills of sale registered in 2001 (9.6, note 5).

An important opportunity

The law relating to security is badly in need of reform and the consultation paper is as thorough a resume of the defects in the current law and of the main strands of opportunity for reform as we could wish for. If the Law Commission can resist the temptation to recommend to the government that we should do anything more than tidy up the law relating to company security and if they can generate a draft statute that does this in a simple and effective, perhaps even elegant, manner they will have done English law a great service.

The potential downside is that nothing happens or that what happens does not adequately reflect the needs of the law in practice. One lesson that we might learn from the lack of progress which, as I mentioned earlier, is so clearly described in the consultation paper, is the relative lack of dialogue between the practitioners, as the Law Commission describes those of us who draft the documents and close the deals, and the academics and lawmakers who devise the laws we implement.

A postscript

Finally, I would like to thank the Law Commission and the Queen Mary Centre for Commercial Studies for organising and hosting on 3 September 2002 what turned out to be a very interesting symposium on the consultation paper. But how heavily weighted the proceedings were towards the academic side of the subject matter and how small, I expect, will be the response to the consultation paper from the practitioners who are too busy implementing, and sometimes wrestling with, the current regime to find the time to help put it into better shape. Both sides of this equation need to do more to ensure that each is aware of the other's views.

CHAPTER 9

Syndicated loans revisited

In one important respect a syndicated loan facility resembles a group of bilateral loan facilities which is made by a group of lenders to the same borrower. In two other equally important respects, a syndicated loan is very different to a group of bilateral loan facilities. Having briefly dealt with the common factor – several liability – I will look at the early development of the international syndicated loan before returning to the other two hallmarks of the syndicated loan: inter-bank and agency issues; and transferability. I have mentioned transferability before (in Chapter 2) and deal with it yet again in Chapter 10, but it is impossible not to mention it when considering the key characteristics of a syndicated loan documented under English law.

Several liability

In a syndicated loan agreement there is always a provision that makes it clear that a lender is not responsible for any failure by any other lender to make the loans it has agreed to make and that neither the arrangers – the banks by whom the transaction was arranged – nor the agent bank (the Agent) has any such responsibility. This is so fundamental an aspect of syndicated lending, and has always been, that it was not surprising when, some 25 or so years ago, a suggestion to the effect that the agent should lend if a syndicate member failed to do so was enough to bring to an end negotiations on a proposed syndicated loan financing for a state agency in a developing economy. The financing was of national importance but politically sensitive and it may be that the suggestion was made in order to crater the deal – if it was, it succeeded, as it was bound to do.

As well as the lenders' obligations to lend being several, so too are the borrower's obligations to repay. Thus it has been the accepted analysis for many years that the debts which are owed by the borrower to the lenders are several and separately enforceable; ie a lender can sue in its own name for a loan (or its share of a loan) which is due but not paid – until recently it was not thought necessary to state this, but the current, LMA-driven, practice is to do so.

The development of the syndicated loan

If syndicated loans share with bilateral loans the several liability characteristic, why would a bank turn to syndicated loans as a mainstream activity instead of concentrating on its bilateral relations with its customers? One way to identify what I believe to be an interesting answer to this question is to ask the apparently unrelated question: are syndicated loans underwritten?

Outside the context of acquisition finance, syndicated loans are not usually underwritten in the sense that a bank or small group of banks commits to a borrower that the proposed loan facility will be made available. Historically, syndicated loans were 'underwritten' on a best efforts basis: the lead manager or managers, the arranger or arrangers – the names have changed over time – would give to the prospective borrower a best efforts commitment to get together a group of banks – the syndicate – which would between them make the facility available. There were exceptions, but the best efforts approach was the norm.

By contrast, in acquisition finance – where the borrower/borrower's parent company needs to know that the requisite funds will be available – a bank or banks may commit not just to gather together a syndicate but actually to make the facility available. This will these days be done on the basis that so-called 'market flex' is there to assist in syndication, market flex being the name given to an arranger's ability (pursuant to its mandate from the borrower to change the pricing and other commercial terms (such as the duration of the loan) in order to achieve successful syndication in changing market conditions.

Return on assets

If the norm was for syndicated loans not to be underwritten, what was the incentive for a bank to seek a mandate to organise a syndicated loan and how did the bank and its customer induce other banks to participate? The answer – or, at least, one answer – is that one of the main drivers in the 1970s and early 1980s was 'return on assets' – regulatory capital requirements were non-existent and 'big was beautiful'. A bank's success was measured by the size of its assets and, in particular, by the level of return on its assets; and being the arranger of a syndicated loan facility was an ideal way for a bank to increase its return on assets.

Arrangers were paid a percentage fee on the amount of their 'best efforts' commitments and the lenders who joined during the syndication process received a lower percentage fee – the arrangers kept the difference. This process, whereby an arranger procures other institutions to fulfil its commitment, whether that is a best efforts or a legally binding commitment, to participate in a syndicated loan facility, is known as 'selling down'.

Because the smaller the amount of a lender's 'take' – its commitment to participate in the facility – the smaller was its share of the fee paid by the borrower, an arranger's total fees will end up as a higher percentage of its eventual 'take' than would have been the case and its exposure to the borrower will be less: more earnings for less risk – irresistible! As a simplified, worked example shows, an arranger can easily increase its return on assets through this process; and everyone is happy, the borrower because it gets its loan and the other lenders because they have an asset which they could not have acquired on their own.

1 Assume that the arranger underwrites 100 million on a 1% fee basis and 'sells down' 80 million on the basis that: a 20 million take earns three-quarters of 1%; a 10 million take earns one-half of 1%; a 5 million

take earns one-quarter of 1%.

2 Assume that in the process of syndication the arranger is joined by 1 new lender at the 20 million level, four at the 10 million level and four at 5 million.

3 As a result, the arranger lends 20 million and earns fees of 600,000 which gives the arranger a return on assets of 3% (instead of 1%) on a lower exposure.

Financing the 'less-developed countries' (LDCs)

The first English law syndicated loan agreement was, I understand from Hugh Pigott, entered into in 1968, but it was at the beginning of the 1970s that the explosive growth in (mainly sovereign) syndicated lending began, only to come to a grinding halt, at least with regard to sovereign debtors, when Argentina defaulted in 1982.

There was in any event a significant need for finance in the emerging economies (known as LDCs – less-developed countries – in those less-politically correct times) of South America, Africa and the Middle East, but in 1973 OPEC dramatically increased the price of oil and suddenly the world's banks were awash in 'petro-dollars' deposited with the banks by OPEC's member countries who, at that time, had neither the skills nor the experience – and perhaps not the appetite – to invest in a broader range of wealth generating assets, whether at home or abroad. Thus, the availability of funds to the LDCs was artificially inflated and the race to grow the biggest balance sheet was on.

It was the major banks who could put together the deals and increase their return on assets in the way I have described. Smaller and/or less experienced banks were the 'participants' in these deals, routinely assuming risks they could not or did not evaluate. If a proposed facility was arranged by one or more of the world's leading financial institutions, this was a sufficient recommendation for many banks and a good reason not to dedicate resources to independent research; besides, this was often their only way in to the market and a golden opportunity to meet the borrowers – to 'press some flesh' (as a former client of mine would put it) – at a level of seniority otherwise unachievable.

By the same token, LDC borrowers knew that if they induced a sufficiently heavyweight 'lead manger' or group of 'managers', then they could get their loan, whether or not it was needed and whether or not it could be afforded – and, for all the lenders knew, a loan the proceeds of which were destined for the coffers of corrupt individuals.

Dangerous strategies

The sovereign debt restructuring era was inevitable and the drive to increase the size of the balance sheet and the rate of return on assets led to some dangerous strategies being tolerated, approved or adopted as a matter of policy:

1 An innovative career development strategy: put loans on the books and move to another bank during the grace period.

2 An imprudent lending strategy: lend dollars to an LDC-based borrower with no foreign currency earnings.

3. A self-defeating credit strategy: shorten maturities as a country's debt burden increases.

It is the last of these strategies which, in retrospect, is the most surprising. Individuals will move on and it is clearly legitimate, if risky, to take on the kind of sovereign risk that exists where your debtor has to buy its foreign exchange from a central bank (which, when the time comes, may have none). But, with the benefit of hindsight, it seems decidedly odd that the banks should have exacerbated their debtors' problems through restrictions imposed as a result of timorous credit policies. The result was that the longer maturities which could have been voluntarily offered were reluctantly accepted as part of the restructuring process – at much lower margins than would have been available had they been freely negotiated at the outset.

There was, however, a silver lining to the sovereign debt cloud. Banks needed time to make provisions – to write down their claims – before they could conclude sovereign debt restructurings. Unless pressing economic and/or political imperatives forced banks into a hasty deal they were happy to take years to do deal. While provisions were being made there was always some trading to be done in a market which was almost entirely unregulated. There was also an interesting accounting angle. As a debtor country's prospects improved, in part as a result of both private and public sector restructuring concessions, the value of the written down debt increased with the result that sovereign debt held by a bank could be sold for a price in excess of its written down value – and any surplus would go straight to profit.

How convenient to have a pool of written down assets which can be sold whenever it is convenient for profit, or an increase in profit, to be reported for a chosen quarter.

Inter-bank and agency issues

Having digressed, interestingly, I hope, it is time to return to what I earlier called the hallmarks of a syndicated loan, starting with the two main inter-bank issues: decision making and sharing.

'Instructing Group' and 'Majority Banks' are the names usually used to identify a group of lenders which, in a conventionally written syndicated loan agreement, is given the power to take important decisions with regard to the loan facility; decisions such as deciding that loans will not be made, or should be 'accelerated', because an 'Event of Default' has occurred. (An 'Event of Default' being, of course, an event which entitles a lender or group of lenders to decline to lend or to call for immediate, early payment of a loan, which is then said to have been 'accelerated'.)

An Instructing Group – my preferred term, being the one I introduced when writing the first standard form English law syndicated loan agreement in 1979 – is these days usually made up of a special majority (66.66% or more by principal amount outstanding) of the lenders, although sometimes 51% (a simple majority) will be used. (This is to be contrasted with the practice in the capital markets where the difficulty, as a practical matter, of getting decisions from a group of bondholders has the resulted in market practices under which major decisions can be taken by a tiny minority of bondholders.)

An Instructing Group will be given a number of specified powers – see below – and when it exercises its powers its decisions will bind all the lenders. However, an Instructing Group will not normally have any power to impose any obligations on any other parties. Syndicated loan agreements do not normally contain any voting procedures, which is surprising given the difficulties which can arise, particularly within a large syndicate, in getting lenders to vote. In the English law sovereign debt restructurings of the 1980s, we invariably included provisions which imposed a deadline on the submission of votes, only votes cast before the deadline being taken into account.

An Instructing Group's powers

A borrower will often require the consent of an Instructing Group for activities such as the creation of security and the disposal of parts of its business or its assets. There will usually be carve-outs allowing small or insignificant transactions to be effected without consent. Where a borrower wishes to do something in relation to which no provision is made for consent by an Instructing Group, the borrower might seek confirmation from an Instructing Group that it will not instruct the Agent to take action as a result of the borrower's carrying out its intentions. A prudent borrower will, however, seek an amendment to the agreement so that it cannot be successfully be argued that the borrower is in default despite there being in place a waiver by the lenders of their rights to take action as a result of the breach.

One of the borrower's concerns would be that a dissenting lender – who had voted against the waiver – might have some cause of action against it, but that ought not to be the case because there will usually be a provision to the effect that any instruction given by an Instructing Group to the Agent will be binding on all the lenders. The borrower might also be concerned that the breach, if not written out rather than being 'waived', could lead to its making or repeating an incorrect representation under some other loan agreement which might give to another syndicate a right to take steps adverse to the interests of the borrower. This is the sort of chain reaction that borrowers fear.

Thus, a contemporary syndicated loan agreement will have an amendment clause which deals with the circumstances in which the Agent or an Instructing Group may or may not agree to amend the agreement. This is a good example of how the LMA has influenced the 'starting point' for syndicated loan documentation – a topic worth a further digression.

One of the most important early decisions taken by the LMA was to involve the debtor side – in the form of the Association of Corporate Treasurers – in the discussions leading to the promulgation of LMA's first standard form syndicated loan facility agreements. The downside to this process, from a lender's perspective, is that standard provisions and approaches originally conceived and agreed to as being appropriate for 'investment grade' borrowers have effectively become the market standard starting point – if not the usual finishing point – irrespective of the status of the borrower. This was the inevitable result of the desire to create an active secondary loan market in London which led to the creation of the LMA. Traders do not mind what it is they are trading or whether it is trading high or low – as long as they are not long or short in the wrong direction.

An Instructing Group's powers invariably include the ability to instruct the Agent to accelerate the loan (or to put it on an 'on-demand basis') and/or to cancel any unutilised commitment to lend. The Agent will usually have a residual discretion to take such action on its own initiative but it is unlikely to exercise this discretion in any but the most unusual of circumstances. If it were to accelerate a loan on its own initiative it would have to be satisfied that if it did not do so there would be some immediate, material prejudice to the lenders.

Is there protection for the minority?

The recent (and important) case of *Redwood Master Fund Ltd v (1) TD Bank Europe Ltd, (2) UPC Distribution Holdings BV and (3) UPC Financing Partnership* [2002] EWHC 2703 (Ch) establishes that there is, but that this does not mean that a disadvantaged minority will necessarily have any right to overturn the majority's decision.

The facts in this case are complicated. Schematically there were three syndicated loan facilities (A, B and C) available to a group which wanted to restructure its loan facilities. Originally, each of a group of banks had a pro rata share in each facility, but as a result of numerous trades there were banks with exposure under only A, only B, only C, only A and B or A, B and C. Pursuant to a decision of an Instructing Group, which was exercising a power to amend the agreements, sums were borrowed under A (a standby facility) to enable prepayments to be made in respect of B and C. As a result of the arrangements which were made, some banks were net recipients of repayments, some had their exposure increased and for others the arrangements were neutral.

The conclusions (in my words) that Rimmer J reached in the course of a lengthy and convincing analysis were that:

- if the agreement so provides, a decision of an Instructing Group can bind all lenders;

- such a power is validly exercised if it is exercised in good faith;

- the result may well be that some creditors are adversely affected because the purpose of majority voting provisions is often to resolve issues where different lenders have different interests.

Thus, there is protection for the minority: an Instructing Group's powers must be exercised in good faith and for the purpose for which they were conferred.

The sharing clause

it is a custom more honour'd in the breach than the observance

Despite the emphasis, as I described at the outset, on the several nature of the commitments made by the members of a syndicate, a syndicated loan agreement will always contain a provision – the so-called Sharing Clause – which provides that principal and interest received from the borrower will, if this is necessary to achieve equal treatment, be shared between the lenders.

The English style clause under which excess receipts are handed over to the agent for redistribution – where 'excess' means the extra recovery made where a lender receives a disproportionately large payment – was something which I developed because there is a problem under English law with the US approach of banks buying and selling participations, ie, in English terms, acquiring or taking assignments of claims on the borrower. The problem with this is that, in practice, such assignments would be effected by means of electronic payments between the banks, but under English law some of these assignments would potentially have to be made in writing. This is because after the first round of assignments, subsequent assignments might be assignments of equitable interests which, under the Law of Property Act 1925, s 53(1)(c), can only be effected in writing – and it would be impracticable to satisfy this requirement. In addition to this, at the time the 'redistribution of payments' approach was introduced, stamp duty would have been payable on the assignments if they were made in writing in order to address the equitable interests issue (although it would not be now in any ordinary circumstances).

The clause tends not to be implemented, but in a restructuring context it can be a powerful disincentive to 'holdouts' – creditors who do not wish to participate in the restructuring – who would like to sue the debtor. If a creditor declines to participate and sues the debtor under a conventional syndicated loan agreement, it could be obliged to share what it recovers with other creditors having a much larger aggregate share of the loan. Contemporary sharing clauses tend to provide that a lender can only benefit if it contributes to the cost and that a lender can not be compelled to participate in an action for recovery, but these provisions do not materially change the dynamics of the situation in a restructuring.

Agency provisions

I have made a few references to the Agent which, as an agent for the lenders, is a conduit for fund flows, handles operational matters and co-ordinates decision making (and, I should add, implements the decisions that are taken). In order to perform its functions, the Agent needs various rights and powers, as well as the benefit of exculpatory provision which are intended to eliminate or reduce various areas of legal risk for the Agent. The Agent also has various specific obligations under the agreement, although, perhaps surprisingly, no express, general obligation to exercise its rights and powers either in the interests of the lenders or so as to implement the transactions contemplated in the loan agreement, is imposed on the Agent. I put this down to the fact that the agency provision in a syndicated loan is largely the product of lawyers who were instructed by the agent banks and who had, therefore, no incentive to add to the agent's burdens.

The Agent's rights

An LMA-style agency clause will usually start with a provision which states that the Agent is authorised by each lender to 'exercise the rights, powers, authorities specifically delegated to it under or in connection with this Agreement together with any other incidental rights, powers, authorities and discretions'. This is an odd piece drafting involving change for the sake of it. It is not at all clear what 'other incidental' means – it suggests that those rights etc which are specifically delegated to it are themselves incidental – which is obviously wrong. What we used to refer to were the express rights and 'all such rights, powers and discretions as are reasonably incidental thereto', but this measured lack of precision was clearly too much for some lawyer (or group of lawyers) unable to understand – or unwilling to accept – the benefits that can flow from the judicious use of uncertainty. The 'grey area' created by the phrase 'reasonably incidental thereto' is potentially very helpful to the Agent. (There are those who cannot abide words such as 'thereto' because they are not plain, modern English, but I do not have a problem with words which serve a purpose and do so clearly and economically.)

The Agent is given the right to assume that no default (on the part of the borrower) has occurred unless it has received notice to the contrary 'in its capacity as agent'. This provision is intended to ensure that an agent which has knowledge of a default in some other way, eg, as a lender to the borrower, is not obliged to take action as agent. There are clearly confidentiality issues for an agent in this position. Finally – and this is, of course, not a comprehensive review of all an agent bank's express rights, I would mention that the Agent is usually given three specific rights which it would not have in the absence of express provisions to that effect, namely: the right to profit from being the Agent without accounting to the lenders for that profit; the right to engage in other business with the borrower; and the right to resign.

The Agent's obligations

The Agent will have certain obligations of a general nature, usually found partly in a clause of this name and partly in the clause dealing with the status of an Instructing Group's instructions (an historic rather than logical arrangement), which will often be no more extensive than those set out in the following three provisions – a surprisingly short list of obligations for the party which has a pivotal role in the day-to-day administration and operation of the facility.

1 The Agent shall promptly inform each Lender of the contents of any notice or document received by it in its capacity as Agent from any of the Borrowers under this Agreement.

2 The Agent shall promptly notify the Lenders of the occurrence of any Event of Default or any default by a Borrower in the due performance of or compliance with its obligations under any Finance Document upon becoming aware of the same.

3 Unless a contrary indication appears in a Finance Document, the Agent shall (a) act in accordance with any instructions given to it by an Instructing Group (or, if so instructed by an Instructing Group, refrain from acting or exercising any right, power, authority or discretion vested in it as Agent) and (b) shall not be liable for any act (or omission) if it acts (or refrains from taking any action) in accordance with such an instruction of an Instructing Group.

As I mentioned earlier there is no express provision obliging the Agent to administer and operate the facility, although there are specific duties to inform lenders if the conditions precedent are satisfied and of their respective participations in any proposed advance. For example, the Agent's input is required to fix interest rates, currency equivalents and the like but the only obligation usually imposed on the Agent is, as indicated above, to inform the lenders of the contents of any notices it receives from the borrower. It is probably the case that if there is provision of this kind which should be there but is not, it can be implied because 'it is necessary in the business sense to give efficacy to the contract', to use the formulation adopted by Scrutton LJ in *Reigate v Union Manufacturing Co (Ramsbottom) Ltd* [1918–19] All ER Rep 143 at 149.

It used to be stated that the Agent shall not be under any obligations other than those for which express provision is made, but this obstacle to the existence of implied obligations for the Agent is apparently no longer included, at least it is not included in the LMA's standard forms. This is another result of the LMA's decision to create standard forms acceptable to investment grade borrowers. However, a provision to the effect that, unless otherwise provided, the Agent's duties are solely mechanical and administrative in nature is still used. This provision, the precise effect of which is unclear, was inserted on the instructions of US banks during the sovereign debt restructuring era. They were in no doubt as to the virtues of this particular grey area which serves to limit the Agent's obligations to a limited class of activities without being unhelpfully specific.

Exculpation and indemnity

Ordinarily, an agent will owe some fiduciary duties to its principal, such as obligations to act in good faith, to keep its own money separate from the principal's and not to profit through dealings with its principal's customer. As well as containing a statement that the Agent is not a fiduciary or trustee, a syndicated loan agreement will specifically address the right of the Agent to engage in business with the borrower and to retain for is own benefit sums it receives for its own account. There is case law that supports the view that a trustee – and thus, by analogy, an agent – can exclude (by clear words) all liability other than liability than for its 'own actual fraud' (*Armitage v Nurse* [1998] Ch 241). Market practice is for liability to be excluded unless caused by gross negligence or wilful misconduct although it is not clear whether English law recognises a difference between negligence and gross negligence. In *Armitage v Nurse* (at 254) Millett LJ said that it would be 'very surprising if our law drew the line between liability for ordinary negligence and liability for gross negligence'. If it does, the benefit for an Agent is likely to be undone by the fact of its being under a greater duty of care as a professional agent than would be the case if it were not a professional agent.

(In the course of his judgment Millett LJ also referred to a remark by the judge (Willes J) in a much earlier case (*Grill v General Iron Screw Colliery Co* (1866) LR 1 CP 600) to the effect that 'gross negligence is ordinary negligence with a vituperative epithet' and to another judicial witticism of a former Lord Justice of Appeal to the effect that 'the main duty of a trustee is to commit judicious breaches of trust', referring to the legal principle that trustees, and fiduciaries generally, can exclude liability for deliberate breaches of their duties if the breaches are committed honestly – see Chapter 13, pages 194–195 for more on this topic.)

A number of exculpatory provisions, together with the stipulation that lenders take their own credit decisions and the inclusion of an express right for the Agent to refrain from taking action unless instructed by an Instructing Group, found their way into syndicated loan agreements in the wake of the so-called 'Colocotronis' litigation in the mid-1970s. This was a dispute between purchasers of participations in loans which had been made to members of the Colocotronis Shipping Group and European American Banking Corporation, which was the lender. Although the position is somewhat different in the case of a syndicated loan facility where the lenders make their own loans rather than buying in to loans made by others, the litigation caused the arrangers of syndicated loans – and the Agent was almost always an arranger or an affiliate of an arranger – to think carefully about the potential for being held responsible by the lenders if the loan went bad. As we have seen, the lenders were not always as well placed as the arrangers to assess the risks of participating in a syndicated loan facility.

(For some contemporary insights into these and other issues which arose in the early days of the international syndicated loan market, see Hugh Pigott's paper 'The Historical Development of Syndicated Eurocurrency Loan Agreements', *International Business Lawyer*, 1982 Vol 10(vi), which is reproduced in the Appendix.)

Transferability

The most recent (relatively speaking – it was introduced about 20 years ago) defining characteristic of a syndicated loan agreement is transferability. Transferability is the name given to the procedures, now invariably incorporated into English law syndicated loan agreements, whereby a lender can 'transfer' all or part of its outstanding loans/ commitment to a new lender. The word 'transfer' is a deliberate misnomer – under English law obligations cannot be transferred (as they can, I understand, under New York law) – which I used to convey (no pun intended) the idea that a stake in a syndicated loan facility was being moved from one lender to another. Because transferability is now an essential part of an English law syndicated loan agreement some consideration of it is essential if the features which distinguish a syndicated loan from a bilateral (or single bank) loan agreement are to be discussed – for a more detailed, contemporary analysis, see Chapter 10.

The importance of the concept – which can also be applied to 'sub-participations' – is that it provides a simple means of enabling lenders to shift not just claims, but also obligations, in such a way that when a lender joins a syndicate through a transfer procedure, it becomes a full member of the syndicate. It has all the rights and obligations it would have had if it had been an original member of the syndicate, including the benefit of indemnities from the borrower and the burden of the sharing clause and certain indemnities in favour of the agent.

Assignment

Under English law, a claim to repayment of a loan, or for payment of interest, is what is known as a 'chose in action' the benefit of which can, subject to any applicable provisions in the agreement, be transferred by assignment. 'Chose in action' is a hybrid, French/English phrase – it loses its charm when translated as 'thing in action' – which literally means something which can only be enforced by a legal action as opposed to a physical act (of taking possession) which would be the case for moveable or immovable property – see Chapter 6 for a discussion of what choses in action are and how they can be assigned.

In order to deal with the fact that under English law such contractual rights can be transferred (by assignment) but related obligations cannot, late 1970s/early 1980s English law syndicated loan agreements used a two-part approach to sales of lenders' interests in syndicated loans:

- an assignment by the seller; and

- a promise by the buyer to behave as a bank which is a party to the agreement.

The idea was to give to the Agent the benefit of an indemnity from the new lender and to ensure that the new lender got the full benefit of the increased costs and tax indemnities given by the borrower (protective provisions as I called them in Chapter 2 – see pages 16 and 19–20) as well as the benefit (and burden) of the sharing clause.

Novation

This two-part 'assignment and assumption' approach was unsatisfactory: the new lender was not truly a party to the loan agreement and, at the time, there were UK stamp duty issues. So 'novation' was used, but in a novel way. Novation is the word used in English law to describe a situation in which C becomes a party to a contract with A in place of B. It is not a complicated idea and has a name more because of the need to fit the process into the English law concepts of consideration, offer and acceptance and privity (see Chapters 1 and 10) than because it is inherently important. In a novation, the departing party (B) is released from its obligations by A at the request of C which is good consideration for the obligations which C assumes towards A. It is important to note that if A agreed to pay £100 to B as payment for B's servicing A's car and the contract was novated so as to become a contract between A and C, a new debt arises, owed by A to C, when the service has been completed – and A owes nothing to B. There is no assignment of a claim from B to C.

If we apply these principles to a syndicated loan agreement, a contract between Borrower, Agent and Lenders, we can see how the objective can be achieved – but how can this be done, on a regular basis if there are, say, 50 lenders each of whom wants to sell (and perhaps buy back) parts of its stake in the facility on a regular basis?

A standing offer to novate

The answer is to employ the fairly old, but extremely helpful, concept of a 'standing offer' to enter into a contract. In the Smoke Ball Case (*Carlill v Carbolic Smoke Ball Co* [1893] 1 QB 256) the company making the offer advertised its 'smoke balls' as a cure for influenza – inhale the vapours, its advertisements said, and you will be cured. As we have seen (in Chapter 1, page 5) the customer followed the instructions, was not cured and was successful in her claim for damages for breach of contract.

The court held that the advertisement was a standing offer to enter into a contract which the customer accepted when she followed the instructions (and her doing so was regarded as valuable consideration). The idea that this approach could be utilised in relation to syndicated loans emerged in discussions I was part of in 1983 or thereabouts and shortly afterwards I decided to draft the necessary provisions – and transferability was born. As long as appropriate, carefully drafted language is used, the loan agreement can constitute a standing offer on the part of all parties – borrower, agent bank, lenders – to accept the substitution of a new lender for all or part of the commitment of an existing lender. In this way a lender's commitments to the borrower and the other parties can be 'transferred' and new lenders can acquire new claims on the borrower and the other parties.

The key objective was to devise a procedure which would be easy to use in practice – the result was a form of 'transfer certificate' to be signed by the 'transferor' and the 'transferee' and delivered to the Agent in order to effect the transfer on the basis that the business deal between buyer and seller was documented separately. Chapter 10 contains a detailed review, from a contemporary perspective, of the commercial and legal issues which led to the use of transfer certificates and the now out of fashion, if not obsolete, transferable loan certificates.

Issues in transferability

Just as with a conventional assignment of all or part of a lender's rights in respect of a loan, there may be a provision requiring the consent of the borrower before a transfer of a loan is made. For the borrower there is a particular concern with regard to the transfer of a lender's commitment to lend (if there is one) from the seller to the buyer.

In the distressed debt market, ie in relation to loans which trade at a substantial discount to par, assignment is the preferred means of transfer. Purchasers of distressed debt are not generally seeking to acquire a commitment to lend nor to assume sharing obligations towards other lenders.

There are two particular issues which arise because the effect of a transfer by novation is to create a new debt. Where the facility is a secured facility, it may be that such a transfer would have a detrimental effect on the security. If the security is created in favour of a trustee, this should not happen because it is the covenant to pay in the security document which is secured, but the position is different where the security is in favour of an agent for the lenders (see Chapter 13, page 200). In relation to loans for which an exchange control consent was required, a similar issue arises. A purchaser would want to be satisfied that the consent would cover the new debts which arise when a transfer by novation is effected.

Two postscripts

1 It is common in the acquisition finance market for an arranger to sign a loan agreement as a single lender on the basis that transfer procedures will be used to bring in other lenders when the deal has been syndicated. If this is to be done effeciently, agency provisions and transfer procedures will need to be incorporated into the loan agreement.

2 The concept of transferability arose in the context of an emerging secondary market in loans. The principles are equally applicable where there is a need to add further borrowers or guarantors to a syndicated facility after the initial parties have signed it. This too is a routine procedure in acquisition finance transactions.

CHAPTER 10

Transferability of loans and loan participations

This chapter deals with the contractual basis of 'transferability' in syndicated loans, a fundamentally important concept which I introduced to the syndicated loan market in the early 1980s. It was written in 1987, but I have included it because although out of date in certain respects, it remains correct with regard to the core concept and is of interest in that when it was written the syndicated loan market was under threat. Accordingly, I have let it stand largely unaltered so that it speaks, in effect, as of Spring 1987; it should not, therefore, be relied on as providing an up to date analysis of any tax, stamp duty or regulatory issues. Text which I have added, or which I have edited in any material respect, appears in square brackets.

The advent of securitisation

On the banking side of the rapidly changing capital markets the emphasis continues to be on 'securitisation'. This is the word which has been coined to describe the shift away from the creation of assets which are to be held until maturity to the creation of assets which are securities or are tradeable as if they were securities.

Although banks continue to make loans with the specific objective of retaining the risks and rewards of those loans until maturity, it is more often their objective to create trading opportunities. For borrowers – or issuers, as one should, perhaps, now call them – one impact of this shift is that the price at which an issuer's debt instruments are traded will determine the cost to that issuer of raising further funds. For lenders there is a continuing need to develop new products which can compete in a rapidly changing market.

The shift from lending to trading has not taken place in one fell swoop. Moreover, the raising of funds through the issue of securities has not, and probably cannot, entirely supplant the other traditional form of fund raising, that is, bank loans. One of the techniques which has given conventional bank lending a new lease of life is the relatively recent concept of 'transferability'. This technique, which has its origins in the syndicated loan market, is one, it can now be seen, which may also be used to give further stimulus to the already active secondary market in loan participations. [In 2003 LMA's participation agreements are indeed transferable.]

Much has been written about the manner in which securitisation has occurred and the forms it takes. The purpose of this article is to consider the extent to which, through the application of the concept of transferability, it may prove practicable to 'securitise' otherwise conventional loan assets.

From loans to securities

During [the years 1982 to 1987, the syndicated term loan all but disappeared in relative terms], its use being reserved for special circumstances such as project finance and secured lending.[1] In its heyday during the 1970s the syndicated term loan was the vehicle whereby a majority of the funds available on the international capital markets were raised and it was sovereign lending which took pride of place. It is not surprising, therefore, that the 'debt crisis' – the incessant rescheduling of sovereign debt which began five or six years ago and is set to continue for years to come – precipitated a decline in syndicated lending and gave its own impetus to the move towards securitisation.

One of the early [mid-1980s] substitutes for the conventional syndicated term loan was the note issuance facility or the multiple option facility, as such arrangements are sometimes described. These are hybrid arrangements which combine securities techniques with the more conventional structures of revolving standby loan facilities. As is mentioned below, elements of 'transferability' are usually to be found in such arrangements.

In its commonest form, a multiple [option] facility offers to the borrower/ issuer a note issuance facility operated through a tender panel mechanism, a short-term advances facility and a committed underwriting (or 'backstop') facility, the analogue of the revolving standby loan facility. The short-term paper issued under the note issuance facility would be issued to bearer and would, therefore, be transferable without more ado. In addition, elements of transferability would be found in relation to the short-term advances and in the backstop facility, where a procedure for shifting the risk of a medium-term commitment is regarded as essential.

[Subsequently], Euro-commercial paper programmes, arranged for an issuer by one bank or a small group of banks, have taken the place of multiple [option] facilities. Such programmes provide mechanisms whereby an issuer can raise finely priced short-term funds without the necessity of entering into the sometimes cumbersome and always complicated two- or three-tiered multiple option facilities.

The absence of fee structures and the other impedimenta of syndicated arrangements further reduce the cost to the issuer of raising funds on the capital market. Thus it is that the multiple facility contains within itself the seeds of destruction of its committed syndicated element.

Back to loans

Euro-commercial paper programmes are entered into by banks on an uncommitted basis. This is to be expected since the issuer's objective of raising funds at the finest price possible will be met by choosing banks whose primary skills lie in placing its paper. It is hardly surprising that many such banks would not be those from whom to seek medium-term commitments – the giving of such commitments is not the ordinary business of an investment bank, whose placing power is its strength.

It is equally unsurprising that the growth in this market for uncommitted facilities has been mirrored by the growth, in relative terms, in the number of committed single bank loan facilities made available by commercial banks. As with all the previously described arrangements which give rise to loan assets or commitments to lend, such single bank committed facilities are today carefully structured so as to create trading or 'asset sales' opportunities. This is essential if the committed facilities are to be competitively priced.

More specifically, such facilities will, more often than not, be structured as revolving credit facilities under which new advances will be made at the end of successive 'rollover' periods – three- or six-month periods being those most frequently found. This type of structure is useful for 'asset sales' purposes since it permits the 'sale' of the risks and rewards of a loan asset on an interest period by interest period basis.

Such 'rollover' facilities, as they are often known, constitute a reversion to a structure largely unused since the early 1970s, one which requires a new, separate advance to be made for each successive interest period. It was towards the end of the 1970s – in retrospect, towards the end of the first phase of the life of the conventional syndicated loan – that steps were taken to render an interest in a syndicated loan itself more readily transferable.

No sooner were these procedures developed than the rapid decline in syndicated lending – after the onset of the debt crisis – came very close to removing the market in which they were intended to flourish. As a result, the impact of such procedures on the then flourishing syndicated loan market cannot now be assessed. However, they have, found new homes in other areas of banking, such as sovereign debt rescheduling and, more recently, in the secondary market in loan assets. These specific developments will be described later; the techniques whereby transferability has been achieved will first be discussed.

Transferability in syndicated loans

In the mid-1970s a syndicated loan agreement would ordinarily have contained a so-called 'Benefit of Agreement' provision in more or less the terms of the following example.

Benefit of Agreement

(A) This Agreement shall be binding upon and inure to the benefit of each party hereto and its successors and assigns.

(B) The Borrower may not assign or transfer all or any of its rights, benefits and obligations hereunder.

(C) Any Bank may at any time with the prior written consent of the Borrower (which consent shall not be required in the case of an assignment to (i) a company which is a subsidiary of such Bank or (ii) a company of which such Bank is a subsidiary or any other subsidiary of that company and shall not be unreasonably withheld in any other case) assign to any one or more banks or other lending institutions all or any part of such Bank's rights and benefits hereunder and in that event the assignee shall have the same rights against the Borrower as it would have had if it had been a party hereto.

(D) Unless and until an assignee has agreed with the Agent, the Managers and the Banks that it shall be under the same obligations towards each of them as it would have been under if it had been a party hereto, neither the Agent, the Managers nor the Banks shall be obliged to recognise such assignee as having the rights again them which it would have had if it had been a party hereto.

(E) Any Bank may disclose to a potential assignee or to any person who may otherwise enter into contractual relations with such Bank in relation to this Agreement such information about the Borrower as such Bank shall consider appropriate.[2]

Such a provision does not (nor was it intended to) promote an active secondary market in participations in respect of the underlying loan. It is not just that, in the case of assignments to unrelated financial institutions, the borrower's consent is required; more importantly, no assignment effected pursuant to the provision could cause the assignee fully to replace its predecessor. This is the case in two particularly important respects:

(1) despite the express language at the end of sub-clause (C), doubt would exist as to the extent to which an assignee could acquire the full benefit of increased costs and tax indemnities;

(2) in so far as the lending banks remain under obligations to the borrower, the assignor (the selling bank) would remain so liable to the borrower and the assignee (the buying bank) would not acquire any obligations owed directly to the borrower.

Resolution of these two issues is essential, from both the seller's and the buyer's point of view, if a lender's interest in a loan is to be readily transferable. The answer to this problem lies in the contractual arrangement known as novation.

Novation

Novation is an arrangement whereby the obligations of one party (the debtor) owed to another (the creditor) are released by the creditor in consideration of a new debtor agreeing with the creditor to assume responsibility for performance of obligations formerly owed by the original debtor. To quote from the judgment in one of the leading cases on this area of English law:

> A debtor cannot relieve himself of his liability to his creditor by assigning the burden of the obligation to somebody else; this can only be brought about by the consent of all three, and involves the release of the original debtor.[3]

In this classical description of novation, a lender with continuing obligations, for example, to lend further money, may be regarded as the debtor and the borrower as the creditor. Thus, the selling bank (the lender) can relieve itself of its continuing obligations to a borrower only if the borrower so agrees and, if the arrangement is one of novation, the borrower will so agree in consideration of a new lender, the buying bank, agreeing to assume those continuing obligations.

In effect, a new contract is entered into by the three parties – the borrower, the selling bank and the buying bank. By the same token, such a three-party arrangement can at the same time be used to cause any outstanding indebtedness of the borrower to the selling bank to be discharged and to be replaced by a new debt which is identical to the old debt save for its being owed to the buying bank. In this case, the agreement by the borrower to repay the new debt which it owes to the buying bank provides the consideration for the original lender's release of the old debt.[4]

For present purposes, the critical element in the brief passage cited above is the requirement that all the parties to the transaction must be involved in the contract of novation. If this principle were applied without modification to a syndicated loan arrangement, the result would be that for a new lender to replace an old lender as to all rights and all obligations, then all the parties to the syndicated loan agreement would have to be actively involved. Such an approach might be legally effective but it is hardly practicable.

The problem to be resolved is, therefore, the following: given that a new lender can be caused fully to replace an old lender by means of a novation, how can this be done in a manner which requires only the active participation of those directly concerned, that is, the borrower, the selling bank and the buying bank? The answer to this question lies in an innovative application of one of the older principles of the English law of contract: namely, that a person may validly and effectively offer to contract with any person who cares to fulfil such conditions as are specified in that offer.

This principle of English law, that an offer may be made 'to the public at large', was established in the case of *Carlill v Carbolic Smoke Ball Co.*[5] This case involved the proprietors of a medical preparation called 'the Carbolic Smoke Ball' who had issued an advertisement in which they offered to pay £100 to any person who succumbed to influenza after having used one of their smoke balls in a specified manner and for a specified period. A user of the smoke hall duly caught influenza and she sued successfully for the £100. In the course of his judgment in the Court of Appeal Bowen LJ said, in the rhetorical manner of English judges, 'Why should not an offer be made to all the world which is to ripen into a contract with anybody who comes forward and performs the condition?'.

Application of this principle to syndicated loan arrangements gave rise to the idea that the parties to a syndicated loan agreement could at the outset offer to accept a limited novation of the original contract, that is, a novation involving primarily the borrower, the selling bank and the buying bank. The result was a 'Benefit of Agreement' provision, the relevant parts of which were as set out below.

Benefit of Agreement
(A) This agreement shall be binding upon and inure to the benefit of each party hereto and its successors and assigns.
(B) The Borrower may not assign or transfer all or any of its rights, benefits and obligations hereunder.

(C) Any Bank may *with the prior written consent of the Borrower (which consent shall not be required in the case of a transfer (i) to a subsidiary of such Bank or a company of which such Bank is a subsidiary or (ii) to any other subsidiary of that company and shall not be unreasonably withheld in any other case)*[6]at any time transfer all or any part of such Bank's rights, benefits and obligations hereunder to a Transferee.

(D) Each of the Borrower and the Banks hereby agrees that after receipt by the Agent of a Transfer Certificate and upon satisfaction of any conditions to which such Transfer Certificate is expressed to be subject:

   (i)   to the extent that in such Transfer Certificate the Bank party thereto seeks to transfer its rights and obligations hereunder, the Borrower and such Bank shall each be released from further obligations to the other hereunder and their respective rights against each other shall be cancelled (such rights and obligations being referred to in this Clause as 'discharged rights and obligations'); and

   (ii) the Borrower and the Transferee party thereto shall each assume obligations towards each other and acquire rights against each other which differ from the discharged rights and obligations only in so far as the obligations so assumed and the rights so acquired by the Borrower are owed to and constituted by claims against such Transferee and not such Bank.

(E) Upon any such transfer taking effect:

   (i)   the Agent shall notify the Borrower of such transfer; and

   (ii) the Agent, such Transferee and the other Banks shall acquire the same rights and assume the same obligations between themselves as they would have acquired and assumed had such Transferee originally been a party hereto with the obligations assumed by it as a result of such transfer.

Such a provision has the effect of causing the borrower and the lenders to offer to accept a new lender (a transferee) in substitution for an existing lender subject only to the selling bank and the buying bank preparing, completing and signing a specified form of 'transfer certificate' and delivering the same to the agent bank.

It is to be noted that the stated effect of such arrangements is that the borrower and the buying bank acquire as between themselves rights and obligations which are no different to the rights and obligations previously arising between the borrower and the selling bank. In addition, it is also expressly stated that the buying bank will have the same rights against, and will owe the same obligations to, the agent and the other lenders as it would have done had it originally been a party to the loan agreement. Subject only to the extent to which such 'transfers' could be affected with or without notification to or approval of the borrower,[7] the provisions set out above provided a mechanism whereby a lender's participation in a syndicated loan arrangement could be transferred at such a price as the selling bank and the buying bank might agree.

However, this early transfer procedure [which is the one still in use] remained somewhat cumbersome. In order for the selling bank and the buying bank to effect a transfer, one of them (no doubt the selling bank) would have to prepare a form of transfer certificate, based on a pro forma set out in a schedule to the loan agreement. In addition, the procedure (in the simple form stated above) did not address such issues as the amounts or multiples in which participations could be transferred nor, for example, the need for a register to be maintained on which the interests of the lending banks party to the loan agreement from time to time could be recorded.

Transferable Loan Certificates

The first opportunity to [address] these and other related issues arose in 1984 in connection with a thoroughgoing readjustment of the terms of an already outstanding US$500,000,000 loan to Ireland. It was this transaction which introduced to the Eurocurrency market Transferable Loan Certificates, usually referred to as TLCs.

As described above, previous transfer procedures made effective use of the English law concept of novation and applied the principle established in the *Carlill* case to create the concept of a standing offer to novate. What was missing was a convenient mechanism whereby a 'transfer' could be effected as easily as if, for example, shares were being bought and sold.

This issue was resolved by the creation of a form of certificate signed by the Borrower and by the agent bank (on its own behalf and on behalf of its principals – the lenders) delivery of which to the agent bank would constitute a standing offer, made by all the parties to the agreement, to accept (by way of novation) a new lender in substitution for a former lender as a party to the agreement.

The crucial statement appearing on the face of each such certificate issued under this arrangement reads as follows:

> Delivery of this Certificate by the Holder to the Transferee constitutes an irrevocable offer by the Borrower, the Holder, the Agent and the other Banks to accept the transferee as a Bank party to the agreement with a Participation of the amount and type for which this Certificate is issued.

Each such certificate was signed [by means of facsimile signatures] by the Borrower and by the agent bank and contained appropriate provisions whereby the 'transfer' of the Holder's Participation – in this case, the lender's right to receive repayment with interest, of a specified repayment instalment of the loan – would take effect on delivery to the agent bank of the certificate further signed by both the 'Holder' and the 'Transferee'. (At the time of a 'transfer', the 'Holder' would be the selling bank – an original party to the agreement or a bank which had become a party as a transferee – and the 'Transferee' would be the buying bank.)

It is not practicable to describe here the details of the provisions in the agreement regulating the issue of TLCs and the transfer procedures, provisions such as those providing for the issue of a new TLC to a transferee and for the maintenance of a register by the agent bank identifying the parties to the agreement at a given time. What can be said is that as long as sufficient care is taken in the drafting of those provisions, TLCs provide a means whereby a new lender can replace a former lender as a party to a loan agreement on a basis which gives the new lender all the rights and all the obligations it would have had as an original party to the loan agreement.

The TLC route has been widely utilised since its creation in 1984 and [had] an established place in the international banking market. It is not, for example, suitable for use in the revolving underwriting facilities which form part of many multiple facilities – the issue, in advance, of TLCs is not practicable – nor will the use of TLCs necessarily be appropriate in relation to secured facilities. The TLC route [was] nevertheless, a useful technique in the syndicated loan market particularly with regard to unsecured single currency loans[8] and [could] be used for more complex arrangements, for example, multi-currency facilities.

In any particular case, the fact that a 'transfer' by novation of debt gives rise to a new debt must be borne in mind. Exchange control or similar regulations, or the existence of security, may make it essential that a debt, once created, must remain. Such considerations led to the use of 'Transferable Loan Instruments' (TLIs) – debt instruments issued in conjunction with novation procedures.[9]

Whatever the respective merits of TLCs, TLIs and other procedures, the foregoing analysis of the legal basis of transferability makes it clear that any loan asset or other debtor-creditor claim can be structured so as to be transferable.

Transferability in the secondary market

Transfers by way of novation can most easily be made in respect of unsecured single currency loans – as mentioned above, it is in relation to such loan assets that the TLC route is most appropriate. The realisation that transferability can, therefore, be introduced into the secondary market in loan assets [was in 1987] a relatively recent innovation.

The previously quoted judicial summary (see [page 136 above]) of the law relating to novation provides the clue as to how the techniques described above might be applied to the secondary market. In order to solve the problem the workings of the secondary market in loan assets must be understood.

One of the most popular and durable of the various asset sales techniques used in London is the non-recourse funding arrangement[10] which is usually referred to as a participation (or, sometimes, a sub-participation). Such arrangements give rise to a debtor-creditor relationship between the selling bank (debtor) and the buying bank (creditor). The distinguishing feature or the debt owed by the selling bank is that its payment is contingent on payment by another (the borrower) of a debt owed to the selling bank. This gives rise to numerous special provisions in a participation agreement, but in all other respects the relationship between the selling bank and the buying bank can be regarded as the same as that which ordinarily exists between debtors and their [creditors, an analysis confirmed by the Privy Council in *Lloyds Bank plc v Clarke* [2002] UKPC 27, [2002] 2 All ER (Comm) 992].

Given that this is the case, the principles underlying transferability of loan assets can be applied to the simple two-party loan contract constituted by a participation agreement. If the debtor (the selling bank), the creditor (the buying bank) and the new buyer so agree, the original contract can be terminated and replaced by a new contract to which only the selling bank and the new buyer are party.[11] A participation agreement which is written with such arrangements in mind can create a very simple procedure analogous to that applicable to TLCs. The first buyer receives a 'Transferable Participation Certificate' (TPC) which, once countersigned by the first buyer and its intended successor (the new buyer) and delivered to the debtor, will cause the novation to occur. In its turn the new buyer receives a TPC and the process can be repeated.

It is thus a relatively straightforward matter to create a transferable participation arrangement which is genuinely tradeable.[12] For the lawyer, one of the problems to be solved in relation to such arrangements is the drafting of the requisite documentation. For example, it is important to remember that on the occurrence of a 'transfer' it is the most recent contract (between selling bank and participant) which is being novated, but the terms of the new contract are identical to those of the first contract made between the selling bank and the first participant. Thus, the TPC will contain a provision to the following effect:

> Delivery of this Certificate by the Holder to the Transferee constitutes, if such delivery is made in accordance with the terms of the Participation Agreement, an irrevocable offer by the Bank to accept the Transferee as the Participant under the Participation Agreement in substitution for the Holder. The Participation Agreement to which this Certificate relates is the agreement made between the Bank and [name of the first buyer] on (date of original contract) or, where applicable, an agreement replacing the same and arising pursuant to the most recent transfer made pursuant thereto.

The development of the TPC brings into sharp focus an issue which inevitably has to be addressed in the context of transferability. If the substitution of a new contracting party, whether a new lender or a new participant, is to be a simple mechanical process, will the debtor (borrower or selling bank) have any control over the identity of its new creditor?

The approach to be adopted on this issue will vary from case to case. A selling bank which carefully controls its exposure, financial and otherwise, to other banks might well approve of the following approach under which the selling bank retains a veto over proposed transfers:

> 'Approved Transferee' means an Eligible Transferee which the Bank has agreed to accept as a new Participant before delivery to the Bank of the Transferable Participation Certificate in which such Eligible Transferee is named as Transferee, and for this purpose 'Eligible Transferee' means a firm, company or corporation which is a bank or financial institution and/or whose ordinary business is or includes the acquisition and disposal of securities and/or the extension of credit.

It might seem that the introduction of a seller's veto on transfers defeats the object of the exercise, but this is not necessarily the case. In the example quoted above, the concept of an 'Eligible Transferee' is included specifically to make the point that the right of veto is not intended to be exercised in the case of a bank transferee save in exceptional circumstances.

Before further legal aspects of TLCs and TPCs are discussed, mention should be made of another business aspect of such arrangements which is a direct consequence of the legal principles involved. As previously indicated, there is sufficient consideration given by the parties to the novation which occurs on a transfer whether or not the transferee pays a fair price (or, indeed, any price) for the asset it is to acquire. Thus, the other parties involved, be it the selling bank or the borrower, the agent bank and the other lenders, need not be concerned with the price paid by the transferee to the transferor. The efficacy of the novation is not dependent on the financial arrangements made between the transferor and the transferee.

Other legal aspects of TLCs and TPCs

The contractual position with regard to TLCs is relatively straightforward, but other legal issues, which affect Transferable Participations as they do TLCs, require consideration. [In this section the law is stated as it was in 1987.]

Perhaps the first question to he asked is whether or not a TLC is a debenture or is otherwise a security. English law knows of no single comprehensive definition of what is or is not a debenture or is otherwise to be regarded as a security [but see Chapter 2, page 12].[13] On the contrary, the meaning of such words is often defined by statute for specific purposes in terms which do not give a general answer to the question.[14] So far as TLCs are concerned, the answer is that a TLC is not a debenture since it is not in any sense an acknowledgement of debt. It (or its delivery) is evidence of (or constitutes) an offer to enter into certain specified contractual arrangements as a result of which indebtedness will arise. Not surprisingly there is no direct authority for this proposition, although there is a wealth of authority for the contrary proposition that a debenture is an instrument whereby a company creates or acknowledges indebtedness [and in practice this is the view which prevails].[15]

The next question to be answered is [whether Stamp Duty Reserve Tax[16] has any application to transfers effected by means of TLCs. The relevant statutory provisions make subject to this tax] certain agreements to transfer chargeable securities. The charge to tax will arise unless within two months after the agreement (a) an instrument is executed pursuant to the agreement and the instrument transfers the chargeable securities to the intended new owner; and (b) the instrument 'transferring the chargeable securities to which the agreement relates is duly stamped in accordance with the enactments relating to stamp duty *if it is chargeable with stamp duty or otherwise required to be stamped*'.[17]

With regard to TLCs, the correct view would seem to be that since no property is transferred on the execution and delivery of a TLC, a 'transfer' so effected is outside the scope of SDRT. If this view were to be incorrect the provisions of the Finance Act 1986, s 87(5), would in any event save the 'transfer' from the charge to tax (subject to observance of the two months' requirement) since the transaction would not give rise to any 'conveyance on sale' giving rise to a charge to stamp duty.

The final aspect of TLCs which may be mentioned at this point concerns the applicability of the Income and Corporation Taxes Act 1970, s 54.

As mentioned above, the relationship between a selling bank and its participant under a participation agreement (whether or not transferable) is a debtor-creditor relationship. With regard to the payment of interest to the Participant, the selling bank is to be regarded as paying interest to the participant in circumstances to which ICTA 1970, s 54(2)(b) will ordinarily apply.[18]

Future developments

Having reviewed the various ways in which transferability can be introduced into otherwise conventional loan assets, by the use of transfer procedures or TLCs, at the primary level, or by the use of transferable participations, at the secondary level, it is time to consider the uses to which these techniques may be put.

Transfer procedures and the use of TLC's are well-established techniques in the vestigial [in 1987] syndicated loan market and in the [then] flourishing market for multiple option facilities [and in 2003 transfer procedures are ubiquitous, but TLCs are no longer used]. In addition, the inclusion in sovereign debt rescheduling agreements of transfer procedures may well [– it did –] become more common. There [was in 1987] a large and fast-growing secondary market in relation to rescheduled sovereign debt which was given fresh impetus by the introduction in sovereign debt rescheduling arrangements of 'debt to equity' provisions.

Such provisions make it possible for the holder of a rescheduled sovereign debt to convert that debt into an equity stake in a company or corporation in the country concerned. In effect, the creditor receives early repayment in local currency which it is then obliged to reinvest locally.

This is not an opportunity which is attractive to bank creditors, but is one which a bank creditor's corporate customers may well find very attractive. For this reason, banks with the appropriate placing power are actively seeking to acquire (or to act as broker in relation to) holdings of rescheduled debt which can in turn be transferred to their corporate customers. It is clear that efficient transfer procedures which have the effect of relieving the bank creditor (whether an intermediary or not) from further obligations in respect of the rescheduled debt will enhance the opportunities available in this market.

The execution by a bank of a series of transferable participation agreements or, perhaps, the arrangement of a transferable syndicated participation agreement, may provide an equally effective (but cheaper) means of 'securitising' an asset, or a pool of assets, as an issue of capital market instruments. This is as yet an undeveloped field of activity, but it is one which promises to make its contribution to the financial engineering which has become the hallmark of today's international banking market.

This was the upbeat conclusion to this paper in 1987 at which time commercial banks were seeking to keep their balance sheets' growth under control, if not actually to reduce the size of their balance sheets. In due course, this gave rise to a securitisation model involving special purpose vehicles and the issue of capital market instruments. Transferable participation arrangements, whether involving the use of transferable participation agreements or simply efficient transfer procedures, could have provided a further means whereby such objectives could be achieved, but the markets developed differently. Citibank's 1986 securitisation of its UK domestic mortgage portfolio by means of the issue of transferable mortgage-backed participation certificates now seems to be just an historical curiosity. That being said, transferability is now – see Chapter 9 – one of the defining characteristics of a contemporary syndicated loan.

1 'The arrangement of syndicated loans fell from $100 billion in 1981 to $20 billion in 1985, while issues of international bonds and floating-rate notes rose from $40 billion to $160 billion'. *Bank of England Quarterly Bulletin*, June 1986, p 209.

2 Such a disclosure clause is, of course, essential if a lender intends to assign or otherwise deal with a loan asset in the secondary market; otherwise the lender may well breach its duty of confidentiality.

3 *Tolhurst v Associated Portland Cement Manufacturers [1900] Ltd* [1902] 2 KB 660 at 688.

4 The author does not share the doubts expressed in 'Selling Loan Assets Under English Law: A Basic Guide', *International Financial Law Review*, May 1986 [p 29].

5 [1892] 2 QB 484; affd [1893] 1 QB 256.

6 The words in italics would have been the subject of a good deal of discussion – to the extent that they benefit the borrower they are to the lenders' detriment.

7 See note 6 above.

8 See note 4 above.

9 For a more detailed review of this topic see 'Developing a Secondary Market in Loan Assets'. *International Financial Law Review*, October 1984 and 'Selling Loan Assets Under English Law: A Basic Guide', *International Financial Law Review*, May 1984.

10 See Maurice Allen, 'Asset Sales- An Analysis of Risk for Buyers and Sellers', [1987] 1 *JIBL*. For an earlier review of the topic see also Martin Hughes and Robert Palache, 'Loan Participations – Some English Law Considerations', *International Financial Law Review*, November 1984.

11 The selling bank gives consideration for the release it receives from the first buyer by assuming new obligations towards the new buyer. The new buyer gives consideration for the selling bank's new obligations by procuring the selling bank's release from its old obligations.

12 A transferable participation is genuinely tradeable in the sense that a buyer can subsequently become a seller – a two-way market becomes possible.

13 The word 'debenture' has, apart from any definition, no precise meaning. It is the name of a genus and not of a species (*Knightsbridge Estate Trust v Byrne* [1940] AC 613, at 621, 628).

14 The Companies Act 1985, s 744 defines a debenture thus: ' ... 'debenture' includes debenture stock, bonds and any other securities of a company, whether constituting a charge on the assets of the company or not'.

15 See for example Pennington, *Company Law*, Butterworths, 1985, p 477; *Levy v Abercorris Slate and Slab Co* (1887) 37 Ch D 260 at 264 where Chitty J. said:

> 'In my opinion a debenture means a document which either creates a debt or acknowledges it and any document which fulfils either of these conditions is a 'debenture'. I cannot find any precise legal definition of the term, it is not either in law or commerce a strictly technical term, or what is called a term of art.'

16 Finance Act 1986, Pt IV.

17 Finance Act 1986, s 87(5) (emphasis added).

18 This brief summary of the [1987] position with regard to Stamp Duty Reserve Tax, Stamp Duty and the Income and Corporation Taxes Act 1970 necessarily simplifies the position. The taxation aspects of a transaction must always be considered on a case-by-case basis [and in the light of current law and practice].

CHAPTER 11

The elegance criterion – an aesthetic approach to legal drafting

> Good drafting skills are not easily acquired – constant practice is required – and even less easily taught. In this chapter I describe an approach to drafting – a methodology – in which keeping the objective in mind can be seen as one of the keys to effective legal drafting. The chapter also contains three drafting exercises – with model answers – which illustrate: the need to express yourself as clearly and succinctly as you can; the importance of getting your ideas well ordered before you start drafting; and the overriding requirement that what you write makes sense in practice.

I have always found it difficult to work out how to teach drafting skills to lawyers because so much, it seems to me, depends on the 'right' choice of word or phrase or sentence structure. The 'knowing how' versus 'knowing that' distinction, as explained by Gilbert Ryle in *The Concept of Mind* (University of Chicago, 1949), is also an issue. It is fine to know that – to have been told that – you should use plain English, use correct syntax and punctuation, be logical, aim for clarity and so on, but knowing that these are objectives to be achieved does not tell you how to achieve them: knowing that is not knowing how. And how can you be expected to remember these and similar rules – 'the usual homilies' as I call them – at 2.00 am in the morning when you have just reached that difficult point that you didn't really understand during the meeting, let alone 12 hours later?

And lawyers are particularly bad at observing even the simplest of rules because they always know better. Thus, however often I mention it, I cannot seem to reduce the prevalence of the dreadful, the hideous, 'lawyer's colon' (as I call it); the colon which is followed by a series of sub-clauses, each ending with a semi-colon but – and this is the problem – containing, as often as not, independent, perfectly formed sentences which end, as they should, with a full stop – oh dear! If this is the substantive structure you want, there is nothing to stop you from saying that: such and such shall be done or dealt with 'as follows'. With as many sentences and paragraphs 'following' the full stop as you please; no colons or semi-colons, save within individual sentences; and syntax which is clear and correct. Punctuation is, as someone once said, 'art not science' – but art, like science, has its rules.

Establishing a methodology

Having said this, perhaps it is really quite simple if you keep in mind what your objective is – why you are doing what you are doing – having absorbed, an approach – a methodology – to the task which will keep you on the right track. In order to develop such a methodology it is helpful to compare some documents which perform different functions (Box 1) and, having done that, to look at who will need to use those documents and when and in what context they will need to use them (Box 2).

Box 1 Different documents

Document	Legal content	Level of usage
Will	High	Once
Mortgage	High	Once
Share Purchase Agreement	Medium	Once
Loan Agreement	Low	Frequent

Take a will, a document with a very high legal content – a will must deal with complex legal issues relating to tax, trusts and probate – and a very low level of usage: you only die once. (I oversimplify. A will may create trusts and interests that last for years. I spent much of my time as an articled clerk – as a trainee solicitor used to be called – dealing with trusts created some 50 or more years earlier by the will of John Joseph Lee deceased. A life tenant died having outlived two generations of relatives, so we had to re-open the estates of her parents, her grandparents and some of her aunts and uncles before we could determine who took the residual estate.)

A mortgage is another example of a document with a high level of legal content. The law relating to the taking and perfecting of security, priorities, powers of enforcement and so on is complex and the issues which arise must be properly dealt with in a mortgage. (For a discussion of the meaning of the term 'mortgage' and other terms with similar meanings, see Chapter 7). And, like a will, a mortgage will only be used once and then only if you default in making the agreed payments. If all goes well and this doesn't happen, both the original mortgage – kept by the bank or building society – and your copy will remain unread. (You certainly won't, if you are a lawyer, bother to read a document whose function you understand and whose terms you cannot influence.)

Moving into the business sphere, a share purchase agreement (an SPA) has a lower but still significant level of legal content, ranging from tax and employment matters to the seller's warranties (as to what it is selling) which form the heart of such an agreement. The level of usage of an SPA (and again I am oversimplifying) is relatively low, certainly once the closing has occurred – the SPA being in part a guide as to how to close the transaction. Otherwise than in its guidebook role, an SPA will only be used in earnest if the purchaser is dissatisfied with what it has purchased and seeks to recover from the seller under the seller's warranties or if the seller has to sue the purchaser for, probably performance related, instalments of the purchase price which the seller withholds.

Last, but not least, we can look at a loan agreement, specifically an agreement for a medium-term, say seven years, loan facility. The legal content in such a loan agreement is relatively low, much of the content being concerned with operational, administrative and credit-related matters such as the borrowing of the loan, its repayment with interest, financial information and conditions, events of default and so on (see Chapters 2 and 9 for more information on the contents of such a loan agreement). But, in marked contrast – deliberate of course – to the other documents we have looked at, a loan agreement will be used very frequently during its life of seven years or thereabouts. Interest has to be recalculated every three or six months (assuming we are dealing with a floating rate loan), financial information has to be delivered (and compliance with financial conditions checked) at least every six months and so on.

Who will need to use these different types of documents and when and in what context?

Box 2 Different users

Document	Users
Will	Lawyers
Mortgage	Lawyers
Share Purchase Agreement	Lawyers and their clients
Loan Agreement	Bankers

Only lawyers will implement the provisions of a will – and, as with your mortgage, you will almost certainly not read your own will because, I am sorry to say, it will probably be written in such obscure terms that try as you might you will not be able to understand what is being said or why – at least, that is my experience. Be that as it may, when the time comes for your will to be used in earnest, it will be a lawyer who uses it. The same is true of a mortgage. In the unlikely event that you default on your home loan, it will be an in-house lawyer at your bank or building society who oversees the enforcement of the security, although that will not require much effort because the legal aspects of enforcement will be minimal (unless extrinsic legal issues, issues unrelated to the mortgage document itself arise, as where one spouse tricks the other into mortgaging their home as security for a hopeless business venture).

With an SPA the position is different. Up to and including the closing phase both lawyers and their clients will be involved in implementing the terms of an SPA. In the case of a loan agreement the position is very different; unless something goes wrong *only* bankers will be using the agreement and the last thing they will want is to have to call their lawyer in order to have a provision explained to them because they cannot work out what it means. In the context of the administration of a term loan, whether single bank or syndicated – see Chapter 2 – instructing lawyers is an unaffordable luxury; or, for the law firm involved, yet another opportunity – or should I say obligation – to provide free advice. What else can you do if you can't provide a loan agreement that can be readily understood by non-lawyers throughout the life of the loan? A loan agreement is, in effect, a code of conduct for a medium term relationship and it should be written accordingly.

Some light relief

At this point in the often repeated training session from which this chapter is derived it was time for a change of tempo, so I will assume that is the case for you, Dear Reader (as Tristram Shandy would say).

One of the objectives we are discussing is clarity and closely allied to this are two related concepts:

— equivocation, which is usually undesirable; and

— ambiguity, which is usually to be avoided.

My favourite example of equivocation (using ambiguous words to conceal the truth or using language evasively or misleadingly) in a loan agreement – indeed, my favourite sentence out of all the dry, turgid sentences, I have had to read in nearly 30 years as a lawyer – appeared in the 'purpose clause' of a loan agreement I was reviewing for one of the lenders; the purpose clause being, as we saw in Chapter 9, the clause which states how the borrower will use or apply the proceeds of the loan.

Read this and take a moment to digest the implications.

> The Borrower undertakes to apply the Loan in or towards payment of the purchase price of two unarmed helicopters.

There is a lawyer somewhere, who, intending to shield a client from allegations that weapons were being financed, managed to make it abundantly clear that this was precisely what was being done. At the time the loan was 'drawn down' (to use the jargon) the guns may not have been fitted, or had perhaps been fitted but not loaded, but that arming the helicopters was what was intended is made absolutely certain by the inclusion of the gratuitous reference to their being unarmed.

My other favourite piece of equivocation appeared in another purpose clause, one that I wrote on instructions from my client, in connection with the financing of the proposed or potential purchase by a stated-owned entity of some very expensive chattels – let's assume that they too were helicopters – where the chattels were not needed but the hard currency proceeds of the loan were needed. The result was the following purpose clause:

> The Borrower shall apply the sums borrowed under this Agreement in or towards the making of down payments for up to the three helicopters.

The loan agreement was signed, the loan was made, but no helicopters were purchased – 'up to three' clearly can, but might not, include zero! The decision makers at my client bank probably thought that there was an intention on the part of the borrower to buy at least one helicopter; the person responsible for the deal knew more about the real intentions of the borrower.

Moving on, but in the same vein, ambiguity will rarely if ever be desirable, even if a degree of equivocation can sometimes be perceived as helpful. My favourite example of ambiguity – allegedly a newspaper headline – is:

> Incest more common than thought in America.

My other favourite – if you can have two favourites – illustrates an important, indeed, I would say fundamental, aspect of language: words only have meaning in a context. With this in mind consider:

> They passed the port at midnight.

This could mean that the chaps were hitting the port late at night (and

– as one should – passing the port to one's left) or that they sailed past Cowes at midnight. If you do not know the context, you cannot tell what the sentence means – and for all you know it has both meanings at once.

The reference to an unarmed helicopter provides its own context, which is why the author's intentions were subverted but the context needed to understand fully the reference to up to three helicopters was extrinsic to the document – some people were aware of it, others were not. For the writer of headlines, context is a problem – they generally have to supply their own context unless supported by a picture.

The basic law of drafting

All of this – at least the serious bits – leads to a rather banal but very important conclusion which, somewhat pompously, I call the Basic Law of Drafting.

> It is always necessary to have regard to the function and purpose of the text which you are drafting.

This is not a hugely original perception; indeed it is rather the reverse. We usually take the context for granted; it would be hard to use the language of a thank you letter in a letter of condolence. However, when writing legal texts it is easy to forget how important the context is to how we say what it is we have to say.

'The Elegance Criterion'

The title of this chapter may have puzzled you. At some point, early in my career, I decided that it was important that what I wrote was elegant – not an aspiration commonly found amongst young lawyers! Translated into the real world this reflected a desire to write sentences, clauses and documents which flowed smoothly and conveyed the information they needed to convey economically, clearly and unambiguously. (There are lawyers who believe that some ambiguity can be helpful in the event that the parties fallout. I do not subscribe to this approach which, wherever it may flourish, is not often to be found in English law financing documents.)

Eventually my thinking on this topic crystallised into 'the elegance criterion'.

If it is not elegant it is wrong.

There is more than a grain of truth in this. If you cannot express the deal – the compromise that was agreed – in a way which satisfies this criterion, either you are getting it wrong or there is something wrong with your instructions or the deal; and, of course, the complex, as well as the simple, can be expressed elegantly (unless it is the exception which proves the rule – US securities legislation). But, beware: the converse is not true – what you have written is not correct just because it is elegant. And to decide whether what you have written is both elegant and correct you have to read it and read it again each time with fresh eyes and an open mind.

Apart from a brief concluding section, most of the rest of this Chapter consists of some guidance on clause construction in legal documents followed by three drafting exercises. The answers to these exercises can be found towards the end of this book. Cheat if you wish, but you should find it more interesting to tackle the exercises before you turn to the answers. Overall the exercises should take about 60 to 75 minutes.

Re-reading without re-thinking is the path to incorrect and inelegant drafting.

Clause construction

A loan agreement's contents – and no doubt the contents of many other contracts – will as often as not be derived from a 'term sheet' or 'heads of terms'. In the context of a term loan it is not unlikely that the relevant term sheet would contain a provision to the following effect.

The Borrower shall not borrow more than $30,000,000.

Such a statement may be adequate at the heads of terms stage, but would fall short of what is required in a loan agreement, which is a contract as opposed to an expression of intent – see Chapters 1 and 5 for discussions of the ways in which contracts are formed and of the difference between contracts and communications which do not create contracts. In a contract there is a need for a greater degree of certainty — for fewer 'grey areas' — than there is in the other contexts. (But, grey areas do have their place — see Box 5 below and also Chapter 9, pages 123 and 125 and Chapter 12, page 167.)

So, in this example, what does 'borrow' mean?

Before we can answer this question, we need to know why the provision is in the heads of terms — in other words, what is the reason for including in a loan agreement a requirement that the borrower shall not borrow more than a specified amount? There are several possible answers to this question (Box 3).

Box 3 Reasons for a borrowing restriction

- To ensure that if there is a breach of covenant the borrower can be sued for damages or an injunction can be sought.

- To protect the lender's position by ensuring that the borrower does not assume too much debt.

- To enable the lender to demand repayment, or threaten to do so, if the covenant is breached.

- To establish common expectations.

The first of these reasons is the least convincing. There may well be a right to sue for damages if the covenant is breached — there should be if the transaction has been managed properly — but this is not why a lender wants the borrower to agree to a restriction on borrowing. Nor will the existence of the restriction prevent the borrower from borrowing too much, although the possibility of the lender's obtaining an injunction if it learns of a potential breach makes this a slightly more convincing answer to the question. More convincing still is the observation that the lender could seek early repayment through acceleration and, in particular, could decline to make further advances if the borrower were to ignore the restriction. However, the real reason for the covenant is to establish common expectations. A wise and/or well advised borrower will not deliberately breach such a covenant, because of the loss of goodwill that could result (and because of the chain reaction effect that I mentioned in Chapter 9 when considering the powers of an instructing group), but will instead approach the lender or lenders, in the latter case through the agent bank, for an amendment to the covenant if it has a decent reason for needing to borrow more than the covenant permits.

Circumstances change in ways that cannot be predicted. The effect of financial covenants such as the one we are considering is to create a framework within which the contractual relationship between the borrower and the lender(s) can develop in a way that reflects such changes but gives to the lender(s) control over whatever contractual variations are required. It is this perspective that leads to the view that the objective is to reduce the number of grey areas and that we need to define "borrow" accordingly. In a loan agreement, as opposed to a heads of terms, the covenant whereby the borrower agrees not to 'borrow too much' might be written in the terms set out in Box 4 on the next page.

Various activities have the same economic effect as borrowing, but some of these activities are a long way from the basic (dictionary) concept of having the temporary use of money or other property. This will be dealt with by means of defined terms such as those set out in Box 5.

A banker's acceptance, under which a company draws a bill on its bank which accepts the bill so that the company can sell the bill in the market, effectively creates a short-term borrowing. The bill is sold at a discount and paid in full by the company at maturity, the discount being equivalent to interest on the discounted principal amount. Similarly, a note purchase facility, in which the purchaser buys an interest bearing promissory note which the issuer redeems with interest at maturity, is a borrowing in all but name.

Under a finance lease or hire-purchase arrangement the lessee/hirer has possession of a capital asset such as an aircraft and the lease/hire payments equate to the sums which would have been payable as principal and interest on a loan equal to the purchase price/initial value of the asset. So too, deferral of the obligation to pay the purchase price of an asset is effectively the borrowing of the purchase price.

Box 4 The covenant

> The Borrower shall not incur or permit to subsist any Financial Indebtedness other than:
>
> (a) any Financial Indebtedness under this Agreement; or
>
> (b) any other Financial Indebtedness the aggregate principal amount of which outstanding at any time does not exceed $30,000,000.

In this expanded version of the heads of terms provision, use is made of the defined term 'Financial Indebtedness', a term which relies on a further definition of 'Indebtedness' (Box 5).

Box 5 Financial Indebtedness and Indebtedness defined

> 'Financial Indebtedness' means any Indebtedness of any person for or in respect of:
>
> (a) monies borrowed;
>
> (b) amounts raised under an acceptance credit or note purchase facility;
>
> (c) the amount of any liability in respect of leases or hire purchase contracts which are treated as finance or capital leases;
>
> (d) the amount of any liability in respect of the purchase price for assets or services the payment of which is deferred for a period in excess of 90 days; and
>
> (e) amounts raised under any other transaction (including, without limitation, a note purchase agreement) having the commercial effect of a borrowing.
>
> [Paragraph (e) deliberately creates a grey area which is included for the benefit of the lender.]
>
> 'Indebtedness' means any obligation (whether incurred as principal or surety) for the payment or repayment of money, whether present or future, actual or contingent.

The technique of embedding definitions within definitions is a pervasive feature of contemporary contracts and finance documents are no exception. However, the constant need to go from one definition to another definition which is embedded in the first can become tedious. The trick is to get the balance right – too many definitions and a document loses its shape, but if there are insufficient definitions needless repetition becomes inevitable.

There is also the question of whether the definitions go at the beginning or the end of a document. I am a 'front ender' but sometimes definitions are found at the back of a document. (I have heard that some lawyers place the definitions in the middle of a document because, I imagine, that reduces – or is perceived to reduce – the average distance from clause to definition and vice versa.)

At this point it is clear that it is time to ask you to do some work, so set out on the following three pages are the exercises I referred to earlier. Model answers to these exercises, together with some notes on these answers, can be found somewhere towards the end of the book. As always, it is important to read the questions carefully.

The objective is to say what needs to be said clearly, unambiguously and (reasonably) briefly. In order to do this you will need to simplify and/or organise the materials in a way which does not result in the loss of relevant information.

Exercise 1

I used to work with someone whose powers of analysis were extraordinary, but whose drafting reflected too closely his detailed understanding of the issues.

An example of what I have in mind would be his version of one of the rules of golf.

If in the course of a round two or more balls are in play at any one time it shall first be established which ball belongs to which player and thereafter the distance of each ball from the hole shall be established and the players shall agree which is the greater distance so as to identify the player whose ball is furthest from the hole at that time and the players shall ensure that this is the ball which is played first.

Please rewrite this in as few words as possible.

Exercise 2

The arrangers of a syndicated loan proposed the following, rather dreadful and very muddled, agency provision. Prepare on behalf of the Agent an improved text covering the same issues as were covered in the arrangers' text.

(If you are not already a banking lawyer, you may find it helpful to read Chapters 2 and 9 before doing this exercise and the following exercise.)

The Lenders each appoint the Agent as their agent so as to take the steps required to implement the transactions described in this Agreement and authorise the Agent to do in connection with such transactions as aforesaid anything which it is necessary to do and accordingly it is agreed that the Agent may exercise such discretion in the interests of the Lenders but notwithstanding the foregoing and subject to the provisions hereinafter mentioned the Agent shall not have any dealings with the Borrower otherwise provided that these presents shall not prohibit the Agent from lending to the Borrower or from taking legal advice in connection with its obligations under this agreement and provided further that the Agent shall not be responsible for the Lenders' obligations. The Agent is empowered to rely on statements made by the Borrower or by the Lenders in relation to its duties as Agent provided that such duties shall include an obligation to account to the Lender for sums paid by the Borrower to the Agent and the Agent shall notify the Lenders thereof. The foregoing rights and duties of the Agent are exclusive and the Agent shall not be liable for any failure to exercise any such right or duty save in the case of negligence or misconduct but the Agent shall protect so far as it can the Lenders' interests.

Exercise 3

Prepare an improved version of the following draft provision for a seven-year loan to the Borrower, a UK company, whose lawyers prepared the draft. Your client is the Lender.

With regard to the financial condition of the Borrower, the Borrower shall endeavour to ensure that the financial condition of the Borrower, as evidenced by its annual financial statements (which the Borrower shall deliver within 90 days after their preparation) adjusted, as the Lender considers appropriate, to take account of changes in circumstances occurring after the date of those financial statements, is such that, provided the Lender has not agreed otherwise, the result of dividing its total liabilities by its total equity is less than two provided that the above mentioned adjustments shall be agreed by the Borrower and the Lender and provided further that the Borrower shall always use current accounting principles.

CHAPTER 12

The Contracts (Rights of Third Parties) Act 1999

The Contracts (Rights of Third Parties) Act 1999 returned to English law the long lost ability for a contract to confer enforceable rights on third parties. The difficulties and injustices sometimes caused by the privity of contract doctrine were perceived to justify this statutory development, but, as has been said before, hard cases make bad law. When this piece was first published in 1999, I remarked that, in the financial markets and elsewhere, the Act is likely to cause as many problems as it solves – and it has.

When the Contracts (Rights of Third Parties) Act 1999 (C(RTP)A 1999) became law, a short statute of only ten sections reintroduced into English law a concept which it had lacked for a very long time. This concept, the idea that someone who is not a party to a contract can obtain a benefit from that contract and acquire the right to enforce its claim, established a foothold in English law in the 16th and 17th centuries, but failed to flourish. It was finally killed off by the decision in *Tweddle v Atkinson* (1861) 1 B & S 393, a case concerning – as did a number of the older cases – an agreement between the fathers of a bride and groom to pay a sum of money to the groom (who was unsuccessful in his action to obtain the promised payment).

The Act came into force on 11 November 1999 and applies to contracts entered into six months or more after that date. It also had immediate effect in relation to a contract entered into during that six-month period if the contract so provided. Although short, the Act raises numerous, difficult issues in the context of the financial markets and elsewhere.

As is to be expected from the product of a 172 page report by the Law Commission (published in July 1996), which was preceded by the Sixth Interim Report of the Law Revision Committee in 1937, the Act raises more issues than can be discussed in a relatively short paper in which the points made, and the examples given, are those which suggest themselves to a banking lawyer. Academics and practitioners in other areas will no doubt identify other issues and see other opportunities.

A three party model

The purpose the Act is to reform the rule of English law to the effect that you cannot take the benefit of a contract unless you are a party to it. This is an old rule which is related to the doctrine of consideration, the doctrine that underpins the English law of contract. The basis of the doctrine is that a binding and enforceable contract can only come into effect if one person (the promisee) has given some 'consideration' (something of value in legal terms) for the promise given by the other party to the contract (the promisor) – see Chapter 1, pages 2–4. Although formerly regarded as part of this doctrine, *Beswick v Beswick* [1968] AC 58 confirmed that the privity rule is a separate rule. The Act does not alter the doctrine of consideration as it applies to contracts generally.

The Act is based on a three party model – see Box A – involving, for instance, a customer, a contractor and a sub-contractor or, to take another example, an insurer, the insured and a member of a class of claimants covered by the policy. This is no doubt because much of the impetus for a change in the law came from the construction industry and from consideration of issues arising in connection with policies of insurance taken out for the benefit of third parties (for example, public liability policies or health cover policies taken out by employers for the benefit of employees). The difficulties faced by the courts in extending the benefit of exclusion clauses to named third parties, affiliates or employees for example, were also an important source of pressure for reform.

Box A

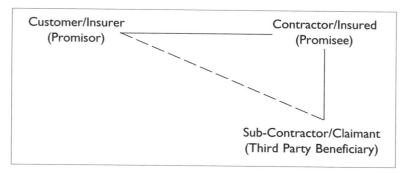

As is often the case with modern legislation, the Act takes no account of the practices of the financial markets, particularly the bond and syndicated loan markets in which the transaction structures are often more complex than the three party model suggests. As a result, the Act is likely to be of only limited value to the financial markets – although see Chapter 4, pages 49–52 – but does have the capacity to cause, in those markets, problems that would not arise without it. This is particularly so in relation to the many financial transactions in which it is envisaged that there will be future holders of debts, whether those debts are constituted by loans or bonds, who are to obtain the benefit of the debtor's promise to pay and other covenants. The Act will have its uses, but care will always be needed to ensure that it does not have unforeseen or unwanted effects.

A right to enforce

The key provision (C(RTP)A 1999, s 1) states that a third party may 'in his own right enforce a term of [a] contract' if the contract expressly provides that he may – C(RTP)A 1999, s 1(1)(*a*) – or the term purports to confer a benefit on him – s 1(1)(*b*). The section creates what is at first sight a rather puzzling distinction between:

(*a*) contracts which expressly refer to a third party having a right to enforce a term of a contract; and

(*b*) (using different terminology) contracts containing a term which 'purports to confer a benefit' on a third party.

It is important to note that the key concept is that of a third party acquiring the right to enforce a term of a contract. Although the language of section 1 makes reference to conferring a benefit on a third party, it is the concept of enforcement which underlies this reference because s 1(1)(b) does not apply 'if on a proper construction of the contract it appears that the parties did not intend the term to be enforceable by the third party' – C(RTP)A 1999, s 1(2). See Box B for the full texts of sub-ss 1(1) and (2).

Box B

> (1) Subject to the provisions of this Act, a person who is not a party to a contract (a 'third party') may enforce a term of the contract if:
>   (a)   the contract expressly provides that he may; or
>   (b)   subject to subsection (2), the term purports to confer a benefit on him.
>
> (2) Subsection (1)(b) does not apply if on proper construction of the contract it appears that the parties did not intend the term to be enforceable by the third party.

The reference to a term which purports to confer a benefit seems to have been made in order to ensure that enforceable third party rights would not arise in circumstances where words which have the apparent effect of achieving this were not really intended to do so. Thus, C(RTP)A 1999, s 1(2) of the Act allows for the inference (or presumption, to use the Law Commission's term) raised by the use of language which is apt to confer third party rights to be negated (or rebutted) if, on a proper construction of the contract, that was not the intention of the parties. If the parties want to be certain of conferring a benefit on a 'third party beneficiary', they must state that the intended beneficiary has the right to enforce the relevant provisions. If, however, no reference is made to enforcement, the parties will only know whether they have conferred enforceable rights on third parties if they are certain of the 'proper construction' of the context – and only the courts can be certain of this, particularly in the light of the decision in *Investors' Compensation Scheme Ltd v West Bromwich Building Society* [1998] 1 WLR 896 – see Chapter 15, page 219.

A two-tier approach

There are a number of reasons which can be put forward to justify the two-tier approach of C(RTP)A 1999. One reason would be that someone may want to state what benefit a third party will get, but leave it to the other contracting party to provide that benefit. For example, a contractual term might state that 'the customer and the contractor intend to ensure that sub-contractors shall be paid on a cost plus 10% basis'. This statement could be a description of the approach the contractor should take in agreeing prices with sub-contractors – a contractual commitment by the contractor to impose the specified cost control regime – or an assurance by the customer to the contractor's sub-contractors as to what payments those sub-contractors will receive. Why is it, however, that a statute should assume that contracts are likely to contain provisions which do not mean what they seem to say? In order to ensure that third party rights are not created by mistake would be one answer. Another answer, one proposed by the Law Commission's report, would be that many contracts will be entered into without the parties focusing on third party rights, so there needs to be a grey area where the judges can exercise their discretion.

This, it may be thought, is an unfortunate approach to take. How much simpler it would have been had the Act said:

(a) that to make a third party's right enforceable you have to say so – as does s 1(1)(a); and

(b) if you don't want the Act to apply you can say so.

Not only would it have been simpler (although simplicity is not inevitably a virtue), it would have been preferable:

(i)   to avoid the need to take a view on the 'proper construction of a contract' save as a last resort; and

(ii) to allow contracting parties to choose whether or not the Act should apply.

As it stands, contracting parties who do not want the Act to apply need to take great care over their choice of language so as to be sure of satisfying the 'proper construction' test knowing, as they do (or should), that the courts can be asked to have the last word on this question.

What we have is an Act which will engender new uncertainties where it need not have done – and for whose benefit? The Law Commission was concerned that if only the first limb were used as the test this would operate 'to the disadvantage of those who do not have the benefit of (good) legal advice'. At the same time, the Law Commission regarded the second limb as 'not producing an unacceptable degree of uncertainty in the law', citing with approval a statement of Lord Wilberforce in *Reardon Smith Line Ltd v Hansen-Tangen* [1976] 3 All ER 570 to the effect that in construing a contract 'the nature of what it is legitimate to have regard to is usually described as "the surrounding circumstances" but this phrase is imprecise: it can be illustrated but hardly defined'. Is this the level of imprecision to which English law aspires and is it the quality of legal advice that contracting parties obtain (or the quality of the lawyers they instruct) which will determine the policies to be adopted when English law is reformed?

Assignees as third party beneficiaries

In order to obtain the benefit of a contractual term, a third party 'must be expressly identified in the contract by name, as a member of a class or as answering a particular description but need not be in existence when the contract is entered into' – C(RTP)A 1999, s 1(3). Rather in the way that trusts work, there is no need to identify a third party by name, although very often this will be desirable in the interests of certainty. Thus, classes of third party beneficiaries can be identified, for example employees or sub-contractors. Again, this approach reflects concerns arising out of the models on which the Act is based: a contractor will probably employ numerous sub-contractors; numerous people could potentially benefit from a public liability policy.

However, it is also the case that the assignees of a party to a contract may form a class of third party beneficiaries and this poses an interesting question. What will be the effect of the Act where the contract would in any event contain provisions aimed at giving assignees rights against a contracting party? Will apparently straightforward statutory provision have the (probably unintended) effect of causing assignees to be third party beneficiaries?

In a loan agreement, it would be usual to find a provision to the effect that '"lender" means the bank and its successors and assigns'. Thus, the repayment clause – the provision obliging the borrower to 'repay to the lender the loan together with accrued interest by equal instalments on ...' – could, it seems, become directly enforceable by an assignee of the lender as a member of a class on which the repayment provision purports to confer a benefit. Such a result would not only be at odds with the well established rule that an equitable assignee of a debt must join the assignor in an action to enforce its claim against the debtor, but would also, it seems, give to the assignee two layers of rights – its rights as an assignee and its rights as a third party.

The language of this example is fairly typical of an informally written, single bank loan agreement, but the same approach is probably to be found in virtually all English law loan agreements.

In many syndicated loan agreements, there will be a provision requiring a lender's assignee to agree to assume the same obligations to the agent and the other lenders as it would have had if it had been a party to the agreement as a precondition to its obtaining the full benefit of the agreement. It is clearly the intention of the parties that assignees which comply with the terms of the relevant provisions should acquire enforceable rights. In particular, the intention is that assignees will be bound by indemnities in favour of the agent bank and by the sharing clause. The Act does not require any such agreement in order for assignees – as third parties – to acquire enforceable rights, although it clearly permits benefits to be conferred on a conditional basis, as where A and B agree that A will pay £100 to C if C marries B's daughter.

In this context, it is also necessary to consider the effect of C(RTP)A 1999, s 1(4) which states that section 1:

> 'does not confer a right on a third party to enforce a term of a contract otherwise than subject to and in accordance with any other relevant terms of the contract'

thus allowing the usual loan agreement terms to apply. Section 1(4) regulates the enforcement of rights which section 1 has conferred and its effect is to ensure that a third party's rights are to be established by reference to the entire contract. What s 1(4) does not do is enable contracting parties who have, intentionally or not, invoked the Act, by using language which purports to confer a benefit on a third party, to exclude the Act simply by saying so.

Protection for third party beneficiaries

For the purpose of exercising its right to enforce its claim, a third party beneficiary will have the same remedies as a contracting party would have had available to it in an action for breach of contract and 'the rules relating to damages, injunctions, specific performance and other relief' all apply – C(RTP)A 1999, s 1(5). Interestingly, s 1(5) gives the third party beneficiary contracting party status only with regard to the remedies available in the context of legal proceedings (and not with regard to so-called self-help remedies), which raises the question of whether a third party beneficiary has the same rights of set-off as it would have had if it had been a contracting party. The Act is silent on the point, as is the Law Commission's report, but the answer (despite the Law Commission's view that a third party right is not a full contractual claim) would seem to be that, for the purposes of set-off, the third party's statutory claim is on all fours with an ordinary contractual claim – both types of claim can be characterised as a right to seek enforcement in the courts.

C(RTP)A 1999, s 1(6) provides that:

> 'where a term of a contract excludes or limits liability in relation to any matter references in this Act to the third party enforcing the term shall be construed as references to his availing himself of the exclusion or limitation.'

This is a complicated way of saying that the 'right to enforce' a term of a contract includes the right to take the benefit of exclusion clauses or other provisions limiting liability, the extension of the benefit of exclusion clauses to third parties being one of the Act's main objectives. As the Law Commission puts it, the tangled case law in this area provides an excellent illustration of the tension between the privity of contract rule and the courts' desire to circumvent the rule so as to give effect to the contracting parties' intentions.

A more innovative set of protections for third party beneficiaries is contained in C(RTP)A 1999, s 2, the objective of which is to allow rights acquired by third parties to be entrenched, on the basis that a right which can be varied or taken away is no right at all. Where a third party has a right to enforce a term of a contract and the right has *crystallised* (not a term used in the statute), the contracting parties may not, by agreement, rescind the contract or vary it so as to 'extinguish or alter' the third party's 'entitlement under that right' without the third party's consent. The idea underlying 'crystallisation' – the term is used in the Law Commission's report – is that a third party is to have its enforceable rights protected from contractual change only where it has agreed to it having them (assent) or has relied on them and the promisor knows (awareness of reliance) or should have expected this (foreseeable reliance).

Importantly, the Act gives to contracting parties the ability to impose a contractual regime in place of the statutory regime. This is permitted by C(RTP)A 1999, s 2(3) which makes s 2(1) subject to any express term under which the contracting parties may by agreement rescind or vary the contract without the consent of the third party or under which the consent of the third party is required in circumstances other than those set out in s 2(1)(*a*), (*b*) and (*c*) – assent, awareness of reliance and foreseeable reliance.

Important omissions

The idea that someone who is not a party to a contract can block its amendment is a novel one so far as simple contracts are concerned. In the context of trusts and deed polls, however, the idea is a familiar one. Not for the last time, C(RTP)A 1999 prompts the question, why is the Act needed or, more accurately, why does it not contain a provision allowing for its exclusion so that in contexts where it is redundant the parties (and their lawyers) do not need to be troubled by it? Another set of questions raised but not answered by the Act in this context is the status of a mutually agreed (by the parties) contractual amendment in respect of which a requisite third party consent has not been obtained. Does this amendment bind the parties to the contract? Does it make a difference if the third party's position is improved by the amendment? That the Act is silent on these issues is a result of a clear policy on the part of the Law Commission to leave issues to the courts. We have seen this in relation to language which 'purports to confer a benefit' on a third party and will meet it again in relation to ss 4 and 5.

The Act is also silent, perhaps not deliberately, about another issue raised by the provisions of s 2. What about amendments which preserve a third party's rights but reduce their value? From a third party's perspective, the requirement that the value of its third party rights should not be impaired by steps taken by the contracting party is what will really matter.

For example, a third party beneficiary which is the 'sleeping partner' in a three party joint venture (and, as a result, not a party to the joint venture agreement) might, after a contractual amendment by the two active parties, find that it retains the right to receive payments pro rata to its equity stake, but that its substantive benefits have been reduced by dilution. Such a third party beneficiary would want the restrictions on the contracting parties' freedom to cancel or vary the contract to be strengthened, if not absolute, ie no termination or amendment without consent. It would certainly not be satisfied with the statutory regime.

From the other perspective, that of the contracting parties, there may be a need to limit or wholly exclude the 'blocking rights' of third party beneficiaries. In practice, care will have to be taken to ensure that third parties cannot block contractual variations and termination where this is not intended (acting for a contracting party) or to protect the third party's rights from being impaired, if this is what is intended (acting for a third party).

Consideration through the back door

The Act contains detailed provisions which specify how and when crystallisation occurs. The approach, as already stated, is that crystallisation occurs when the third party beneficiary gives its assent to the rights or relies on the rights and the promisor knows or should have expected this. It is not clear, however, why the third party beneficiary cannot have its rights protected from the outset. If the contracting parties have said that there should be enforceable third party rights, or are to be taken to have intended that there should be, should not the promisor be held to its commitment (for which it must have received good consideration if the issue is to arise at all)? The law of contract has as one of its foundation stones the concept that the parties to a contract are bound by what they say, but this principle is not being applied where third party beneficiaries are concerned not, at least, until the third party has done something to deserve the benefit of the contract.

What, in fact, is happening is that the third party beneficiary is being required to provide consideration through the back door. Initially, the third party's rights are of little value because they are subject to rescission or amendment until the third party has either agreed to have the rights or has altered its position because of their existence; only after crystallisation has occurred will those rights be of value. It is as if it were thought unfair for a third party to acquire something of value without in some way paying for the privilege – in a manner understood by the eye of the law. What is more, both assent and reliance presume knowledge, so the third party's rights cannot become protected until it knows of them. Where contracting parties really want to make a binding commitment to a third party they may conclude that the use of a trust will serve their purpose better.

The crystallisation conditions

A third party's right to enforce a contractual term will have crystallised if the third party has 'communicated his assent to the promisor' – C(RTP)A 1999, s 2(1)(a)– or 'the promisor is aware that the third party has relied on the term' – s 2(1)(b)– or 'the promisor can reasonably be expected to have foreseen that the third party would rely on the term and the third party has in fact relied on it' – s 2(1)(c).

As already stated, these provisions have the effect that the intended beneficiary must have done something and the promisor must have a certain state of knowledge if the third party's rights are to exist. (Again, this can be contrasted with a trust under which, to oversimplify, the necessary intention and certainty in the terms of the trust are really all that is required.) Various difficulties arise – for third party beneficiaries and for contracting parties – under these provisions, such as knowledge (or lack of it) of the term, the burden of proof and the concept of a reasonable expectation of foreseeability.

The concepts of reliance and a reasonable expectation of foreseeability will give rise to plenty of debate, but particular difficulties flow from the critical importance of the third party's knowledge (or lack of it) of the relevant contractual term. If the beneficiary is not aware of the contractual provision, it can't have blocking rights, because it can neither agree to or rely on a term of which it is ignorant. The result is that the contracting parties will know whether or not a third party has blocking rights (and may, therefore, have to be approached if the contract is to be successfully amended) only if they know whether the beneficiary knows about the contract.

This is not a good position to be in if certainty is desired and the uncertainty will be compounded if it is also necessary to worry about the proper construction of the contract! If, for example, its contract of insurance were silent on the point, a liability insurer would not know who could exercise blocking rights in respect of the policy unless it knew to whom the insured had disclosed the terms of the contract. If, in addition, the person who wrote the contract had inadvertently failed to refer to the enforceability of any third party claims, the insurer might be unable to determine the scope of its liability. Insurers will want their insurance contracts to deal with these issues.

The basic tests for crystallisation having been established, five further subsections of s 2 are required to explicate the concept. These subsections deal with how assent may be given and create powers for a court or arbitral tribunal to dispense (on terms which may include compensation to the third party) with the need for consent where the third party cannot be found or is mentally incapable or it cannot be established whether or not there was reliance.

Protection for the contracting parties

The Act now turns, in s 3, to providing protection to the promisor, but again on the basis that the contracting parties may substitute their own contractual regime for the statutory one – s 3(5). Thus, s 3(1)–(4) seek, in relation to defences, set-offs and counterclaims, to put the promisor in the position it would have been in had the third party been a contracting party, but allow the contract to increase or reduce the defences, set-offs and counterclaims available to the promisor. In a similar vein, s 3(6) is intended to prevent a third party from enforcing a term, in particular a term purporting to exclude or limit liability, if the third party could not have done so had it been a party to the contract. Again, there is the emphasis on the extension of the benefit of exclusion clauses to third parties.

So far as the promisee is concerned, the Act provides only that 'section 1 does not affect any right of the promisee to enforce any term of the contract' (s 4), leaving it to the courts to develop and work out how the promisee stands in relation to the third party and other promisees. One of the promisee's rights preserved by s 4 is the promisee's right to sue the promisor for failing to perform its obligations to the third party. For example, if a sub-contractor is not paid, it may fail to provide services to the contractor/promisee which may as a result receive reduced payments from the promisor. It would also seem to be the case that, subject to the general law on exclusion clauses and fundamental breach, the promisor can exclude liability for its failure to perform its obligations to the third party.

Judicial reduction of claims

Where a third party beneficiary sues the promisor, the court or arbitral tribunal will have a discretion to reduce an award to a third party if 'the promisee has recovered from the promisor a sum in respect of:

(a) the third party's loss in respect of the term [the subject of the action]; or

(b) the expense to the promisee of making good to the third party the default of the promisor' (C(RTP)A 1999, s 5).

The ability of the court or other tribunal to reduce an award to the third party could disadvantage the third party if the promisee becomes bankrupt before paying sums recovered to the third party. Once again, it is left to the courts to work out the consequences of this provision, in particular whether a third party has in any particular case a claim *in rem* or *in personam* against the promisee.

C(RTP)A 1999, s 5 could also cause problems in relation to assignments. The current position is that once an assignee has given notice to a debtor/promisor, only the assignee can give a good discharge for payment by the debtor/promisor and the assignor/promisee will (almost certainly) hold a sum paid to it in error on trust for the assignee/third party. It seems, therefore, that situations will arise where an assignee's (old) rights as assignee conflict with its new (and less favourable) statutory rights as a third party beneficiary. Although it might be thought unlikely that the discretion would be exercised in such a way, the Act's silence with regard to assignees – they seem not to have been considered – means that it could be. A recipient promisee's liquidator might well consider asserting that an assignee has acquired statutory third party rights and both that s 5 applies and that it overrides any implied trust that might otherwise have arisen. Mistaken payment to the wrong person may not be an everyday occurrence in all contexts, but it is quite common, for example, in relation to impaired sovereign debts. As already mentioned, similar concerns arise in relation to bond issues and syndicated loans (where both assignments and transfers by novation could be adversely affected). Buyers of debts and other assignees will want to ensure that they do not acquire statutory benefits (and disadvantages) 'on a proper construction' of the relevant contract.

Excluded contracts

C(RTP)A 1999, s 6 sets out to create some exceptions to the basic rule that the Act will apply to all contracts. However, s 6 does not say that the Act does not apply to the contracts it specifies. Instead, it provides that s 1 confers no rights on a third party 'in the case of the specified contracts'. This approach reinforces the conclusion that the Act is intended to apply to all contracts, so that whenever benefits are purportedly conferred on a third party, the courts can be invited to determine the outcome. Contracts to which the Act will not apply include a contract on a bill of exchange, promissory note or other negotiable instrument (see Chapter 3, page 31), a Companies Act 1985, s 14 contract (Memorandum and Articles of Association), contracts of employment and contracts for the carriage of goods (except that a third party may take the benefit of a term excluding or limiting liability). The contracts excluded from the ambit of the Act are ones where the position of third parties is too well established to justify any change (for example, the position of successive holders of negotiable instruments) and/or for policy reasons third parties should not take benefits under such contracts, for example contracts of employment. Contracts for the carriage of goods provide an example of contracts to which both considerations apply.

Supplementary provisions

C(RTP)A 1999, s 7 contains some supplementary provisions of which the first is particularly important and particularly difficult. Section 7(1) states that 'section 1 does not affect any right or remedy of a third party that exists or is available apart from this Act' and was inserted, in the words of the Law Commission, 'to preserve the statutory and common law exceptions to the third party rule'. The Law Commission was faced with a dilemma when it came to deciding how to ensure that the Act was compatible with the many ad hoc exceptions to the privity rule that already exised, some being statutory and others being the result of judicial initiative and invention. The final decision was to make no attempt to list the exceptions, but to insert a provision – now s 7(1) – which would leave those exceptions unimpaired and the courts free to develop the law.

What, in practice, the courts may do is to restrict some exceptions in the light of the new regime introduced by the Act – and this is where the problems start. The Act does not specify in which exceptional circumstances the provisions of the Act will or will not apply and, if a list of exceptions cannot be formulated, it probably could not do so. The only alternative would be to say that the Act should not apply where satisfactory provision is already made for third party rights and that would clearly not be a satisfactory approach. Instead of saying where the Act will or will not apply, s 7(1) purports to protect all the exceptions, but its effect may be to cause a potential third party beneficiary to acquire both the benefit and the burden of the new statutory regime (including ss 2 and 5) as well as its rights under the 'old law'.

The remaining provisions of C(RTP)A 1999, s 7 are more straightforward. Section 7(2) provides that a third party beneficiary shall be denied the benefit of the Unfair Contract of Terms Act 1977 reasonableness test where liability for negligence is excluded (unless the claim is for death or personal injury). Sections 7(3) and (4) provide that the Limitation Act 1980 and the Arbitration Act 1996, Part I, shall apply and s 7(5) states that a third party is not to be treated as a contracting party simply because for certain purposes the Act says the position is to be determined as if it were.

Two key provisions

On the basis of the foregoing analysis, two of the provisions of the C(RTP)A 1999 are of particular relevance to the bond and loan markets. Firstly, if the Act necessarily applies to the trust deeds and deeds of covenant which are commonly used in English law bond issues and to syndicated and single bank loan agreements:(a) care will have to be taken that unwanted 'blocking rights' do not arise under s 2; and (b) the position of loan assignees and transferees may be adversely affected by C(RTP)A 1999, s 5.

Other issues arise, but these are easily dealt with once it is established whether or not the Act necessarily applies or can be excluded. For example, there are many third party indemnities in bond documentation and syndicated loans usually contain at least one such indemnity in favour of the agent bank, its directors, employees and agents. So too many financial contracts are expressed to be made for the benefit of the parties and their successors and assigns; the assignment issue will be relevant in all such contracts.

The Act contains no provision for its exclusion. The starting point, therefore, is that in relation to a contract (and a trust deed is a contract) which purports to confer benefits on third parties (the bondholders) the Act will apply. Section 1(4) has been considered and rejected as a provision which might be used to exclude the Act. Does s 7(1) have the effect of excluding trust arrangements from the Act (bearing in mind that what the Law Commission intended is now irrelevant)? It is impossible to be certain, but it seems as likely as not that, as well as preserving the rights of the beneficiaries of a trust, s 7(1) does not prevent the benefit and the burdens of the statutory regime from applying to the beneficiaries.

What is certain is that the risk of 'blocking rights' arising under C(RTP)A 1999, s 2 is too great for anyone to want to run the risk that they might arise in their statutory form. The only safe course of action will be to assume that the Act applies and make sure that an appropriate contractual regime of blocking rights is substituted for the statutory regime. Most trust deeds contain provisions dealing with amendments; these provisions should by now have received close scrutiny. (Potential assignees under a loan agreement could also acquire 'blocking rights' unless these are written out by the loan agreement.) There will also, if it is thought appropriate, be the possibility of using the Act to permit deeds of covenant to be amended, something which is not presently considered possible.

Turning to loans and C(RTP)A 1999, s 5, the question is whether a debtor who wrongly pays an assignor after it has received a notice of assignment from an assignee can be required to pay the full amount to the assignee, as is currently the case. Here, again, it is not certain that the issue is one which s 7(1) addresses, at least not directly, since it preserves rights from attack by s 1 when it is s 5 which will do the damage. Again, only the courts can decide, although it must be more likely than not (in this instance) that the rights of assignees will be preserved, perhaps on the grounds that once an assignee has given notice to the debtor, it is no longer a third party (so that s 5 will not apply). Nevertheless, it would be prudent for assignment provisions in loan agreements – particularly single bank loans where there is no agent bank to take the blame – to make it clear that when an assignee has done what is required by the terms of the agreement, it shall be regarded as a party to the loan agreement. (Since this is the intended effect of transfer procedures, transferees' rights ought not to be affected by the Act and, by definition, a transferee has the (contractual) 'blocking rights' of a lender in any event.)

Freedom of contract denied

The main features of C(RTP)A 1999 are easily summarised – see Box C on the next page – but not surprisingly any such summary glosses over the practical difficulties which will flow from the Act and it is hard to resist the conclusion that a long awaited development in English law will cause as many problems as it solves.

There are three main conclusions to be drawn.

1 The absence of a provision allowing for the exclusion of the Act and excessive reliance on judicial discretion have combined to produce an Act which reduces the freedom to contract despite the purported desire to respect 'the autonomy of the will of the parties' – see para 1.1 of the Law Commission's report.

2 Rather than providing solutions, the Act's reliance on judicial

discretion and its apparent intention to benefit those without access to (good) legal advice, by allowing them the opportunity to obtain benefit of the doubt where third party rights may have been created, has resulted in a high degree of uncertainty which may well place an unnecessary burden on the courts. This too is contrary to the Law Commission's aim to 'save the taxpayer the needless litigation caused by the complexity of the [pre-Act] law' – see para 1.8 of the Law Commission's report.

3 The Act's shortcomings highlight the need for practitioners to monitor legislative developments. All too often – and the Act is no exception – modern legislation is written and enacted in ignorance of market practices.

Box C

1 The benefit of a contract can be extended to a third party, but only a reference to the third party's right to enforce creates certainty.

2 A class of third parties may benefit (and assignees could be such a class).

3 A third party beneficiary's consent may be needed to amend the contract, unless the contract contains a provision to the contrary.

4 Unless the contract says otherwise, a contracting party will have the defences and set-offs *vis-à-vis* a third party beneficiary that it would have had if the third party had been a contracting party.

5 Double recovery can be prevented by the courts.

6 The Act does not apply to negotiable instruments or to a company's Memorandum and Articles.

A footnote

It is interesting to note that the Law Commission's report contains a footnote (on p 139) to the effect, in the context of the second limb of

C(RTP)A 1999, s 1, that if the parties to a contract intended an established (statutory) exception to the privity rule to apply, they would not have the requisite intention to cause the new, statutory regime to apply, with the implication that as a result the exception would govern the outcome rather than the Act. It is a pity that no support for this view is to be found in the language of s 1 or anywhere else in the Act.

CHAPTER 13

Trusts and trustees in secured and structured finance

> A particular objective I have in his chapter is to explain why it is that wherever possible there should be a trust (and a trustee) at the heart of every English law secured (syndicated) or structured financing, including a secured restructuring, whether a bond or a loan restructuring (or both). To many, perhaps most, finance lawyers trusts are a bit of a mystery – and this can cause problems. In the capital markets area there is often a role for both a professional trustee and for a dedicated trust lawyer (trustee's counsel) or, in the context of CDOs, for the use of trusts as a means of transferring the benefit of underlying obligations. In the banking area, the trustee will nearly always be a commercial bank with no 'trustee department' (and no trustee's counsel).

This dichotomy between the approach taken in capital markets transactions and that taken in banking transactions is commercially driven, but one result is that a commercial bank trustee is likely to agree to things that professional trustee would not agree to. It may or may not be desirable for market practice to change – and as lawyers we may or may not wish or be able to effect any such change – but we should, at least, understand the issues in this area of legal risk. Just as important, there may be serious 'local law' issues where there is a need to take security in favour of a trustee over property in jurisdictions other than

England and Wales – it is a bit late to make the point that all these essays are written from an English law perspective, but better late than never.

In order to explore these issues it is helpful to start at the beginning by answering the question – what is a trust and how is a trust created? – and then to consider the role of the security trustee (which will lead to a discussion of certain issues arising out of subordination arrangements) and some of the structures which may be used where a trust and a trustee are used.

Trusts and their creation

As well as looking at what trusts are and how they are created, I will briefly contrast trust structures with agency structures. In jurisdictions where trusts are not recognised, recourse is often had to agency structures as an alternative, despite the fact that the two structures have little in common, so it is important to understand the differences between them.

What is a trust?

To paraphrase Underhill and Hayton (*Law of Trusts and Trustees*, 16th edn, 2003, p 3), a trust is an equitable obligation which obliges the trustee to deal with the trust property (which the trustee owns) for the benefit of other persons (the beneficiaries); and to quote from the same page 'any act or neglect on the part of the trustee which is not authorised or excused by the terms of the trust instrument, or by law, is called a breach of trust'.

A trust is very different from a contract (but, as I mention in passing in Chapter 12, page 178, a trust deed is a contract (in so far as the parties assume obligations towards each other) to which the *Contracts (Rights of Third Parties) Act 1999* applies (see, for instance, Underhill and Hayton, pp 168–9). A contract is a bargain for which, under English law, consideration is needed (see Chapter 1, pages 2–4). A trust, on the other hand (to mention just two of the distinguishing features identified by Underhill and Hayton on pp 10 and 11), may arise without there being any consideration and the beneficiaries of a trust do not have a right to damages for breach of trust but (instead) the right to call for an account and to have the trust fund put into the state it would have been in but for the trustee's breach. If this right is exercised, the accounts will be adjusted – strangely, the term used is 'falsified' – so that the correct amounts and assets are shown in the accounts. The trustee can then be obliged to reconstitute the fund and, if there has been any negligence on its part, to supplement the fund so as to compensate for the consequences of its negligence. A further consequence of a wronged beneficiary's claim not being a claim for damages for breach of contract is that the common law rules which can limit damages – rules as to causation, foreseeability and remoteness – do not apply.

(As I said in Chapter 3 – about bills of exchange – 'there is no point in my attempting to provide anything like a comprehensive treatment' of the law [of trusts] 'because there is far too much detail and the subject is exhaustively treated in the standard works'; and, as I said in Chapter 1, 'without such works pieces such as this could not be written'. I have used Underhill and Hayton as my guide in writing this Chapter, but as always the most insight (and entertainment) is to be gained from the cases – as long you ignore the headnotes.)

Creating a trust

Under English law there are only two ways in which an express trust can be created *inter vivos* – ie otherwise than pursuant to a deceased person's will. Usually, the 'settlor', the owner of one or more items of property, creates the trust by transferring that property to the trustee to hold on the desired trusts – or, and this is an important distinction, by doing everything in his power to transfer title to the property. This principle was established in *Re Rose* [1952] Ch 499, [1952] 1 All ER 1217, prior to which the requirement was that the settlor had to do 'everything, which, according to the nature of the property, was necessary to transfer the property' – a stricter regime which had prevailed since *Milroy v Lord* (1862) 4 De GF & J 264. In *Re Rose* a trust over shares was created when the settlor handed to the trustee the share certificates and share transfer form even though legal title vested in the trustee only when the company subsequently registered the transfer. Alternatively, an owner of property can declare itself trustee of the property for the benefit of others, but – and this is important in practice – the proposed beneficiaries of a trust *cannot* create the trust or appoint the trustee. Only the owner of property can create a trust over that property. (This is not quite true. If someone enters into an agreement to hold future or after-acquired property on trust, that person will be regarded as a trustee when he or she acquires or becomes the owner of the property – *Re Lind* [1915] 2 Ch 345.)

On the other hand, the trustees of a trust or the beneficiaries *can* appoint additional or successor trustees under an express or necessarily implied power – there are other circumstances in which new trustees can be appointed but we need not concern ourselves with these. A new trustee will have the same powers, authorities and discretions as an original trustee where those powers, authorities and discretions are 'incident to the office of trustee' rather than personal to the original trustee (*Re Smith* [1904] 1 Ch 139). Because such powers of appointment are construed narrowly, if the power to appoint new trustees is vested in 'the continuing trustees' they cannot all resign at once and appoint new trustees under one deed on the grounds that a trustee who is about to resign is not a continuing trustee; thus such a process would have to be carried out in stages – see *Re Coates to Parsons* (1886) 34 Ch D 370 (to be contrasted with *Re Glenny and Hartley* (1884) 25 Ch D 611) where the contrary, and more convincing, view is expressed).

Very helpfully, the effect of the Trustee Act 1925 (TA 1925), s 40, is that where a new trustee is appointed and the contrary is not stated, any property subject to the trust shall vest in the persons who are the trustees after the appointment has taken effect – and this occurs 'without any conveyance or assignment', ie no transfer or assignment takes place and none is required. There are, however, three exceptions: leases where consent or a licence is required for an assignment; shares which are registered or only transferable under a statutory procedure; and (I will quote rather than paraphrase the following slightly obscure provision) 'land conveyed by way of mortgage for securing money subject to the trust, except land conveyed on trust for securing debentures or debenture stock'. There are, it appears, some uncertainties with regard to the effect of TA 1925, s 40 (see Underhill and Hayton, pp 777 and 778), in particular as to whether the section will cause an equitable interest to vest in the successor trustees because, as we all know, LPA 1925, s 53(1)(c), specifies that an equitable interest can only be transferred in writing. It seems to me that the stipulation that property vests 'without any conveyance or assignment' deals with this issue.

A digression

Returning to the way in which trusts can be created, there is a fairly recent case on this which provides a good excuse for a brief digression. In *T Choithram International SA v Pagarani* [2001] 1 WLR 1, PC it was held that an effective transfer of property to the trustees of a charitable foundation – one of whom was the settlor – occurred when the settlor declared, so soon after the creation of the trust as to make it fair to regard the sequence of events as being part of one transaction, that he was giving property of his to the foundation ('I now give everything to the trust'). In the course of the judgment Browne-Wilkinson LJ noted that the facts raise a new point – on the rules of equity with regard to complete gifts – and memorably stated that: 'Although equity will not aid a volunteer, it will not strive officiously to defeat a gift', a proposition which paves the way for the innovation which his judgment introduces.

The first half of this assertion is, as the judges say, trite law; the second, it seems to me, could be construed as a disguised way of saying that 'fairness' is a principle of equity, which, I would suggest, it is not. Browne-Wilkinson LJ goes on to say that there 'can in principle be no distinction between the case where the donor declares himself to be the sole trustee for a donee or a purpose and the case where he declares himself to be one of the trustees for that donee or purpose'. In both cases his conscience is affected and it would be unconscionable and contrary to the principles of equity to allow such a donor to resile from his gift.

Thus, 'in the absence of special factors where one out of a larger body of trustees has the trust property vested in him [unless, presumably, vested in him otherwise than as trustee] he is bound by the trust and must give effect to it by transferring the trust property in to the name of all the trustees'. The result of all this seems to be that if you cause yourself to become a trustee you can then orally give your own property to yourself as trustee without the need to take any steps at all to transfer title to the property from yourself in your personal capacity to yourself as the trustee.

Another digression

Shortly after writing the previous paragraph, I read *Re Lind* (cited above) which supports the proposition that if you agree to sell or mortgage property you do not own, when you do come to own the property you hold it on trust for the buyer/mortgagee (as long as the original agreement was one in respect of which specific performance would be available). What *Re Lind* makes clear is that for a very long time the fundamental principle of Equity (at least in relation to trusts) is not fairness but doing the right thing, doing what ought to be done – being a good chap, one might say.

The most interesting passage in *Re Lind* consists of an analysis of two cases I have mentioned elsewhere: *Holroyd v Marshall* (1862) 10 HL Cas 191, in which Lord Westbury LC stated the principle that a vendor/mortgagor becomes a trustee on acquiring the property the subject of the sale/mortgage; and *Tailby v Official Receiver* (1888) 13 App Cas 523 in which it was stated by Lord Macnaghten (as paraphrased by Swinfen Eady LJ in *Re Lind* at p 359) that long before *Holroyd v Marshall* was determined 'it was well settled that an assignment of future property for value operates in equity by way of agreement, *binding on the conscience of the assignor,* and so binding the property . . . on the principle that equity considers as done that which ought to be done' (emphasis added).

This is the core concept, one which is consistently and frequently invoked by the judges, as it was by Browne-Wilkinson LJ – if a person's conscience is bound, equity will intervene.

(It is hard to believe that in 1915 someone (Hugh Lind) was able to mortgage 'a possibility of becoming possessed in the future of a share of his mother's personal estate', a possibility which existed only because his mother was of unsound mind and had not made (and was unlikely to make) a will. For all I know, it may still be technically possible to mortgage such a 'spes successionis' – the hope of an inheritance – but I very much doubt that there are any lenders in this market.)

Certainty

In order to create a trust, the settlor must, with reasonable certainty, display an intention to create a trust and describe the trust property, the intended beneficiaries and the purpose of the trust (which must be administratively workable). A particular uncertainty arises where a settlor seeks to create a trust over an unspecified portion of a given species of property, say a fifth of the shares he owns in a company or three of her ten cases of Chateaux Margaux 1990, without specifying which particular shares or cases they are. An attempt to create a trust in this manner will fail because the specific shares the subject of the intended trust cannot be identified. As Lord Mustill said in the Privy Council case *Re Goldcorp Exchange Ltd* [1994] 3 WLR 199 at 208 (also cited as [1995] 1 AC 74 90-92 and [1994] 2 All ER 806, PC) – a case concerning a New Zealand company which sold unascertained bullion to eager investors but never allocated anything to anyone – 'It makes no difference what the parties intended if what they intend is impossible, as is the case with an immediate transfer of title to goods whose identity is not yet known'. (The Court of Appeal decision to the contrary, *Hunter v Moss* [1994] 3 All ER 215, is unconvincing and probably wrongly decided.)

The courts will need to take a pragmatic approach when faced with trusts of dematerialised securities such as shares held in a system such as CREST or bonds held in Euroclear or Clearstream. In such circumstances the settlor will own no shares or bonds at all; it will simply have an interest in its broker's block holding of shares in the clearing system and if it wants to create a trust over some only of the shares or bonds it owns will have no choice but to take the 'unspecified portion' approach. No doubt a declaration of trust over a specified number of shares will be treated, as Underhill and Hayton suggest (on p 79) as creating a trust over the settlor's equitable interest in its broker's holding (which itself will be an equitable interest in some other entity's account with the clearing system – see Chapter 4 for an explanation of the structure of a contemporary bond issue).

Declarations of trust in CDOs

As briefly mentioned above, an owner of property can declare itself a trustee of the property for the benefit of others. This approach is frequently used to transfer the benefit of loans in the context of a CDO (an issue of collateralised debt obligations). In a CDO, the benefit of the underlying obligations is transferred to a special purpose vehicle (SPV), a company located in a jurisdiction with convenient corporate, tax and securities laws, which issues notes to investors, usually in different classes payable in a specified order of priority, the lowest ranking being, in effect, equity rather than debt. The SPV's obligations under the notes will be secured by the SPV's interest in the underlying obligations, the security being created in favour of a trustee under a security trust deed. A convenient means of transferring the benefit of a loan to an SPV is a declaration of trust by the lender to the effect that it holds the benefit of the loan on trust for the SPV absolutely. In many cases this may be the only available method because the loan agreement contains a prohibition on assignments or transfers (see Chapters 2, 9 and 10) without the consent of the debtor and it is commercially impracticable or undesirable for consent to be sought.

Doubts about this method of transfer, which was becoming more frequently used despite these doubts, were dispelled as a result of a dispute between two internationally famous boxing promoters, Don King and Frank Warren, whose disagreement over the ownership of some extremely valuable promotion and management contracts was resolved by the Court of Appeal in *Don King Productions Inc v Warren* [2000] Ch 291, CA. In his judgment, which now seems less surprising than it did in 2001 (but is still correctly characterised as a lifeline to banks seeking to securitise their portfolios – see Chapter 6, page 80), Lightman J confirmed not only that a trust of a contract or the benefit of a contract can exist – which we all knew – but also that a clause prohibiting assignment [or, we can infer, requiring consent as a precondition to assignment] 'is prima facie restricted to assignments of the benefit of the obligation and does not extend to declarations of trust', citing in support of this proposition that other important case in this area, *Linden Gardens Trust Ltd v Lenesta Sludge Disposals Ltd* [1994] 1 AC 85, which is best remembered (or at least hard to forget) as '*Lenesta Sludge*' – see Chapter 6, pages 79–80.

Trust v agency

An approach which, in the context of secured financing, is often seen as an alternative to the trust route (especially where it is perceived that in some other jurisdiction there are local law reasons for not using a trust structure – about which more later) is agency. This is rather odd because the two concepts are fundamentally different, as I will briefly explain.

An agency relationship is one under which one person (the principal) appoints another person (the agent) to represent it. As Sir Roy Goode puts it, the principal appoints the agent 'to bring about, modify or terminate legal relations between the principal and one or more third parties' (*Commercial Law*, 2nd edn, 1995 p 166). As put more simply on p 7 of Underhill and Hayton, agency is a relationship where one person 'has express or implied authority to act on behalf of another ....and consents so to act'. This latter description better describes, for example, the role of the agent bank in a syndicated loan (see Chapter 9) which is to facilitate the implementation of contractual arrangements rather than to create them.

If an agent bank can be said to facilitate the implementation of a contract by representing the lenders in their dealings with the borrower, the same cannot be said of a trustee. A trustee does not represent its beneficiaries; it cannot commit them nor speak for them and when it enters into a commitment it is personally liable (albeit with the right to be indemnified out of the trust property). Property rights may or may not be involved in an agency arrangement, but it is the essence of a trust that property rights are involved: a trust is always a trust of property or rights in or to property. Thus, in the 'base case', the settlor transfers property to the trustee in order to create the trust (and, as we shall see, the trustee needs to concern itself with the implications for itself of holding the trust property).

The role of a security trustee

Leaving aside for the moment jurisdictions where this may not or will not work, the effect of a trust structure is that each security interest the benefit of which is to be acquired by the creditors – whether noteholders or lenders – will be created in favour of the security trustee. With regard to each item of security there will be a transfer of title to or the creation of a security interest in favour of the security trustee – see Chapter 7 for a discussion of the difference between these two ways of taking security. At the same time the security trustee needs to be given a wide range of powers and protections because, as we have seen, any act or neglect on the part of a trustee which is not authorised or excused by the trust or by law is a breach of trust. These powers and protections will be established in a deed, usually called a Security Trust Deed or an Intercreditor Deed. It is almost always as convenient to deal with such matters in a single document which is separate from the documents whereby the security is created as it is helpful to minimise the extent to which inter-creditor issues might confuse matters on enforcement.

Where there are to be different layers of debt or classes of creditors, the deed will contain provisions which are designed to regulate priorities as between those classes of creditors, such as the junior and senior lenders (in an acquisition finance transaction) or the holders of various classes of notes (in a structured finance context). The trustee in its personal capacity will usually seek to be the creditor which gets paid first.

Subordination

Subordination is the name given to any attempt (successful or not) to cause a creditor or group of creditors to cede priority in the winding up of a debtor to other creditors of that debtor. The obvious way to do this is to provide that the security trustee distributes receipts in a certain order by means of an 'application of proceeds' clause which is often, particularly if it is complex, referred to as a 'waterfall', the analogy being with one of those fountains with various levels arranged so that water reaches a given level only when the higher levels are full. However, in an English winding up – at least, before the coming into effect of the Enterprise Act 2002 – creditors (save for preferential creditors and those who make recoveries through enforcing security) must be paid on a 'pari passu' basis with the result that it is possible, where there is a shortfall in the security, that such a contractual waterfall might be wholly or partly disregarded by a liquidator in an English winding up of the debtor.

That secured creditors are free to regulate between themselves the relative priority of their security and thereby bind the debtor was confirmed by the Privy Council in *Cheah Team Swee v Equiticorp Finance Group Ltd* [1991] 4 All ER 989, in which Lord Browne-Wilkinson observed that 'Their Lordships' conclusions accord both with what they understand to be the generally accepted view of the law affecting subordination of debts and the law of the United States: see Corpus Juris Secundum § 218; *Putnam v Broten* (1930) 60 ND 97. It is manifestly desirable that the law on this subject should be the same in all common law jurisdictions' – see the remarks of Colman J noted on page 14.

(A further digression is in order here. As a result of the EC Regulation on Insolvency Proceedings (Council Regulation 1346/2000 which came into force on 31 May 2002, the place where the primary winding up proceedings in respect of an insolvent company, whether EC incorporated or not – see *Re BRAC Rent-a-Car International Inc* [2003] 2 All ER 201 – will (unless that company is a bank or an insurance company, for which different regimes will apply) take place where that company's 'centre of main interests' is to be found. The term 'centre of main interests' is not defined but will be where a company's registered office or seat is located unless there is evidence that the company regularly conducts the administration of its business from some other place. For this reason it is important when considering the effectiveness of subordination provisions to think in terms of an English winding up of a company rather than of the winding up of an English company.)

Because of the potential vulnerability of contractual subordination, financing institutions have looked for other ways in which to subordinate creditors' claims. One approach is to give the financing creditors whose claims are to be subordinated – the junior creditors – claims which are inevitably going to be paid after the claims of the other financing creditors. This can be done by means of a combination of contractual subordination and what is called structural subordination – causing the junior creditors' claims to be claims on a company of which the debtor is a subsidiary and dealing contractually with the payment of inter-company indebtedness. This element of contractual subordination means that the pari passu rule still has to be dealt with, as it will where structural subordination is not thought to be appropriate and the senior creditors rely solely on contractual subordination.

Turnover trusts

The solution which is adopted is to specify that the junior creditors will 'turnover' to the security trustee any payments they receive and that pending such 'turnover', payments received will be held on trust for the security trustee and the other creditors. It is sometimes suggested that such 'turnover trusts' as they are called create security which is registrable under the Companies Act 1985, s 395, but in my view this is not the case.

The property the subject of the trust (which is created by the creditor's declaration) is 'cash at bank' – an equitable interest in the bank account into which the payment to the creditor was made – not a claim on the payer – and the trust is declared not to secure the creditor's obligation to pay the amount in question to the security trustee nor to provide security for the debtor's indebtedness to the creditors, but in order to segregate that amount from the creditor's 'own' assets. As often as not the creditor will be a bank and banks do not secure their obligations – obligations owed, in effect, to other banks – in this way nor do they use their assets to secure a borrower's indebtedness to other banks. (And where the creditors are not banks, the segregation objective fully explains the use of the trust device.)

In neither case is there is any intention on the part of the creditor to create security – and thus there is no security. (See Goode, *Commercial Law*, 2nd edn, 1995, p 664 for a different analysis (which he has now modified – see Goode, *Legal Problems of Credit and Security*, 3rd edn, 2003, para 1-81 on pp 56 and 57) and see also his statement on p 676 with regard to the need for there to be an intention to create security if security is to be created.) The rights of the security trustee which arise as a result of the creditors' declarations are, of course, not merely contractual, arising as they do under a trust, but this does not mean that those rights constitute security.

Powers

The trustee will usually have the power to agree with the debtor to the making of any modification to the deed which in the opinion of the security trustee is 'not materially prejudicial to the interests of the creditors' or which is 'of a formal, minor or technical nature or is made to correct a manifest error'.

The trustee will also have a wide range of other discretions, for example to employ agents and experts, to deposit documents for safekeeping, to convert sums from one currency to another, to delegate, to appoint co-trustees and to take any appropriate action in the event of enforcement. The instructions may be from an 'Instructing Group' or the 'Majority Banks' in a banking transaction – as to which, see Chapter 9 – or take the form of a resolution of the noteholders in a capital markets transaction. Philosophically, professional trustees regard it as their role to perform mechanical and administrative functions and are reluctant to accept wide discretionary powers, although in practice they often have quite extensive discretions.

Protections

One of the reasons that a trustee can live with the discretions they end up with is that a trustee has – or should have – the right not to exercise its discretions, in other words the ability 'to sit on its hands', unless – to use the usual phraseology – indemnified and/or secured to its satisfaction; this is a right a security trustee would not want to be without. Further protection is provided to a trustee by provisions which entitle it to rely on external information or communications such as notices or instructions received (which it may treat as genuine and duly authorised) and opinions or advice received from a lawyer or other expert. A trustee will also be exonerated from numerous responsibilities which might otherwise be implied. Thus, taking a few routine provisions as examples, a trustee will not be liable: for the efficacy or validity of the documents; for any failure to file or perfect the security; for any person's credit worthiness; or for any other person's performance of its obligations.

Some responsibilities, referred to by Millett LJ in *Armitage v Nurse* [1998] Ch 241 as forming an 'irreducible core of obligations owed by a [trustee] to the beneficiaries' cannot be excluded because if the beneficiaries have no rights enforceable against [the trustee] there are no trusts but, he went on to say, these core obligations do not include the duties of skill and care, prudence and diligence. 'The duty of the [trustee] to perform the trusts honestly and in good faith for the benefit of the beneficiaries is the minimum necessary to give substance to the trusts, but in my view it is sufficient.'.

In today's financial markets it is usual for a trustee to have the benefit of an indemnity from the debtor for any and all claims, costs and liabilities it may incur which arise otherwise than as a result of its 'gross negligence or wilful default', although the use of 'gross' as a qualifier does sometimes give rise to debate. (It is not clear whether English law recognises a difference between negligence and gross negligence. In *Armitage v Nurse* (at 254) Millett LJ said that it would be 'very surprising if our law drew the line between liability for ordinary negligence and liability for gross negligence'.)

It is also common practice not to seek to exclude the liability of the trustee but instead to make it clear that the trustee is protected if acting on appropriate instructions and, as already mentioned, to refrain from acting without instructions. These market practices are to be contrasted with the 'core obligations' principle that I just mentioned pursuant to which a trust deed may exclude a trustee's liability for even a wilful default as long as that default is committed in good faith and in the honest belief that the trustee is acting in the interest of the beneficiaries.

(It was at this point that Millet LJ quoted the remark (which I also quote in Chapter 9) allegedly made by 'the late Selwyn LJ' to the effect that: 'the main duty of a trustee is to commit *judicious* (his emphasis) breaches of trust'. However, in a more serious vein, Millett LJ went on to say (at 256) that 'the view is widely held that [contemporary] clauses have gone too far, and that trustees who charge for their services and who, as professional men, would not dream of excluding liability for gross negligence should not be able to rely on a trustee clause excluding liability for gross negligence.)

At law, a trustee has the right to be indemnified against (and has a lien on the trust property for) all expenses properly incurred and this includes the right to be reimbursed for paying calls on shares (*James v May* (1873) LR 6 HL 328), this being no more than 'the ordinary right of a trustee to be indemnified by his cestui que trust' (the beneficiary). In practice the trustee would want to have the right to decline to pay any calls unless and until put in funds.

Taking the security

In an English law security document the 'transfer' of property to the trustee will more often than not be effected by the granting of a security interest by means of a charge, but in a legal mortgage of property other than land, eg chattels (but beware the Bills of Sales Acts) or choses in action, there will be an outright transfer of the property with the usual 'proviso' for redemption – see Chapter 7 for a discussion of concepts and terminology in this area and note that in the case of land special rules apply under the Law of Property Act 1925. Where the security is being created outside England, the security will be granted in the manner appropriate under local law and all the usual issues which arise in relation to the taking of security will need to be considered and addressed where security is created in favour of a trustee.

It is not my aim in this Chapter to discuss such matters in any detail, but I should point out that where security is taken in other jurisdictions, as is often the case in acquisition finance or in a restructuring, unexpected issues may arise. Thus, to take some examples from a recent restructuring: holding land as security may result in environmental liability for the trustee, particularly if it becomes a mortgagee in possession; there may be a duty on enforcement for a trustee to have regard to the interests of a company of whose shares it is a pledgee; or a trustee may be liable for the acts of an attorney it appoints for the purposes of enforcement even if the attorney exceeds its authority.

Security structures

In the final section of this chapter, I will look at some frequently encountered security structures, starting with 'the base case' – see below – in which the security is granted to a trustee to hold on trust for the creditors. It is quite common (at least in acquisition finance) for such a trustee to be called the 'security agent' – when 'security trustee' would be more natural – whether or not a trust structure is being used; this is because, as we shall see, trust structures cannot always be used and an agency structure is the usual alternative. It is a usage which is convenient if, as is often the case, trust and other structures are used in the same transaction where several jurisdictions are involved.

THE BASE CASE

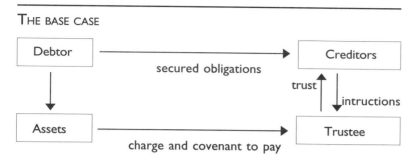

(A covenant to pay is a covenant to pay to the Trustee on its demand all the secured obligations.)

To an English lawyer this is a very familiar structure. Debts are owed by a borrower or an issuer (the debtor) to a group of banks or bondholders (the creditors) in respect of loans or bonds. In an acquisition finance transaction or a structured finance transaction there would probably be various layers – senior, mezzanine and junior – of debt or numerous classes of notes – and security might well be given by guarantors, perhaps subsidiaries or affiliates of the debtor, as well as the issuer or borrower, over property in a variety of jurisdictions and of various kinds – land, shares, contracts or whatever. An important feature of this basic structure is the "covenant to pay" all the secured obligations, whether of the debtor or of other debtor side parties, which will be given by every party on the debtor side and contained in each and every security document and guarantee.

A 'covenant to pay' is simply a promise by a person who is giving security – we can call each such person a mortgagor – to the person to whom security is being given – the trustee – that the mortgagor will on demand of the trustee pay to the trustee all the obligations (the secured obligations) of the issuer/borrower and every other mortgagor to the creditors, the trustee included, as and when those obligations fall due. Apart from causing time to run, for limitation purposes, only when demand is made – the clock would otherwise start in relation to each secured obligation as and when that obligation became due – the effect of a covenant to pay is that whatever security the mortgagor is providing secures, when the time for enforcement comes, the obligation (to pay all the secured obligations when they fall due) that results from demand being made by the mortgagee.

Except with regard to 'accessory security' (see below) this analysis ought to apply where security is being taken in another jurisdiction irrespective of whether that jurisdiction does or does not recognise trusts. In other words, it ought not to be relevant to the validity of the security, accessory security aside, that in a local winding up of the trustee the security would potentially be available to the general creditors of the trustee, which is the main result oft he trust not being recognised. The security trustee will have taken full (or legal) title to the security and its relationship with its beneficiaries should not affect the position. It is different with so-called 'accessory security', which is security in respect of which the holder of security must be the creditor or creditors, directly or through an agent, and cannot be a trustee. This requirement exists in some jurisdictions in relation to certain types of security, but is by no means a universal requirement.

Parallel debt

For reasons which I find hard to understand, there is a practice – unrelated to the accessory security issue – of either dropping or not relying on a covenant to pay in jurisdictions where trusts are not recognised and substituting a so-called 'parallel debt obligation', which is described as a covenant by way of an abstract acknowledgement of debt to pay to the trustee sums equal to the secured obligations as and when they fall due. There are two things that distinguish this from a covenant to pay. Firstly, it purports to create an immediate debt whereas a covenant to pay is an obligation to pay on demand such that a debt will arise when demand is made (as the limitation point illustrates), but I have not heard it argued that this is where the problem lies, that there must be an immediate debt if the security in question is to be valid. Secondly, there is a perceived need for the inclusion in a parallel debt provision of statements to the effect that if either the real debt or the abstract debt is reduced then the other is to be regarded as having been reduced by the same amount. Since this goes without saying with a covenant to pay – which is a promise to pay what is owed, no more, no less – the reasons for the parallel debt approach remain mysterious to me.

My best guess – but it is a guess and I may well be wrong – is that the idea results from a misunderstanding of a remark by Philip Wood in section 7-31 on page 115 of *International Loans, Bonds and Securities Regulation*, Sweet & Maxwell, 1995. In the context of transfers by novation (see Chapters 2, 9 and 10) and security arrangements, he states that any concerns resulting from the fact that transfers by novation create new debts 'can be avoided by initially granting the security ... in favour of a trustee to secure *a parallel obligation* (my emphasis) from the borrower to the trustee to pay the debt and on terms whereby the trustee holds the benefit of the security for [original and future lenders]'.

All you parallel debt supporters out there, Philip was, I believe, simply describing a covenant to pay structure – a parallel obligation, not a fictitious parallel debt – in typically colourful terms. Philip goes on to mention, quite separately, that trust structures are 'not usually available if the secured assets are situate in countries which do not recognise the trust. This is because mortgages over land, for example, must be registered in the name of the actual creditor – not the trustee'. I think Philip has been misunderstood both with regard to the covenant to pay/ parallel debt point and with regard to the extent to which trust structures can be used in jurisdictions where trusts are not recognised. The need in certain jurisdictions – Italy is one – for mortgages over land to be granted to actual creditors is not a consequence of the non-recognition of trusts; it is simply the case that the two issues commonly crop up in one and the same jurisdiction; as it happens Italy does recognise trusts being one of the few 'civil code' countries to have ratified the 1985 Hague Convention on the recognition of trusts.

For me this whole story is an example of a relatively recent tendency to place too much reliance on books which seem to provide all the answers and too little on personal research and analysis. Lawyers these days find themselves obliged to put so much emphasis on what I call processing, 'turning' documents over more frequently and speedily, that there is less and less time for reflection.

Agency structures

Another, more convincing, but still problematic, security structure which is used where a trust structure cannot be used – and, is of course, the usual route in many jurisdictions – is the agency approach under which security is given to an agent for the creditors, as in the following diagram.

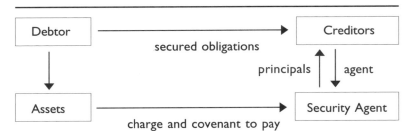

This structure has the same basic outline as the trustee structure. There is a covenant to pay the Security Agent, which is effectively a promise to pay the creditors because the Security Agent is the agent of the creditors. The same basic agency structure appears in various guises; for example:

in Germany the security agent holds 'accessory security' for the benefit of the creditors who authorise it to exercise its powers as mortgagee;

in Italy each creditor appoints the security agent as its 'common representative' with the power to exercise rights and remedies;

in Mexico each creditor appoints the security agent as its agent and grants to it a mandate to execute the security documents and perform the security agent's obligations under those documents;

in Brazil each creditor appoints the security agent as its attorney-in-fact.

From the English law perspective, the difficulty with all these approaches is that each of the agent's principals, ie the creditors, would have an undivided interest in the security. They would all be co-owners of the security, with the result that when a creditor assigns all or part of its claim on the debtor, the assignment will be of an undivided interest in both the debt and the security.

It can be anticipated that in different jurisdictions this will give rise to different issues, including re-registration in the name of the new owners. On the other hand, if creditors transfer their interests, in whole or in part, by means of transfers by novation, the secured debt will be partially discharged and a new secured obligation will arise – and this may lead to problems if, for example, the debtor is in financial difficulties. By contrast, a trust structure permits interests to be traded, by assignment or novation, without disturbing the underlying security which secures the covenant to pay in favour of the trustee – see Chapter 9, page 129.

CHAPTER 14

An introduction to letters of credit

This topic is an enormous black hole – a concept explained in Chapter 1 – but it is one which we all need to explore to some extent. Letters of credit are so widely used that a finance lawyer is bound to meet them at some stage, whether as part of a structured trade finance transaction, as a payment mechanism in an asset finance transaction or as a substitute for a guarantee in a structured capital markets transaction. Of all the topics I have dealt with, this is the most difficult to condense. Letters of credit are operated by banks and their customers on a daily basis in relation to contracts the value of which must be enormous – astronomical used to be the term – and rely on the 'strict compliance' of contractual, shipping and other documents to the terms of the credit. So minimal is the room for deviation, and so rife are the opportunities for fraud, that a real document must be accepted even if, on its face, it does not conform to the terms of the credit, but a forged document which, on its face, does conform will be treated as valid unless the fraud is known to the bank to whom the document is presented.

There are two types of letter of credit: documentary letters of credit and standby letters of credit. Documentary letters of credit are used to finance international trade. Goods are shipped to the buyer and the seller presents the shipping documents not to the buyer, but to the buyer's bank (or to that bank's correspondent bank) which, if the documents are in order, pays the seller and is reimbursed by the buyer (or its bank). A standby letter of credit is a substitute for a guarantee. The beneficiary will present not shipping documents but a statement that a sum is due by reason of another party's performing or failing to perform its obligations under a contract.

Documentary letters of credit

The structure of a documentary letter of credit is best explained by reference to a diagram.

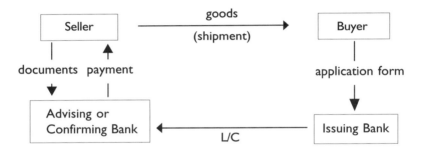

The underlying contract is, I will assume, a contract for the sale of goods between a seller and a buyer. The buyer — known as 'the applicant' — will request its bank to open a letter of credit and will be requested by the bank to sign the bank's standard application form which, when signed, will create an obligation on the part of the applicant to reimburse the bank for any sums it pays out and any related costs and expenses. The form will usually permit the bank to call for cash collateral to cover the total amount that could become due from the applicant. When the paperwork is in order, the applicant's bank — now the 'issuing bank' (sometimes the 'opening bank') — will issue (or open) the letter of credit.

The letter of credit could be in favour of the seller — known as 'the beneficiary' — but in an international context it will usually be issued in favour of another bank in the country of the seller. This bank may be an 'advising bank' — which informs the seller of the terms of the credit without assuming any financial commitment – or it may be a 'confirming bank' – which means that it assumes a commitment to pay out under the letter of credit. The advising bank will often be the issuing bank's correspondent bank in the country of the seller and may be (but need not be) the bank through whom the issuing bank pays the seller.

Assuming the correct documents are tendered in accordance with the terms of the credit – a major assumption as we shall see, the issuing bank is obliged to pay the seller where the letter of credit is issued directly to the seller or is 'advised' by another bank, but where the letter of credit is 'confirmed' by another bank, the confirming bank is obliged to pay and the issuing bank is obliged to reimburse it. The observation most often made about the role of banks in relation to letters of credit – and only banks issue letters of credit – is that banks deal only with documents, not with goods. Goods are sold by sellers to buyers, but payment occurs solely as a result of the delivery of documents by the seller to the buyer's bank.

Letters of credit are sui generis

There is no consideration to support the existence of a contractually binding obligation on the part of the bank, whether it is an issuing bank or a confirming bank. It has been said that a letter of credit is an offer which is accepted by the seller's presenting documents (see *Elder Dempster Lines Ltd v Ionic Shipping Agency Inc* [1968] 1 Lloyd's Rep 529) but this analysis does not explain why a letter of credit is irrevocable once issued. If the offer and acceptance analysis applied, an issuing bank could revoke the letter of credit at any time before acceptance of the offer by the beneficiary, but this is not the case. As is pointed out on p 95 of *Documentary Credits* by Jack, Malek and Quest (3rd edn, 2001), which I will refer to as '*Jack on Documentary Credits*' (or simply '*Jack*'), the alternative to regarding a credit as being effective upon being advised is that the credit becomes binding when the beneficiary has done some act in reliance upon it, but this would introduce an undesirable element of uncertainty.

(I have referred a number of times to my use of standard works as sources of information on a given topic. With regard to the subject matter of this Chapter, my guides have been *Jack on Documentary Credits* and Goode,

Commercial Law, 2nd edn, 1995 ('Goode'), which provide interestingly different approaches.)

The only convincing reason why letters of credit are contractually binding on the parties (and why they are irrevocable when issued, per Goode, p 986, note 64, or when advised to the beneficiary, per *Jack on Documentary Credits*, p 95, para 5.3) is that this is the position which the courts have accepted for 200 years or so since 'Lord Mansfield … fashioned the law merchant (*lex mercatoria*) to the needs of the 18th Century industrial revolution' (per the US Court of Appeals for the 2nd Circuit in *Alaska Texfile Co v Chase Manhattan Bank* 982 F 2d 813 (1992)). The law merchant being, as Goode describes it in the opening pages of *Commercial Law*, essentially the law of international trade which, as interpreted and understood by the English courts, was eventually integrated with the common law through the efforts of Chief Justice Holt and Lord Mansfield.

Letters of credit are autonomous

'The fundamental principle governing documentary letters of credit … is that the obligation of the issuing bank … is independent of the performance of the underlying contract for which the credit was issued.' (*Bank of Nova Scotia v Angelica-Whitewear* [1987], 1 SCR 59 at 81, Can SC per Le Dain J) or, as Goode puts it (p 987): 'One of the primary functions of the letter of credit is to create an abstract payment obligation – shades of parallel debt here (Chapter 13, pages 198–199) – independent of and detached from the underlying contract of sale between S and B from the separate contract between B and IB'.

Another way of saying this, as I have already mentioned, is that the parties deal in documents and in documents alone. If the documents provided by the beneficiary to the bank conform to the terms of the credit, the bank must pay irrespective of the seller's performance or failure to perform. The main exception to this is fraud, whether relating to the letter of credit or the underlying contract. Where the bank is on notice of fraud on the part of the beneficiary or its agent, it is entitled (and obliged) to withhold payment. I will look at this in more detail later. Other defences – per Goode, p 989 – available to the bank are: misrepresentation – a bank may rescind a letter of credit which it was induced to issue by misrepresentation (*Rafsanjan Pistachio Producers*

Co-operative v Bank Leumi (UK) plc [1992] I Lloyd's Rep 513); mistake – as where a letter has been issued to the wrong person who knows that this is the case; and illegality – in the place for performance of the bank's obligations.

On the latter point, it is, of course, only illegality in the place for performance of a letter of credit that can provide a defence to a party who has agreed to procure the issue of, or to issue, a letter of credit. In *Toprak Mahsulleri Ofisi v Finagrain Cia Commerciale Agricole et Financiere SA* [1979] 2 Lloyd's Rep 98 the Court of Appeal confirmed this, applying the principle which had been established in *Kleinwort Sons & Co v Ungarische Baumwolle Industrie Akt* [1939] 2 KB 678. More revealing (and more entertaining) than the decision (which on the facts was more or less a foregone conclusion) is the brief concluding statement of Cummimgs-Bruce LJ, who, concurring with Roskill LJ and Lord Denning MR, simply said 'I agree with both judgments', and added (with reference to the unsuccessful plaintiff's counsel) 'On the liability issue I would only add that Mr Johnson's powerful arguments only demonstrated the truth of the adage that no case, however impossible, is unarguable'.

The UCP

Almost all documentary credits are expressed to be subject to The Uniform Customs and Practice for Documentary Credits (1993 Revision) ICC Publication No 500, known as the UCP, which was first published in 1933. 'The traditional view in England (Goode, p 984) is that the UCP are simply a set of standard rules having no legal force except so far as incorporated by reference into the contract between the parties concerned'. Goode himself (p 985) thinks that rather than just being a set of model rules 'they are strong evidence of banking custom and practice, which themselves will readily be treated by the court as impliedly incorporated into the various documentary credit contracts as established usage'. And to take this further, Goode says, when the UCP are revised they create market practice so that documentary credit parties must be taken to have intended to contract by reference to the UCP even where one party is not aware of the UCP (see *Harlow & Jones Ltd v American Express Bank Ltd* [1990] 2 Lloyd's Rep 343, a case relating to the Uniform Rules for Collections).

The UCP apply to documentary credits and, to the extent applicable, to standby credits where they are incorporated into the text of the Credit (Article 1) – this and all subsequent references to Articles are to Articles of the UCP – and provide in Article 2 that a credit (documentary or standby) is an arrangement whereby an issuing bank at the request and on the instructions of a customer or on its own behalf: is to pay (or accept and pay a bill drawn by) the beneficiary; authorises another bank to do so; or authorises another bank to negotiate, in each case against stipulated documents, provided that the terms of the credit are complied with.

The obligation of an Issuing Bank (to simplify somewhat) is, if the stipulated documents are presented and the terms of the credit are complied with, to pay at sight or at a specified later date (or dates), or to accept and/or pay drafts drawn by the beneficiary, the amount due or covered by such drafts in accordance with the terms of the credit (Article 9a). A Confirming Bank assumes obligations to the beneficiary which are the same as those assumed by the Issuing Bank (Article 9b). Thus, a credit may provide for sight payment, deferred payment, acceptance (of a bill of exchange) or for negotiation – in the latter case the bank must pay the holder in due course of the documents called for by the credit, one or more of which may be a bill of lading. (A bill of lading is a document which constitutes an acknowledgement by a carrier that it holds the goods covered by the bill of lading for whoever holds the bill of lading and the holder of such a bill has constructive possession of those goods which it can transfer by transferring the bill of lading. Thus, a bill of lading resembles a bill of exchange and may, by its terms, be negotiable or non-negotiable. For further insight into the many legal and practical issues arising in connection with the documentation for international sales of goods, refer to Goode, Part 7, pp 875–1133.)

Types of documentary credit

Documentary credits can be classified in a variety of ways. Thus a credit may be: revocable or irrevocable; negotiable or non-negotiable; confirmed or unconfirmed; payable at sight or at a later date, the latter being called a deferred credit; or transferable or not. I will deal briefly with these various types of credit.

·

Irrevocable and revocable credits

Most documentary credits are irrevocable. Article 6 provides that a credit should clearly indicate whether it is revocable or irrevocable and that in the absence of such indication the credit shall be deemed irrevocable. A revocable credit, on the other hand, can be amended or cancelled by the issuing bank 'at any moment and without prior notice to the Beneficiary' (Article 8a). Thus a revocable credit is of little use to a beneficiary as it can be revoked even after the documents have been presented. The issuing bank must, however, honour any obligations it may have to a bank which is a 'nominated bank', this being the bank which the issuing bank has specified as the bank to whom the documents must be presented and which is authorised (Article 10b.i.) 'to pay, to incur a deferred payment undertaking, to accept Drafts or to negotiate'. Unless it is a confirming bank – see below – a nominated bank is not under any liability to take any of these steps, but is entitled to be reimbursed by the issuing bank if it does (Articles 10c and 10d).

Negotiable and non-negotiable credits

A credit may be expressed to benefit only the named beneficiary or it may be expressed to benefit anyone who becomes a bona fide holder of the documents called for by the credit. This may be helpful to the beneficiary where the credit does not provide for immediate payment because it can sell the documents to a bank for cash, thus getting immediate payment, albeit at a discount. As the UCP puts it in Article 10.b.i, in a freely negotiable credit any bank can be the nominated bank. Whether a credit is negotiable is a matter of construction, something which should be straightforward but often is not. A complicating factor is the use of the term 'negotiation', which is a term defined in Article 10.b.ii to mean 'the giving of value [for drafts and/or other documents] by the bank authorised to negotiate'. In a credit, a reference to negotiation may be a reference to the giving of value in this way by a bank named in the credit or it may indicate that the credit can be regarded as being negotiable. There is apparently, no consensus on whether the 'default position', if a credit is silent on the point, should be that credits are not negotiable or whether current practice leans towards credits being negotiable rather than not – see Jack, pp 33–35, note 1 on p 35 in particular. This means, of course, that a credit should always deal with the point.

Unconfirmed and confirmed credits

A credit which is not confirmed can be regarded as the base case – the issuing bank opens the credit and requests the bank it selects as the advising bank to inform (advise) the beneficiary of the opening of the credit. The advising bank acts as the agent of the issuing bank both in receiving the documents which are presented and in paying out against them, but it has no obligation to the beneficiary. Thus, the issuing bank will be bound as against the beneficiary even if the advising bank advises the credit incorrectly, eg, by failing to stipulate that a specified document should be presented. If, however, the advising bank decides to pay the beneficiary, the issuing bank will be entitled to reject the documents it receives as being incomplete. If in such circumstances the credit stipulates that payment should be made – and is made – by the issuing bank or a nominated bank, will the applicant (the buyer) have to reimburse it even though, because the credit was wrongly advised, the documents are not what the applicant specified when it requested the issuing bank to open the credit?

The answer ought to be 'no' (with the result that the issuing bank's remedy is against the advising bank) but if it is a bank other than the issuing bank which pays, ie the nominated bank, the wording of Article 18 casts doubt on this by stating that where a bank utilises the services of another bank for the purpose of giving effect to the applicant's instructions it does so '*for the account and at the risk of the applicant*'. This leads to the odd result that an applicant would not be liable to reimburse the issuing bank which had itself advised a credit incorrectly, but would be required to reimburse an issuing bank which instructed another bank to advise the credit even if that other bank advised the credit incorrectly. Jack argues (para 4.20, pp 87 and 88) that the true effect of Article 18 "is only to prevent the issuing bank from being liable in respect of the errors of a correspondent bank unless the issuing bank has itself been negligent", but the wording of the article itself provides little support for this clearly sensible conclusion.

A confirming bank, by contrast, adds (as we have seen) its own undertaking – to pay (or accept bills) against compliant documents – to that of the Issuing Bank. Article 9.b states that a "confirmation of an irrevocable credit by another bank ("the confirming bank") upon the authorisation or request of the issuing bank constitutes a definite undertaking of the confirming bank, in addition to that of the issuing bank, [to pay, accept bills etc]". Thus, there is a contract between the beneficiary and the confirming bank which, again, is formed without there being any consideration. So-called 'silent confirmations', in which, at the seller's request but not at the issuing bank's request, an advising bank guarantees payment under the credit to the seller, are not uncommon. Such an arrangement is outside the UCP so there is no right to be reimbursed by the issuing bank for an advising bank which agrees to provide a silent confirmation (unless it happens to be the nominated bank and entitled to reimbursement in that capacity).

Sight and deferred credits

A sight credit is one under which payment is to be made on presentation of the documents, time being allowed for examination of the documents. Under a deferred payment credit, payment is due after a specified period from the date of presentation of the documents. In order for the buyer to get hold of the goods the subject of a deferred payment credit, the issuing bank will have to relinquish possession of the documents before it has become obliged to pay the seller and, thus, before it is entitled to be reimbursed by the buyer. It is in such circumstances that the issuing bank may take from the buyer a 'trust receipt' under which the buyer agrees to hold the goods and their proceeds on trust for the issuing bank. A trust receipt operates to preserve whatever security the issuing bank had over the goods the subject of a credit, a principle confirmed in *North Western Bank, Ltd v Poynter, Son, & Macdonalds* [1895] AC 56, but rather better explained in *Official Assignee of Madras v Mercantile Bank of India Ltd* [1935] AC 53, in which Lord Wright pointed out (at 63) that where for a specific, limited purpose documents of title to goods (in that case railway receipts for consigned goods) were given back to the pledgor by the pledgee, the pledgee 'did not part with possession of the goods or receipts in the juridical sense of that word; they merely parted with the custody, by entrusting the receipts to the [pledgor] as their agents or mandatories'.

A trust receipt is, however, only as good as the bank's customer is honest: a dishonest customer can create a valid security interest in the goods if, being a mercantile agent, it is treated as being in possession of the goods with the consent of the owner within the Factors Act 1889, s 2(1). This is a provision which creates one of the exceptions to the nemo dat rule and under which – see the judgment of Sir Wilfred Greene M.R. in *Lloyd's Bank Ltd v Bank of America National Trust* [1938] 2 KB 147, CA, at 162 – 'owner' may mean the two persons – you probably didn't know this was possible, but you do now – between whom ownership is divided and who would in combination be in a position to give express authority with regard to a relevant dealing in the goods, one having 'the right to possession, which is one of the incidents of ownership, and [the other having] all the other rights incident to ownership'.

A bill of exchange may well be one of the documents to be presented under a letter of credit, whether a sight bill, which is payable on presentation, or a bill payable at a fixed time after acceptance. Commercially, a credit which calls for the latter has the same effect as a deferred payment credit but is referred to as an acceptance credit; an acceptance credit is said to be 'available by negotiation' where it is contemplated that the correspondent bank will purchase the bill at a discount which reflects the tenor of the bill and prevailing interest rates.

The use of bills of exchange in a letter of credit complicates the operation of the credit and the contractual relationships between the parties since all the rights and remedies which bills give rise to will be superimposed on the rights of the parties under the UCP and otherwise. Thus, Jack is surely correct in recommending (para 1.22, p 10) that 'bills of exchange should not be included among the documents required by a credit without reason' – and I will use that instruction as an excuse to move on to another topic.

Transferable credits

Under a transferable credit (see Article 48), a beneficiary can request the nominated bank to transfer the credit to the beneficiary's supplier, but the nominated bank is not obliged to do so. The reason that a seller would want this to be done is that it provides a means whereby the seller can pay its supplier. I met this procedure some time ago in a structured trade finance transaction in which a commodity trader (which was acting as a conduit for a medium-term loan to the supplier) was the beneficiary of transferable letters of credit covering sales to its customers which it transferred to the supplier after deduction of its 'trading margin'.

In the absence of such contractual arrangements, all that a beneficiary can do is to request the nominated bank to transfer the credit – it can't insist that this happens. The leading case in this context is *Bank Negara Indonesia 1946 v Lariza (Singapore) Pte Ltd* [1988] AC 583, the end result of lengthy litigation and notable because: at first instance the judgment made no reference to the UCP; in the hearing in the Privy Council no cases were cited in argument or referred to in the judgment; and the Privy Council was forced to decide that on the first issue of the two main issues they had to consider 'it would be unsafe for them to form a concluded opinion ... without the assistance [which they had not received] of expert evidence on relevant banking practice'. What can one say?

A credit must be described as being transferable if it is to be transferred. For this reason and because the use of a transferable credits carries with it a risk of disclosure of the supplier's name to the ultimate buyer, a seller may prefer to use back to back credits. These are credits where the documents required by one credit may, possibly with the substitution of invoices and other documents, be used to obtain payment under another credit, as where a seller asks the issuing bank – the seller becomes the applicant – to open a credit in favour of its supplier. This may obviate the disclosure risk, but the seller's bank will, if the supplier's documents are in order, have to pay under the back to back credit even if its customer, the seller, cannot get paid under the original credit. This is a risk that would not exist if a transferable credit were used. In *Mannesman Handel AG v Kannlasen Shipping Corpn* [1993] 1 Lloyd's Rep 89, a bank was held not to be acting in accordance with a Swiss law requirement to act in good faith where it declined to pay under a back to back credit because of discrepancies the reasons for which it was well aware of. This is a decision on a point of Swiss law which is more informative about the role of expert witnesses as to the law of other jurisdictions and how the courts respond to what they have to say than it is about letters of credit.

Revolving and other credits

For the sake of completeness I will mention a few other types of credits without going into any detail. A revolving credit can, as the name suggests, be utilised more than once on whatever terms are set out in the credit; for example, utilisation might be possible as soon as documents have been presented subject to a limit on the size of the shipments to be financed. There are also two more colourful types of credit, or, more accurately, of provisions found in letters of credits for particular commodities. A 'Red Clause Credit' – the relevant provision used to be printed in red – allows a seller to make a drawing before the goods have been shipped. There is a risk here for the buyer who will be obliged to reimburse the issuing bank even if the goods are never shipped. This type of credit, which will usually call for delivery of security for the issuing bank in the form of a warehouseman's warrant or receipt, is most often found where the export of wool from Australia, New Zealand or South Africa is being financed. A 'Green Clause Credit' is essentially similar but the goods are held in storage in the name of the bank rather than in the name of the beneficiary. This approach apparently has its origins in the Zaire coffee trade.

Documents

Article 13.a of the UCP provides that banks must examine all documents 'with reasonable care to ascertain whether or not they appear, on their face, to be in compliance with the terms of the Credit', compliance of the stipulated documents being 'determined by international standard banking practice as reflected in [the UCP], and that documents "which appear on their face to be inconsistent with one another will be considered as not appearing on their face to be in compliance with the terms and conditions of the Credit"'. This would seem to be a clear and straightforward proposition which leaves little room for debate, but the reality is very different.

In January 2003 the ICC issued a 100 page publication, called 'International Standard Banking Practice for the Examination of Documents under Documentary Credits (ISBP)' (ICC No 645) which deals with the day to day implications of the compliance requirement. The ISBP does not amend the UCP – it 'explains, in explicit detail, how the rules are to be applied on a day-to-day basis'. The ISBP is intended to resolve issues arising out of the existence of differing practices in different countries, but it recognises that 'the law in some countries may compel a different practice than that stated here' (Introduction, p 8). Clearly, I cannot make a serious attempt to deal with such a large topic in the course of this Chapter, but I can at least identify some key issues.

Strict compliance

One general principle is that the documents presented by the beneficiary must comply strictly with the terms of the credit see *Equitable Trust Co of New York v Dawson Partners Ltd* (1926) 27 Ll L Rep 49 at 52, where this fundamental principle was held to mean that a requirement for delivery of a confirmation from 'experts who are sworn brokers' was not satisfied by a confirmation from one such broker – thus entitling the buyer to reject the documents and to decline to reimburse the issuing bank – even though this requirement had been communicated by means of a code which made no distinction between the singular and the plural. The issuing bank was not helped by the coding error because it was committed by its correspondent bank. Another basic rule is that original documents are required – a rule which gives rise to problems in the age of emails and the pdf despite the detailed stipulations in Article 20.b of the UCP. In *Kredietbank Antwerp v Midland Bank plc* [1999] Lloyd's Rep Bank 219, CA, the Court of Appeal held that a bank cannot reject a document just because it is not marked as 'original' if in fact it is the original, albeit an electronically generated original – Article 20.b provides that a document will be regarded as original if a carbon copy or generated electronically if it is marked as such and signed if necessary.

Fraud

The basis of the decision in the *Kredietbank* case makes good sense but reflects an interestingly different approach to that taken in relation to documents which although appearing to be correct are in fact, and unbeknown to the parties, forged (and thus a 'nullity'). In this context – the context being the 'fraud exception' – it is the appearance that matters, not the true status of the document, because 'banks deal in documents and questions of apparent conformity' – Potter LJ in *Montrod Ltd v Grunkotter Fleischvertriebs GmbH* [2001] EWCA Civ 1954 [2002] 1 All ER (Comm) 257 at 274. Fraud is a constant problem for banks engaged in letter of credit business and as a result there is a plethora of cases to deal with; again, I can only sketch out some core principles.

A letter of credit gives rise to obligations which are separate from and independent of both the underlying commercial contract and the contract between the applicant and the issuer – this is the so-called 'principle of autonomy'. However, where the seller acts fraudulently, eg, in presenting false documents, an issuer which becomes aware of this may be relieved of its obligation to pay even though the documents appear on their face to be in compliance with the terms of the credit. See *United City Merchants (Investments) Ltd v Royal Bank of Canada* [1983] 1 AC 168, HL, in which the nullity point – what is the result where, unbeknown to the beneficiary or the bank, a document is presented which is itself a forgery or otherwise fraudulent (eg a signature is forged) – was left undecided. A bill of lading had been deliberately (but not by or on behalf of the beneficiary) backdated so as to comply with the terms of the credit. As a result, the bank was relieved of its obligation to pay because it learnt of the fraud and was thus able to contest the point. In the more recent *Montrod* case, the Court of Appeal held that knowledge of fraud (on the part of the beneficiary or the bank) is essential if the fraud exception is to apply; in the absence of such knowledge an apparently conforming document is to be regarded as in fact conforming even though fraudulent.

(This is not a view shared by Goode pp 1007–1010 or by Richard Hooley in his articles in the March and April 2003 issues of Butterworths Journal – and they have a point. I have this recollection, whose source is too old for me to trace its origins, to the effect that a forgery is a nullity for all purposes. In the context of bills of exchange, for instance, forgery is one of the few available defences to a holder in due course's claim on a bill – see Chapter 3, page 33.)

In the *Montrod* case, an inspection certificate (for a consignment of frozen meat) was inadvertently signed (by the seller) without due authority. The Court of Appeal upheld the first instance decision on this point of Judge Raymond Jack QC, who had stated that the 'nullity exception' did not form part of English law. However, where a seller, for the purposes of drawing on a credit, fraudulently presents to the confirming bank documents that contain actual or implicit misrepresentations of fact, the courts will not compel the issuing bank to pay because 'the courts will not allow their process to be used by a dishonest person to carry out a fraud' – Lord Diplock in the *United City Merchants* case. This continues to be a developing area of law, a black hole into which I will go no further.

To pay or not to pay

A bank is entitled to reimbursement even where the documents presented by the beneficiary are fraudulent or presented fraudulently as long as the bank has inspected the documents with reasonable care and has determined that on their face they are in compliance with the terms of the credit. However, a bank should not pay – and will not be entitled to reimbursement – if it is clear and obvious to the bank that there is fraudulent conduct – see *Czarnikow-Rionda Sugar Trading Inc v Standard Bank London Ltd* [1999] 2 Lloyd's Rep 187 at 203 per Rix J. (In the US the bank has the option to pay if it does so in good faith – UCC 5-109(2).) An issuing bank may invite its customer – the applicant – to injunct it where fraud is suspected or the applicant may take the initiative and seek injunction(s) preventing payment or, perhaps, the presentation of documents by the beneficiary. Although there is a Court of Appeal case (*Themehelp Ltd v West* [1996] QB 84) in which an injunction restraining a beneficiary from demanding payment [under a performance guarantee] was upheld, this is regarded as anomalous in that it is contrary to the autonomy principle and has the effect of preventing payment in circumstances where the issuing bank itself would not have had the benefit of the 'fraud exception'; thus the decision effectively extends the fraud exception to fraud in the underlying transaction.

With regard to a bank, the evidence (as to the fraud and as to the bank's knowledge) must be clear – the alleged defrauder should have been challenged and failed to provide an adequate answer: 'If the Court considers that on the material before it the only realistic inference to draw is that of fraud' then fraud there is. (Ackner LJ in *United Trading Corpn SA v Allied Arab Bank Ltd* [1985] 2 Lloyd's Rep 554n at 561.)

A longer than usual postscript

I had thought that I might deal with standby letters of credit in this Chapter, but I soon realised that if I did, I would also have to deal with what are often called 'demand guarantees' – such things as advance payment guarantees and performance bonds – and that I would need another chapter in which to do this; but since I have already used up the time I have available for this project, all they are going to get is this rather extended postscript.

Standby letters of credit

Standby Letters of Credit originated in the United States as a result of its being illegal for national banking associations to issue guarantees. A standby letter of credit is a simplified form of credit – falling within the UCP – in respect of which the two basic elements in any letter of credit are present: the issuer is obliged to pay against appropriate documents; and the principle of autonomy applies, so that an issuer is not concerned with underlying contractual arrangements. The difference between documentary letters of credit and standby letters of credit is that standby letters of credit are used not to effect payment of the price payable under a contract but either as a guarantee of a debt or to impose a sanction in the event of a default by a contracting party. Thus, a very common use of standby letters of credit is as a substitute for a conventional guarantee.

There are, however, very significant differences in the relation between the parties where a standby letter of credit is used in this way. As we saw in Chapter 5, a conventional guarantee creates a relationship of suretyship, with all the consequences that flow from that. Where a standby letter of credit is used, there is no such relationship – the issuing bank has not become liable for another's debt, it has assumed its own primary obligation; it has no rights of subrogation – instead it has direct recourse to the applicant.

The UCP are written so as to be capable of applying to standby letters of credit although in 1998 the ICC adopted a set of International Standby Practices (ISP98). It remains to be seen which code will be preferred in the long term. In any event, if either code is to be used, this must be expressly stated in the credit.

Demand guarantees

Demand guarantees – so named to distinguish them from conventional guarantees – are instruments under which the issuer (a bank) will become obliged to make a payment to the beneficiary if the issuer's customer defaults in the performance of a contractual obligation, usually physical performance rather than payment, the usual context for these instruments being construction contracts where the contractor is the bank's customer.

There are three main types of demand guarantee to describe, but first a warning: a similar type of protection for the beneficiary is sometimes given by a form of contract embodied in a deed under which a bank or, more likely, an insurance company will, together with its customer, enter into a suretyship guarantee (see *Trafalgar House Construction (Regions) Ltd v General Surety & Guarantee Co Ltd* [1996] AC 199, in which Lord Jauncey of Tullichettle endorses the observations of Lord Atkin in our old friend *Trade Indemnity Co Ltd v Workington Harbour and Dock Board* [1937] AC 1 – see Chapter 5, page 65 – where he says, at 209, 'I find great difficulty in understanding the desire of commercial men to embody so simple an obligation in a document which is quite unnecessarily lengthy, which obfuscates its true purpose and which is likely to give rise to unnecessary arguments and litigation as to its meaning'.

Confusingly, instruments which are in substance 'demand guarantees' may be called guarantees or bonds. A Bid Bond will oblige the issuer to pay a percentage of the contract price (say 5%) if a successful bidder for a contract decides not to enter into the contract; an Advance Payment Guarantee will oblige the issuer to pay an amount equal to the advance payment if a contracting party which has received an advance payment fails to take the steps, eg, mobilisation of labour and machinery, that it was required to take by the contract; and a Performance Bond will require the issuer to pay five, perhaps ten, per cent of the contract price if the contractor fails to perform its obligations properly.

As you can see, there are plenty of issues in relation to demand guarantees, so many that I had better stop now. As my final observation on the topic, I will mention *Edward Owen Engineering Ltd v Barclays Bank International Ltd* [1978] QB 159, in which the Court of Appeal, led by Lord Denning MR, confirmed that even though the beneficiary had committed a serious breach of contract – by failing to ensure that the letter of credit whereby the price was to be paid was confirmed – Barclays' customer was not entitled to an injunction which would prevent Barclays from paying under its performance guarantee. If you are a bank which issues a demand guarantee, your word is your bond.

CHAPTER 15

Areas of legal risk in sovereign-linked credit derivatives

> **Although much has changed in the derivatives markets since this piece was first published in 1999, the general thrust of this paper remains as pertinent now as it was then. In the course of a discussion (illustrated by a case study) of the application of credit events to sovereign reference entities, I seek to make four main points. First, it seems to me that ISDA's credit events, although recently revised, are not easily or effectively applied to sovereign entities. Secondly, I make some suggestions as to how disputes relating to credit derivatives might be resolved, dispute resolution procedures of the kind in use in credit derivative contracts four or five years ago having fallen out of favour and recourse to the courts proving to be unsatisfactory. Thirdly, I will argue that legal risk is not well handled by treating the simple as if it were complex and the complex as if it were simple. And finally, I suggest a rather different way of resolving the difficulties inherent in applying credit events to sovereign entities.**

The economic crises which occurred in Asia and Russia during 1998 gave rise to serious legal problems in the derivatives markets, particularly in relation to credit derivatives. Specific areas of concern included the formulation of credit events with regard to sovereign entities and the implementation of the then current dispute resolution procedures and the concept of publicly available information.

The dispute resolution procedures have since been dropped by ISDA but not replaced, recourse now being had to the courts to resolve disputes – and this approach is not without its problems, as Schuyler Henderson firmly pointed out in his May 2003 article in Butterworths Journal, 'When is an option not a contingency' (2003) 5 *JIBFL* 178, in which he reviews the decision in *Nomura International Plc v Credit Suisse First Boston International* [2002] EWHC 160 (Comm). This is a decision which could be said to subvert the intention of the parties, but it has to be remembered that a contract means not what you meant it to say but what the judges think the words you used 'must reasonably be understood to have been intended to say' (per Lightman J in *Don King Productions Inc v Warren and others* [2000] Ch 291 at 311, explaining and applying Lord Hoffman's dictum, in *Investors' Compensation Scheme Ltd v West Bromwich Building Society* [1998] 1 WLR 896 at 913, that 'The meaning which a document (or any other utterance) would convey to a reasonable man is not the same thing as the meaning of its words. The meaning of words is a matter of dictionaries and grammars; the meaning of a document is what the parties using these words against the relevant background would reasonably have been understood to mean'.

It cannot be assumed that the judges will have the market insights that will enable them correctly to infer what the parties intended to say. It is correct, as I mention in Chapter 11, that words only have the meaning they have by reference to the context in which they are used, as in 'they passed the port at midnight', but it follows from this that if you are to understand a document correctly, you must understand the context correctly. Ironically, Lord Hoffman's next sentence reads: 'The background may not merely enable the reasonable man to choose between the possible meanings of words which are ambiguous but even (as occasionally happens in ordinary life) to conclude that the parties must, for whatever reason, have used the wrong words or syntax', a statement which sits nicely with the first of the four fundamental errors identified by Schuy in the *Nomura/CSFB* judgment which is that 'The court's reading … is not a possible reading if the rules of punctuation and grammar are followed'.

Credit events and sovereigns

The 1998 economic crises raised questions regarding the management of legal risk in the derivatives market as well as suggesting that there was a need to look afresh at the basis on which credit events are written, particularly in relation to sovereign-linked credit derivatives.

A credit default swap, which is but one type of credit derivative contract, is – assuming for the sake of convenience that it is one which requires cash settlement – a contract whereby one party (the seller) agrees with another party (the buyer) that if any one or more of an agreed set of events (credit events) affects a specific debt obligation or set of obligations of an issuer, or the issuer itself (the reference entity), the seller will pay to the buyer an amount calculated by reference to the notional amount of the swap and any concomitant drop in value of one such obligation or a number of them (the reference obligations). In return for this commitment, the buyer will agree to pay the seller a modest fee on a regular basis during the life of the swap, the duration of which will be agreed at the outset. Put in more straightforward, if slightly inaccurate, terms, the seller will compensate the buyer for a notional loss suffered by reason of a deterioration in the creditworthiness of the issuer. (There need not, probably will not, be any actual loss; it is for this reason that it is generally accepted that credit default swaps are not contracts of insurance.)

The specific areas which I will consider are:

(a) the formulation of the credit events;

(b) the use of 'publicly-available information' as a means of determining whether or not a credit event has occurred; and

(c) the type of provision which is made for the resolution of a dispute as to whether or not a credit event has occurred.

Credit events

The credit derivatives market is no longer in its infancy, as could be said four years ago, and the 2003 ISDA Credit Derivatives Definitions (the Definitions) are firm evidence of this, providing a new suite of standard credit events which reflect the experiences of the market in recent years. The credit events in a conventional, corporate issuer swap would include some or all of: bankruptcy; failure to pay; obligation acceleration; obligation default (meaning that an obligation has become capable of being declared due and payable as a result of a default or the occurrence of an event of default); failure to pay; repudiation/moratorium; and restructuring – see Article IV of the Definitions. Despite the progress which has been made it continues to be the case that sovereign-linked credit default swaps will contain credit events which originated in a corporate context. This was one of the sources of the problems which were encountered in the late 1990s and could still be again.

Sovereigns are different

Corporate issuers of public debt are almost always subject to a domestic insolvency regime. In addition to this, the assets of a corporate issuer in some other jurisdiction can often be made subject to a local insolvency or bankruptcy procedure. There will be procedures under which creditors may file claims and procedures for the valuation of claims. There will be provision for a tribunal of one sort or another to determine who gets paid what and, in due course, to wind up or terminate the existence of the corporate entity the subject of the proceedings. It is very different where an issuer is sovereign. (It is also likely to be more or less different where the issuer is quasi-sovereign, for example, a legally distinct entity which is owned by a sovereign, but I will confine myself to sovereigns as such.). A key distinguishing feature of a sovereign debt default is that there is no applicable insolvency regime, which is one of the reasons why a sovereign debt restructuring is very different from a corporate restructuring.

There is always pressure on a distressed corporate debtor either to develop a viable workout programme under protective bankruptcy legislation, for example 'administration' in the UK or 'Chapter 11' in the US, or to reach agreement with its creditors. If a solution is not developed or agreement is not reached, a corporate debtor can be wound up, its existence terminated and its management's jobs lost (if the original management has survived that long). As has been said before, countries do not go bankrupt and the pressures to reach agreement with creditors are very different. It is usually said by external creditors to recalcitrant sovereign debtors that a voluntary solution needs to be agreed so that the country can return to the international capital markets. The truth is that a country can remain absent from these markets almost indefinitely. The need to have access to the international markets is a political one, not an economic one, and the management (in the form of the Minister of Finance) is more likely to lose its job through offering terms which are perceived as being too generous than by failing to reach agreement with external creditors. Thus, a restructuring event which has been developed from a set of corporate events may well fail to catch a deterioration in a sovereign's creditworthiness which it was intended to. Worse than this, from the perspective of a market which needs certainty in these areas if disputes are not to impede its operation, ill-suited restructuring events may make it impossible to be sure whether a credit event has or has not occurred. This is what happened in 1998.

A case study

What follows is a hypothetical case study which is closely based on real life experiences, but in which the names and circumstances have been altered to protect the innocent.

1 In January 1998, two financial institutions, Shortbank and Longbank, entered into a pair of credit default swaps in respect of which the reference entity was the Republic of San Seriffe and the reference obligations were the US$750 million 9% Republic of San Seriffe bonds due 3 June 2006.

2 Shortbank was the seller in the first of the swaps to mature (which was of one year's duration). Longbank was the seller in the other swap, which matured four years later. In each case the seller was the 'calculation agent'.

3 Within three months of the onset of its debt crisis, the Republic of San Seriffe contacted one of its core relationship banks, HelpyouBank, and indicated that it could not pay the coming year's maturities on its commercial bank debt.

4 HelpyouBank quickly arranged for the formation of a creditor committee which met the Republic's Minister of Finance a month later.

5 The press reported the meeting and quoted the Minister as saying that the Republic was seeking a rescheduling of its commercial bank debt and meanwhile was going to stop servicing current maturities.

6 In July 1998, both Longbank and Shortbank contacted their lawyers. Longbank asked its lawyers to demonstrate that a credit event had occured. Shortbank asked its lawyers to demonstrate that no credit event had taken place.

Conflicting contracts

The lawyers were confronted with a not wholly unprecedented problem. The swaps had been documented under non-standard, ISDA based contracts but, unfortunately, the two banks had sent each other their preferred forms (which had quite different credit events) and there was a dispute as to which form governed the swaps. Both banks' lawyers decided to analyse both forms to see which favoured their clients.

The outcome of the dispute which was to ensue would depend in part on the following three credit events, the first being Longbank's restructuring event (Box 1), the second Shortbank's restructuring event (Box 2) and the third a 'payment event' (Box 3), which was the same in both forms.

Box 1

Longbank's restructuring event

Restructuring means that a moratorium is proposed or a suspension of payments is declared in respect of any indebtedness or obligation of the Republic.

[Under the Definitions a credit event will not occur unless, amongst other things, 'a moratorium, standstill, roll-over or deferral, whether de facto or de jure', is declared or imposed and a failure to pay or a restructuring (in either case of any amount, however small, has occurred) (s 4.6(*a*)).]

Box 2

SHORTBANK'S RESTRUCTURING EVENT

Restructuring means that a waiver, deferral or rescheduling of any obligation of the Republic, the effect of which is that the terms of such obligation are materially less favourable from an economic, credit or risk perspective to a holder of such obligation.

[Under the Definitions there is a restructuring only if one (or more) adjustments to the terms of an obligation occurs or is agreed or announced (or otherwise decreed) in a way that binds all holders (s 4.7(*a*)) – and such events are not relevant unless they 'directly or indirectly result from a deterioration in the creditworthiness or financial condition' of the reference entity.]

In the real world a swap would contain both forms of restructuring event, but the pretence that one bank wanted to rely on one of them and one on the other serves to underline how a particular phrase may be seen as supporting a commercial aim even though an objective analysis would suggest otherwise.

Box 3

PAYMENT EVENT

Failure to pay means, after giving effect to any applicable grace period (under any terms in effect at the trade date), the failure by the reference entity to make, when due, any payments equal to or exceeding the default requirement under any obligations of the Republic.

Longbank's restructuring event

The first event could be said to describe quite accurately the early stages of a sovereign debt rescheduling. Whatever words are used by the sovereign and its creditors (be they London Club, Paris Club or others) at the beginning of a sovereign debt rescheduling or restructuring – the two words have the same meaning in this context – one of the first steps is almost always a cessation of payments of principal. However, Shortbank argued that since no formal *declaration* had been made, the de facto moratorium or suspension of payments imposed by the Republic did not constitute a credit event. Because Longbank's exposure as seller had three years to run, it had a hard decision to make. Should it declare an event where it was seller (knowing that it could not force Shortbank to do likewise) or should it sit on its hands and hope that no formal declaration was made after the expiry of the shorter-term swap but before the expiry of the longer one?

(The reason Shortbank could not be forced to declare an event is that it was the calculation agent and, in accordance with usual practice, was entitled to make that determination in its sole discretion.)

Shortbank's restructuring event

The second event posed a different problem which arose a few weeks later when the Republic announced it had reached agreement with the Paris Club for a rescheduling of the current year's maturities. Leaving aside for the moment the difficulties posed by the materiality requirement, when does a Paris Club rescheduling happen? Is it when an outline agreement is struck in Paris and evidenced by a 'minute' or 'procés-verbal' or is it when bilateral agreements, which implement the terms of the outline agreement, are signed between debtor and creditor countries?

Longbank's lawyers argued that, because immediately after the meetings in Paris the Republic's Minister of Finance had announced that the Republic had 'agreed a rescheduling with the Paris Club', there had been a rescheduling within the terms of the Shortbank restructuring event. They pointed out that the parties to the Paris Club discussions, the Republic of San Seriffe and its governmental creditors, all regarded a rescheduling as having been agreed at those discussions and that the IMF had publicly referred to the Republic's Paris Club rescheduling as being an important step in the Republic's progress towards achieving the economic objectives which had been agreed with the IMF. If these parties think there has been a rescheduling, there must have been one, Longbank's lawyers said.

However, Shortbank's lawyers took the view that no rescheduling could be said to have occurred until at least one bilateral agreement had been signed between the Republic and one of its Paris Club creditors. They argued that what had been achieved in Paris was no more than an agreement to agree. In any event, they added, even if there were a rescheduling as a result of what was agreed in Paris, the 'materiality' requirement of Shortbank's restructuring event was not satisfied. The requirement was that the new terms of the rescheduled obligations are less favourable (than the previous terms, presumably) from a risk perspective to a holder of such obligations. This was not the case, the lawyers argued. Since the Republic had agreed to payment terms which it could comply with, as the IMF confirmed, the risk, that is the risk of default, was reduced by the rescheduling.

An unresolved dispute

Not surprisingly, Longbank did not think much of this argument and, anyway, regarded its restructuring event as the one the parties had agreed on. Shortbank, for its part, disagreed and invited Longbank to invoke the swaps dispute resolution procedures (which, fortunately, were the same in both parties' preferred forms).

Since the payment event was also identical in both forms of contract, why was the dispute between Longbank and Shortbank not resolved by reference to this event? To answer this question, we need to look at the concept of publicly available information.

Publicly available information

The difficulties arising out of the need to apply the typically brief description which constitutes a credit event to a complex set of circumstances is compounded by the use of the concept of 'publicly available information'. This concept, an established market practice which can still be applied if the parties so agree (s 3.2 of the Definitions), embodies the idea that circumstances can only constitute a credit event if information which reasonably confirms the occurrence of such credit event has been published in (usually) not less than two internationally recognised sources of published information.

When a sovereign reschedules, the economic reality is readily apparent and the process is well understood by those involved. It is, however, a matter of chance whether a rescheduling will take a form or be described in terms which neatly and unarguably fit within the terms of a relatively briefly defined credit event. It is also a matter of chance whether the media will find relevant the same specific characterisations of the process as may be singled out in that credit event.

With regard to the payment event in a credit default swap, the usual requirement is that a payment default is relevant only if in excess of a specified amount (the default requirement). However, when a sovereign default is reported, it is likely that the amount of individual non-payments will not be information that ever reaches the public domain. Why would the amount of a single missed payment be of interest where a country is defaulting on the totality of its current debt obligations?

In practice, the effect of the 'publicly available information' requirement is that what will trigger a conventionally written credit default swap will be the media's perception of what needs to be reported rather than what is actually going on. It is not clear that this is what the parties to a swap intend or what the market wants.

In 1999 I said that 'to exaggerate only slightly, there is a real risk that the market may adopt documentation practices the result of which will be that credit default swaps are not triggered by a deterioration in creditworthiness [of the reference entity] but simply by accident'. It is good to see that the Definitions – s 4.7 (b) (iii) – recognise the importance of this concept, because otherwise the occurrence of a credit event might depend, amongst other things, on how a sovereign chooses to announce the reality of a crisis-driven rescheduling and how the media choose to report that reality. I also observed that 'a slight sense of unease about this as a basis for a significant financial market is not reduced by the inclusion in swap contracts of dispute resolution provisions which are calculated to deny reality the victory it deserves'. It is, equally pleasing, therefore, to see that provisions of this kind are no longer promulgated by ISDA.

Dispute resolution provisions

The central problem with a dispute resolution provision of the kind used in the swaps entered into by Longbank and Shortbank (see below) is the requirement that a dispute should be resolved by a disinterested third party which is itself, or is the affiliate of, a dealer in obligations of the type represented by the reference obligation. Not surprisingly, it soon became that in a time of crisis there are no such disinterested third party dealers or, if there are, they do not want to get involved. In 1999, my conclusion was that 'as a result, it is likely that the next generation of dispute resolution provisions will take a different approach' – it is, I think, still interesting to look at why this was so.

The Dispute Resolution Provision – an indicative example of a 1999 provision

In the event that a party (the 'disputing party') does not agree with any determination made (or the failure to make any determination) by the calculation agent or the other party (the 'determining party'), the disputing party shall have the right to require that the determining party have such determination made by a disinterested third party that is a dealer in Derivative Obligations and that is, or whose affiliates are, dealers in obligations of the same type as those under the bonds but is not an affiliate of either party. Such dealer shall be selected by the calculation agent in its reasonable discretion after consultation with the parties. Any exercise by the disputing party of its rights hereunder must be in writing and shall be delivered to the determining party no later than the tenth London banking day following the London banking day on which the determining party notifies the disputing party of any determination made (or of the failure to make any determination). Any determination by a disinterested party shall be binding in the absence of manifest error and shall be made as soon as possible but no later than within five London banking days of the disputing party's exercise of its rights hereunder. The costs of such disinterested third party shall be borne by (i) the disputing party if the disinterested third party substantially agrees with the determining party's determination or (ii) the non-disputing party if the disinterested third party does not substantially agree with the determining party. Determinations as to any amounts due shall (if possible) be calculated retrospectively with reference to the actual amount that was due on any cash settlement date and shall not account for subsequent changes with respect to the bonds. Interest on any amounts due that are subject to dispute shall be paid from (and including) the date of non-payment to (but excluding) the date such amount is paid, at the termination rate. Such interest will be calculated on the basis of daily compounding and the actual number of days elapsed. 'Derivative Obligation' means any privately negotiated forward, swap or option on one or more rates, currencies, commodities, equity securities, debt instruments, economic indices or measure of economic or credit risk or value, or any similar transaction.

The effect of these provisions, in circumstances where no disinterested third party could be found, was to make it difficult to find any forum in which a dispute could be resolved. The English courts would be reluctant to get involved where contracting parties have chosen their own dispute resolution procedure and, in any event, one or both parties might be reluctant to have the dispute resolved through judicial proceedings. This poses a dilemma for both parties: if the courts are not to be used, but the agreed procedure fails, what is to be done? The answer, in practice, was that the parties needed to agree on an alternative forum for resolution of the dispute or to reach agreement between themselves. Thus, ironically, the one thing the disinterested dealer approach does not do is to resolve the dispute. What it does is to create another level of disagreement. My conclusion was that an alternative approach is urgently required – given the dissatisfaction that apparently exists with regard to the decision in the *Nomura/CSFB* case, it still is.

It seems to me that in a market where the business people and their lawyers are so far ahead of the courts, which they surely are given that by and large people either do derivatives all the time or they don't do them at all, there is a need for the market to set up its own forum for dispute resolution. The problem is, of course answering the question: who will have both the expertise and the independence to be a member of such a tribunal? However difficult the question, it needs to be answered.

Time limits

By the then applicable market standards, the time given to the disputing party in our hypothetical dispute to invoke the dispute resolution procedure – ten London business days – is generous; less time would have been allowed in many deals. More critically, the provisions require that a determination of the dispute be made within five London banking days of the exercise by the disputing party of its right to invoke the procedure. Again, experience made it clear that five working days is not even enough time in which to establish the absence of a disinterested dealer, let alone to resolve a dispute over whether or not a sovereign has defaulted or is or is not in the process of restructuring its external debt.

This was particularly true where discussions were based on the sort of provisions described earlier. However, even if more appropriately worded provisions are used, it is arguable that the timetable is far too compressed. The adoption of a compressed timetable is based on the view that the market will not function efficiently if weighed down by unresolved disputes. The problem with this approach is that in difficult cases compressed timetables do not resolve disputes, instead they force one or other disputing party to find ways of delaying the process so as to procure a means of establishing an acceptably objective and informed dispute resolution process.

An impartial tribunal

Re-reading the conclusion I reached in the Spring of 1999, I am struck by its continuing relevance. What I said was as follows.

> 'Where large sums of money are at stake and most, if not all, market participants face the same set of issues, speedy but potentially clumsy dispute resolution is not what the market needs. On the contrary, what is critical is that, as already suggested, decisions are taken (and seen to be taken) on an informed basis by an impartial tribunal. Decisions taken in any other way, decisions which may set market-wide precedents, will operate to the detriment of the market and will serve to increase legal risk rather than assist institutions in its management.'

The key word in this proposal is 'informed' – the derivatives market is almost entirely opaque to anyone, myself included, who is not a regular participant in it. (This is not because it is difficult, but because it is, to be frank, irrelevant to most people, perhaps most lawyers, most of the time. It is a private world with private rules which just happens to be rather important.) In the article which I referred to earlier, Schuyler Henderson said 'Perhaps the court did not follow the precise language because it missed the commercial rationale of the characteristic and supplied its own instead ... and this is the fourth error ... [made] perhaps a mistake based on [its] misreading of the relevant definition ... and its unnecessary and uncommercial restrictive analysis of what a contingency is'. Again, the only conclusion we can draw is that there is a need for decisions to be taken on an informed basis by an impartial tribunal. This is a challenge which ISDA needs to accept.

One possibility would be a fairly large standing committee of, say 25 acknowledged experts from the same number of firms, some being bankers and some being lawyers, which would consider and vote, anonymously, on issues put to it, the anonymity of the parties to the dispute also being preserved. If to their knowledge some of the committee members' firms were involved in an issue, they would not be permitted to disclose this, directly or indirectly, nor to withdraw – as this would give the game away – and it would be unlikely that one or two individuals would materially affect the outcome of the committee's deliberations. Alternatively, ISDA could retain, at enormous expense, a panel of long serving lawyers – who have time to write pieces such as this and articles such as Schuy's – and who, being briefed on a continuing basis as to what the market is seeking to achieve, can chair informed, speedy and decisive arbitration sessions (to be known as ISDAs) which will swiftly and expertly determine any disputes which arise.

Management of legal risk

It was clear, I ventured to say at the time, that in the late 1990s legal risk in the derivatives market manifested itself in at least three ways:

- key concepts (payment default and restructuring) had been defined inappropriately or unhelpfully;

- an established technique (publicly available information) produced results at odds, it would seem, with the purpose of the contracts in which it was employed; and

- concepts designed to resolve disputes (the disinterested dealer and the compressed timetable) produced the opposite result.

The consequences of the events of 1998 and their aftermath also suggested that there is a more general area of legal risk which deserved attention then and still does so.

Simplicity and complexity

The drive towards standardisation, as I said in 1999 and can say again now, has led to the existence of a surprising, if not dangerous, relationship between form and substance with respect to a wide range of derivative contracts, particularly credit derivatives such as credit linked notes. Very many derivative transactions are very simple, straightforward swaps, forward contracts and the like. Despite this, the market standard documentation continues to grow in complexity (although this does not trouble the market professionals who view a mastery of the intricacies of ISDA as simply a starting point).

At the same time, one of the virtues of the ISDA approach is that it can handle very complex transactions. Thus, traders, lawyers and transaction management teams have become used to using a relatively complex set of contractual rules and provisions to handle both the simplest and the most complex transactions.

This has unforeseen consequences. Simple transactions are documented in a complex fashion; this may be unnecessary but it is not a fundamental problem. Worryingly, however, very complex transactions are processed as if they were simple just because the complex documentation they require is structurally identical to that which is used for things that really are simple. As a result, complex transactions involving genuinely difficult documentation may be handled inappropriately. The time allowed by the market for institutions to prepare and review documentation of this kind is often no more than the time allowed in the context of very simple trades.

A group of associated risks, for example, sovereign risk, currency transfer risk, regulatory risk, counterparty risk and delivery risk may be very easily described in commercial terms. It may then seem that it is correspondingly straightforward to prepare or review the confirmation or contract which is to document a trade based on an assessment and pricing of these risks. In fact, as lawyers and transaction managers working in these areas are well aware, it can be very difficult to pin down these types of risk in a contractual document. If asked to prepare or review such a document in the space of two or three hours, the likely response will be to the effect that 'that is impossible, but if you insist ...'.

Causing the complex to be treated in this way and to be processed as if it were simple is probably not the best way to manage legal risk.

This was a conclusion suggested and supported by the events of 1998. Are there other inferences which might be drawn from those events in relation to sovereign-linked credit derivatives?

Seeing the wood for the trees

The earliest credit default swaps were documented by contracts which were no more than two pages in length, the operative provision being along the following lines: 'if [sovereign] defaults on any public bond issue or reschedules all or part of its external debt, Party A will pay to Party B ...'.

It is not certain that any credit default swap was written in quite such simple terms, but why not? If traders can discuss a trade in plain (and simple) English, why cannot the resulting contract be written in similar terms? The answer, as every finance lawyer knows, is that simple concepts and everyday phrases contain a wide multitude of risks which it is the lawyer's job to identify, analyse and eliminate (or if not eliminate, pass on to the other side). Why cannot this be done? An outsider might ask. Why not document trades in the simple terms in which they are made? The answer, of course, is that to do so would be to encourage uncertainty and the result would be a multitude of disputes and this would impair the efficient operation of the markets. (See Chapter 11 for a discussion of uncertainty and the 'grey areas' which are inevitably present in any contract.)

At this point déja vu looms, the circle has turned. The certainty which was sought through detailed, lawyer-written documentation has been lost through the use of intricate, market standard documentation and this in turn has lead to an increase in legal risk, an increase which threatens to overwhelm the commercial risks which the parties intended to assume.

An alternative approach

If a fundamental objective is to preserve an active market in which disputes are infrequent and for the most part easily settled, it may be that a different approach should be taken. One basis for an alternative approach is to be found in the disinterested dealer approach (and, incidentally, is supported by the concept of 'publicly available information'). Perhaps what the market wants is a system under which the existence or absence of a sovereign credit default is determined not by the facts but by the market's perception of the facts. If the only credit event in a credit default swap stated that a credit event is to be regarded as having occurred if and only if the market believes the relevant sovereign to have defaulted or to have commenced restructuring, disputes might be few and far between.

Stated in this way, the idea seems rather outlandish, but if restated to refer to a sovereign's standing on a credit deterioration index, the appearance of normality returns. All that is needed is for the market to agree to how the index should be constituted and who should maintain it. This may or may not provide a solution to the problems faced by participants in the sovereign-linked credit derivatives market. But one way or another, a middle way needs to be found between the simplicity of the concept of sovereign default and its elusiveness in contractual terms.

[The original version of this Chapter was published in Butterworths Journal (1999) 4 JIFBL 128 and also as Chapter 3 in Credit Derivatives: Law, Regulation and Accounting Issues, edited by Dr. Alastair Dawson, Sweet & Maxwell, 1999.]

Model answers to the Chapter 11 exercises

Read these only if you have completed the exercises in Chapter 11. These are 'model answers' – there is no 'right answer' to any of the exercises, but there are many bad ones.

Model answer (with notes) to Exercise 1

The exercise was as follows.

I used to work with someone whose powers of analysis were extraordinary, but whose drafting reflected too closely his detailed understanding of the issues.

An example of what I have in mind would be his version of one of the rules of golf.

If in the course of a round two or more balls are in play at any one time it shall first be established which ball belongs to which player and thereafter the distance of each ball from the hole shall be established and the players shall agree which is the greater distance so as to identify the player whose ball is furthest from the hole at that time and the players shall ensure that this is the ball which is played first.

Please rewrite this in as few words as possible.

This is the model answer

[When the balls are in play,] the ball farthest from the hole shall be played first.

(see rule 10-2b of the rules of golf)

NOTES

The answer I prefer omits the words in square brackets, but most of the people who have done this exercise have felt that some introductory words are necessary, eg 'during a round of golf' or, as in the model answer, 'when the balls are in play'. And, to be fair, the rules themselves provide a context in this way, using words similar to those in the model answer. It is not very difficult to answer this exercise correctly. It is obviously as unhelpful as it is inelegant to describe in detail the mechanical steps to be taken in order to implement a rule if what you are trying to do is to state the rule itself.

Apart from the obvious points that brevity is almost always desirable and that clarity, not obscurity, is the aim, this exercise neatly illustrates that what we write has no meaning without a context and that there can be different views as to how much context to provide. I am inclined to think that here the question provides the context – what you were asked to do was to write one of the rules of golf. But, on the other hand, some of those rules relate to matters that occur off the course, so the context needs to be set. As I said earlier, drafting is art not science.

(At this point I have always recounted how many years ago I met the host at a neighbours' party and his response – I had seen a plethora of books on golf on his library shelves – to my opening remark along the lines of 'I see you are interested in golf' was to say 'I write the rules'. He was the legal adviser to the rules committee at The Royal and Ancient!)

Model answer (with notes) to Exercise 2

The exercise was as follows.

The arrangers of a syndicated loan proposed the following agency provision. Prepare on behalf of the Agent an improved text covering the same issues as were covered in the arrangers' text.

The Lenders each appoint the Agent as their agent so as to take the steps required to implement the transactions described in this Agreement and authorise the Agent to do in connection with such transactions as aforesaid anything which it is necessary to do and accordingly it is agreed that the Agent may exercise such discretion in the interests of the Lenders but notwithstanding the foregoing and subject to the provisions hereinafter mentioned the Agent shall not have any dealings with the Borrower otherwise provided that these presents shall not prohibit the Agent from lending to the Borrower or from taking legal advice in connection with its obligations under this agreement and provided further that the Agent shall not be responsible for the Lenders' obligations. The Agent is empowered to rely on statements made by the Borrower or by the Lenders in relation to its duties as Agent provided that such duties shall include an obligation to account to the Lender for sums paid by the Borrower to the Agent and the Agent shall notify the Lenders thereof. The foregoing rights and duties of the Agent are exclusive and the Agent shall not be liable for any failure to exercise any such right or duty save in the case of negligence or misconduct but the Agent shall protect so far as it can the Lenders' interests.

This is the model answer

1 Each of the Lenders appoints the Agent to act as its agent in connection with this Agreement and the transactions contemplated herein and authorises the Agent to exercise such rights, powers, authorities and discretions as are reasonably incidental thereto.

2 The Agent may accept deposits from, lend money to and generally engage in any type of banking or other business with the Borrower.

3 The Agent may rely on any communication believed by it to be genuine and may in its sole discretion and at the cost of the Lenders instruct lawyers or other advisers in connection herewith.

4 The Agent shall account to each Lender for such Lender's share (if any) of any payment made hereunder by the Borrower to the Agent on behalf of the Banks.

5 The Agent shall not be liable for any failure on the part of the Borrower or any Lender to perform its obligations hereunder nor shall the Agent be under any liability as a result of taking or omitting to take any action in relation to this Agreement save in the case of its gross negligence or wilful misconduct.

NOTES

The starting point for this exercise was a chunk of text – it merits no more flattering a description – in which apples, pears and oranges were all mixed up and muddled up. Again there is an obvious point to be made, which is that it is important to get your ideas in order before you start drafting – and constantly to review your conclusions as you go.

It is often necessary to start again when drafting from scratch; something to beware of is the temptation to continue trying to get what you have already written to work when what you really need to do is to start again.

All that the model answer does is to split up the original text into five paragraphs:

(1) appointment of the agent;

(2) what the agent may do in relation to the borrower;

(3) discretions the agent has;

(4) obligations the agent has; and

(5) what the agent shall not be liable for.

In a sense that is all there is to it. However, there are some points of law and practice lurking in this exercise.

1   Without its principal's consent an agent cannot safely engage in profitable activities with its principal's customers, so it has always seemed prudent (when acting for the agent bank) to say that an agent bank can carry on banking and other business with the borrower.

2   In practice, the agency clause in a syndicated loan will not include a provision that the agent bank must at all times act in the interest of the lenders or that it must perform the functions it is expected to perform – rightly or wrongly, these things are taken for granted – but there will be a few specific requirements for the agent to satisfy (see Chapter 9).

3   An agent will never – at least, not in my experience – assume any responsibility for the performance by any other party of that party's obligations. As I mention at the beginning of Chapter 9, I well remember a significant, potential loan transaction for an emerging economy that didn't happen because the borrower insisted that my client, the agent, should make up any shortfall resulting from a lender's failure to lend.

The final observation that this model answer prompts me to make is that it is always important to allow a text to breathe, to make sure that there is plenty of white space on the page so that the reader can easily see what subject matter is on a particular page – lots of space and plenty of paragraphs is what is required. As Marshall McLuhan said in the 1960s – 'The Medium is the Message'.

By way of contrast, this is not an approach that generally commends itself to practitioners of law in the US where the practice is to fill every page with as many words as possible and to avoid indents and paragraphs like the plague.

(As a not wholly relevant aside I would mention that legal writing in the US more closely resembles by far English prose as it was written in the early 18th century than does contemporary English legal writing. If you compare the US Foreign Sovereign Immunities Act of 1976, the only US statute I know reasonably well, with something written by Richardson, Defoe or Sterne – and my own prose style owes a lot to Sterne – you will see what I mean.

This is not surprising. Many of the 'Americanisms' which surprise the English – diaper being the obvious one – are in fact words which were in use in England at or about the time the Mayflower set sail. The best example is of course 'solicit'. English solicitors are so called because they used to solicit work for the attorneys. In England the usage has changed; attorneys are now called barristers and being a solicitor is a reasonably honourable activity, at least in the eyes of a solicitor. In the US, 'attorney' is still the word that is used to describe a lawyer and soliciting is an unsavoury activity which is prohibited on beaches and elsewhere!)

Model answer (with notes) to Exercise 3

The exercise was as follows.

Prepare an improved version of the following draft provision for a seven-year loan to the Borrower, a UK company, whose lawyers prepared the draft. Your client is the Lender.

With regard to the financial condition of the Borrower, the Borrower shall endeavour to ensure that the financial condition of the Borrower, as evidenced by its annual financial statements (which the Borrower shall deliver within 90 days after their preparation) adjusted, as the Lender considers appropriate, to take account of changes in circumstances occurring after the date of those financial statements, is such that, provided the Lender has not agreed otherwise, the result of dividing its total liabilities by its total equity is less than two provided that the above mentioned adjustments shall be agreed by the Borrower and the Lender and provided further that the Borrower shall always use current accounting principles.

This is the model answer

I   Unless and to the extent that the Lender shall have otherwise agreed, the financial condition of the Borrower, as evidenced by financial statements of the Borrower prepared on the same basis as its Financial Statements 2002, shall at all times be such that its Total Liabilities are equal to no more than twice its Total Equity, for which purpose:
   (a) 'Total Liabilities' means [   ];
   (b) 'Total Equity' means [   ]; and
   (c) 'Financial Statements 2002' means the audited financial statements of the Borrower for its financial year ending 31 December 2002.

2   Within 90 days after the end of each of its financial years the Borrower shall deliver to the Lender financial statements for such financial year, such financial statements to be:
   (a) prepared on the same basis as the Borrower's Financial Statements 2002; and
   (b) audited by a firm of accountants acceptable to the Lender.

NOTES

These exercises were originally written for young lawyers who were about to qualify into a banking group and had, therefore, had at least one banking 'seat' during their time as a trainee solicitor. This is why this particular exercise is as much about problems that arise in writing and applying financial conditions as it is about drafting issues – and by now it more or less goes without saying that while the starting point was a complete mess, the answer should be well organised and easy to follow, as is the model answer.

(Turn over the page for the substantive points.)

What are the substantive points?

1   The first is whether a financial condition, is a term which requires a borrower to maintain a certain financial condition – and is therefore to be written as a covenant – or whether a financial condition should be viewed as a statement of a condition to be satisfied and thus written as if it were an event of default – for commentary on covenants and events of default see Chapters 2 and 9.

     The answer to this question is that there are good reasons for writing financial conditions as objective conditions. As mentioned in the Appendix, in 1975 a celebrated default occurred when a major borrower, Burmah Oil was in breach of its financial covenants through no fault of its own. The cause was a sudden depreciation in the value of shares in British Petroleum – in which Burmah Oil had something like a 40% stake – which led to a very large drop in the value of Burmah Oil's net worth and a consequential breach of its debt to equity covenant.

     Although the point does not seem to have been made at the time, it seemed to a number of us that there was risk that in such circumstances the borrower could argue that it should not be regarded as being in breach of a covenant as a result of circumstances beyond its control. Perhaps not the strongest of arguments but one which is certainly circumvented if the relevant financial condition is written as a condition which is to be satisfied and it is stated that failure to satisfy it is an event of default. (A financial condition could be written as an event of default but this would be awkward in presentational terms.)

2   Other difficulties with financial conditions stem from the fact that financial statements are needed to determine whether a given financial condition is or is not satisfied – but financial statements are always historic, so by the time a financial statement has been prepared, the borrower's financial condition has changed! Can a lender accelerate a loan on the basis of non-compliance with a financial condition if the borrower asserts that the breach revealed by its recently delivered statements has been cured – and what evidence of the 'cure' would a court require or accept? I do not know the answers to these questions.

3   Another difficulty relates to the basis on which a borrower's financial statements are prepared. If two years after a loan agreement is signed

a lender wishes to determine whether a given financial condition is satisfied, it needs to be provided with financial statements which are prepared on the same basis as the 'original financial statements' (in other words, those on the basis of which the condition was agreed), but the borrower will have been required by its auditors/best practice to prepare its most recent statements on the basis of current accounting practice! What is to be done about this? In the absence of 'same basis' statements the lender cannot effectively police the financial conditions.

A possible compromise is to agree that the borrower will prepare what we might call 'translation statements' showing what the value or amount of relevant items would have been had the original accounting principles been used, but this will only happen in a deal that is important enough for the borrower to give the lender enough leverage to insist on what will be a costly and time consuming exercise for the borrower. The Borrower's lawyers' suggested compromise – that adjustments should be agreed between the borrower and the lender is clearly not a solution from the lender's perspective.

APPENDIX

The historical development of syndicated eurocurrency loan agreements

Hugh S Pigott, London

(Presented at the Fifth Conference of the Section on Business Law of the International Bar Association, Budapest, Hungary, October 1981)

1. The origins of the Eurodollar market

To explain the origins of the Eurodollar market, I do not think I can do better than to quote the following extract from a lecture given in New York in 1977 by Alexander D. Calhoun, Jr.

"The origins of Eurodollars were partly economic and partly regulatory. Eurodollars resulted from the large quantities of Dollars which the United States spent abroad for foreign aid, for defence, for investment and increasingly, since 1960, for imports. Some of these Dollars came back to the United States to pay for exports and for investment; but, as the 1960s gave way to the 1970s and the United States continued to run substantial deficits in its balances of trade and payments, increasingly substantial quantities of Dollars accumulated abroad.

Domestic United Sates regulatory policy which prohibited the payment of interest on demand deposits and limited the rates of interest payable on time deposits also contributed to the flow of Dollars abroad at such times as they could earn a higher rate of interest there. This tendency for Dollars deposited abroad to produce a more favourable return as compared to the same Dollars deposited with their domestic offices was reinforced from the standpoint of the American banks by additional regulatory policy which imposes reserve requirements on domestic deposits but not on deposits in branches of American banks abroad and which imposes federal deposit insurance assessments on domestic deposits but not on the same deposits when placed in and payable at branches of American banks abroad.

The innovation of lending these foreign Dollar deposits was initiated in London from the middle 1950s as the system of foreign exchange controls inherited from the World War II and early post-war years was progressively relaxed. In 1957, this market was used to fill the gap created by the British balance of payments crises and tight restraints on sterling loans; conversely, in 1959 tight money in the United States led some banks and borrowers to seek Dollars from this market in London.

Thus, an infant Eurocurrency market was in being and operating by 1964 when the Interest Equalization Tax was enacted, and 1965 when the Foreign Direct Investment Regulations and the Federal Reserve Board's Voluntary Foreign Credit Restraint Program effectively cut off both foreign and American enterprises from the United States capital markets insofar as their needs for their operations outside of the United States were concerned. From 1963 to 1976 the Eurodollar market expanded from a few billion Dollars to over $200 billion; and the foreign branches of American Banks increased from around 150 to almost 700."

2. Fundamental principles

There are certain principles which apply to all syndicated Eurocurrency Loan Agreements. By far the most important of these, which is absolutely fundamental, is that the banks' "profit margin" (i.e. the interest it receives less its cost of funds) must remain constant and never be eroded. In a loan which bears interest at a fluctuating or floating rate, this margin is usually expressed as a fixed percentage per annum above the rate at which prime banks lend Eurocurrency deposits to each other for short periods. ("LIBOR")

The life of the loan (which may be, say 7 years) is divided at the option of the borrower into successive periods of months, (usually of 3 or 6 months duration) which are known as Interest Periods. A separate rate of interest is fixed for each Interest Period, by reference to LIBOR for that period. The theory behind this method of rate-fixing is that each lending bank funds the loan it has made to the borrower by borrowing a deposit of the same currency and amount in the London Interbank Market for the relevant Interest Period. At the end of each Interest Period the bank repays the deposit (plus interest at LIBOR) and borrows another deposit in the London Interbank Market for the next Interest Period, and so on. Whenever a bank actually does this – and there is a high degree of matching in the market today – the Applicable Margin above LIBOR would represent precisely the pre-tax profit made by the lending bank from the interest it receives on that loan.

In practice, of course, banks obtain the funds they need for lending in a variety of ways:

(a) from their shareholders in the form of share capital or subordinated loans;

(b) from the public in the form of floating or fixed rate notes or bonds;

(c) from customers in the form of current or deposit accounts; and

(d) from other banks throughout the world in the form of deposits.

Accordingly, LIBOR will not reflect a bank's actual cost of funds if this is calculated on a global basis. It also follows that the average cost of funds will vary from bank to bank. For example a bank with a large number of non-interest bearing current accounts in the currency in question may find its cost of funds cheaper than that of a bank with few current accounts. Similarly, a bank which starts life with a very large issued share capital will initially have a low average cost of funds.

The concepts which I have been describing result in the appearance of certain clauses which are now standard and will be found in nearly every syndicated loan agreement.

As they are usually the most difficult to draft (and sometimes the most difficult for a borrower to understand) I think it may be helpful if we examine some of them in detail. I am thinking of three in particular:

• The Increased Costs Clause

• The Taxes Clause

• The Alternative Interest Clause

3. The increased costs clause

A typical increased costs clause is set out in Appendix A. The purpose of this clause is to preserve the profit margin of each bank in circumstances where, due to requirements of a central bank or other monetary authority, a bank's funding costs are increased.

It is hard to anticipate what these requirements may be in the future. One is guided, of course, by the restrictions imposed by the U.S. Federal Reserve Board and by the special deposit and reserve asset requirements of the Bank of England (which relate to sterling lending in the United Kingdom), but you have to take into account the possibility that quite different kinds of control may in the future be imposed in other jurisdictions. And in this connection you must remember that in major transactions the syndicate may be composed of banks whose offices are scattered all over the world.

You will see that the clause will apply if the increased funding cost arises either from:

(a) a change in law or a change in the interpretation of law; or

(b) compliance with any request from or requirements of any central bank or other fiscal, monetary or other authority.

The reason the word "request" is there is that the credit controls imposed by the Bank of England are not, strictly speaking, legally binding regulations but take the form of a letter from the Bank of England to each bank requesting it to comply with the particular control. For example the Supplementary Special Deposits Scheme introduced in December 1973, which became known as "the Corset", begins with the words:

> "The Bank ask (sic) that banks and deposit-taking finance house should be prepared to place with the Bank non-interest-bearing Special Deposits in relation to the growth in each institution's interest-bearing resources on the following bases….."

The Increased Cost Clause provides for three kinds of increased cost:

(i) a cost incurred as a result of having agreed to make advances under the loan agreement. This envisages a credit control which would impose increased costs on banks by virtue of their commitment to lend.

(ii) An "increase in the cost to a Bank of making, funding or maintaining all or any of the advances comprised in a class of advances formed by or including the advances made or to be made by it under the loan agreement". That rather tortuous language was devised to cover the situation where it is not possible to allocate a specific increased cost to a specific loan. For example, in the Bank of England's Supplementary Special Deposits Scheme (which is no longer in effect), sterling lending was controlled by reference to the average rate of growth in a bank's lending over a previous rolling three month period. If the allowed rate of growth (initially 8%) was exceeded the bank would have to place with the Bank of England non-interest bearing supplementary deposits of the following amounts:

Amount of Excess	Amount of Deposit
1% or less	5% of excess
More than 1% up to 3%	25%of excess
Over 3%	50% of excess

I remember that I was, shortly after the introduction of the Scheme, negotiating an increased cost clause for a bank which had, before the Scheme came into force, committed to lend a large sum to a borrower which would, when borrowed, take the bank over the rate of growth permitted by the Scheme. It was a tough battle, but the borrower eventually agreed to accept responsibility for the increased cost.

(iii) The third kind of increased cost envisaged by the clause is where a bank becomes liable to make a payment calculated by reference to the advances made or to be made by it under the agreement. This anticipates some sort of levy charged on the amount of the advances, like, for example, the United States interest equalisation tax (now deceased) which was a tax on the capital value of debt-instruments acquired. By increasing the investors' necessary outlay while leaving the nominal rate of return on the investment unchanged, its effect was to depress the investor's real rate of return.

A lot of time and ingenuity is spent on drafting provisions such as these which are often the subject of intense and bitter negotiations between lenders and borrowers. Borrowers do not wish to concede to lenders the right to charge what they like: lenders argue that, unlike borrowers, they are in ordinary circumstances locked in by these loans and that, as long as they charge on a cost-plus-margin basis, they have the right to include in the cost all costs, no matter how incurred, other than overheads and overall net income taxes.

4. The taxes clause

Like the Increased Cost Clause, this clause (a specimen of which is set out in Appendix B) is designed to preserve the banks' margin.

It envisages the imposition of two possible taxes:

(a) a withholding tax, that is a tax levied by deduction at source; and

(b) a tax imposed on or in relation to sums received by a bank under the agreement, which I shall refer to as a "receipt tax".

A withholding tax is normally dealt with by the grossing-up of the payment from which the tax is deducted so that after the appropriate deduction the bank receives a net sum equal to the sum which it would have received had no such deduction been required.

The clause goes on to provide that the borrower shall notify the Agent of the imposition of any withholding tax and shall deliver to the Agent a receipt for each withholding of tax. This, of course, is to provide evidence that the tax – for which the bank would be liable – has actually been paid and also to enable the banks to claim any tax credits to which they may be entitled.

At this point in the negotiations a borrower will usually ask that a provision be inserted whereby a bank which obtains a tax credit in these circumstances, should pay to the borrower an amount equal to the benefit of such credit on the footing that otherwise the bank will have received not only its cost of funds plus margin but also the tax credit.

It is difficult to resist such an argument on the grounds of pure morality but the practical difficulties it imposes are immense and for these reasons many banks steadfastly refuse to give in to such a request as a matter of policy. The real problem lies in the impossibility of allocating a particular benefit to a particular loan. Suppose a bank has made a series of loans to say, Italy and a withholding tax is imposed. The tax credit will be claimed on a global basis but if the bank has insufficient profits in its country of incorporation to use the tax credit to the full how does it decide which tax credits to use?

5. The alternative interest clause

The Clause set out in Appendix C is one attempt to find a solution to the problems caused by two quite different situations:

(a) firstly, where it is impossible to calculate LIBOR because none of the Reference Banks is offering dollar deposits to prime banks in the London Interbank Market. This, of course, would mean that the mechanism for interest calculation had totally collapsed; and

(b) secondly, where LIBOR (calculated by averaging the rates quoted by the Reference Banks) does not accurately reflect the rates at which a percentage of the banks (usually 35% or more in value) can obtain dollar deposits on the London Interbank Market. This has happened once in my experience when some years ago the Japanese banks in London found that they had to pay higher rates than other banks for their dollars.

In either situation the next Interest Period is shortened to 1 month and during such period the rate of interest is the Applicable Margin plus the average of the cost to each bank of funding its portion of the loan from whatever source it may select.

So long as the situation continues the interest rate is fixed in the same way at monthly intervals.

If either situation occurs, the Borrower is obliged at the Agent's request to enter into negotiations to see if a substitute basis for interest determination can be agreed. In the absence of agreement, the Agent is given power to call the Loan.

I should like now to turn to the major changes in the form of syndicated Eurocurrency loan agreements which have come about as a result of catastrophes in the market place.

6. The colocotronis litigation

Part of this litigation (which was settled before coming to trial) was between several participating banks and European American Banking Corporation ("EABC"). EABC had made a series of single-bank loans to companies in the Colocotronis Group which it then proceeded to participate among various North American banks.

When the borrowers defaulted, the participant banks alleged that EABC in soliciting the plaintiffs' participation in the Colocotronis loans represented, *inter alia*, that:

1. EABC had thoroughly investigated the borrower and would continue to maintain close contact with it.

2. The cash flow from certain charterparties (the principal source of repayment of the loans) would be sufficient to maintain the loans current.

3. Proceeds of the charterparties would be segregated from other assets of the Colocotronis companies.

4. The Colocotronis companies were generally credit worthy.

According to the complaint, none of these presentations was true.

In addition, the complaints alleged failure to disclose various conflicts of interest on the part of EABC and various specific financial arrangements that it had with the Colocotronis companies.

Based on the foregoing allegations, the complaint claimed actionable violations of the U.S. Securities Acts violations of the state securities laws of New York, New Jersey and Michigan, fraudulent misrepresentation under common law doctrines, negligent misrepresentation and breach of fiduciary duty.

Notwithstanding that the Colocotronis litigation related to a lending transaction which was quite different from syndicated loan (where all the lenders are parties *ab initio*) and involved alleged breaches of the U.S. Securities Act arising from the manner in which the single bank loan was subsequently participated, as you may imagine the news of the allegations caused a considerable degree of apprehension in the London

Eurocurrency market place. Banks who were already acting as agents nervously examined the agency clauses in their loan agreements and those who were about to act as agents asked their lawyers to write into their agency clause language which would give them the maximum possible protection.

It was, I believe, an over-reaction but it resulted in considerable expansion of the standard form of agency clause.

In particular there was a move towards taking away from the Agent the responsibility of exercising any right or discretions under the loan agreement by providing that the Agent could refrain from exercising them unless instructed by an Instructing Group.

There was introduced a disclaimer of responsibility on the part of the Agent for the accuracy and/or completeness of the Information Memorandum which is a document containing detailed information about the borrower which is circulated to the syndicate members before they agree to join the syndicate. It is, of course, one of the principal sources of information on which a syndicate member forms its credit decision.

There was also introduced a disclaimer of responsibility on the part of the Agent for the enforceability of the Loan Agreement.

Finally it became usual to provide that each bank was, and would continue to be, responsible for making its own independent appraisal of the credit-worthiness of the borrower.

How far these protective clauses are effective in English law completely to protect an Agent is another matter. When I investigated the position some time ago, I reached the conclusion that it was probably not possible to exclude:

(a) negligence in the performance of specific duties; or

(b) failure to use the same care and skill as if the Agent were the sole lender.

7. Burmah Oil

In January 1975 Burmah Oil got into grave financial difficulties because of the catastrophic drop in the market value of its shareholding in British Petroleum, which caused it to be in breach of covenants in various eurocurrency loan agreements to maintain certain financial ratios. If not remedied within thirty days, this breach would cause the loans to become immediately due and payable at the option of the lending banks.

As a result of pressure from those banks, Burmah Oil was forced to obtain the guarantee of the Bank of England for its loans and, as a quid pro quo, to sell its shares in BP to the Bank of England for £179 million at a price of £2.30 per share when the market value was £2.54 per share.

On 3rd June, 1981, the biggest commercial case ever to be heard in the High Court began. Burmah Oil was demanding from the Bank of England the return of some 311 million BP shares – currently valued at about £1.2 billion. Burmah Oil claimed that the sale was: "Unconscionable, inequitable, unreasonable and unfair" and that the Bank of England took unfair advantage of the company's weakness at the time. On the first day of the trial Mr. Justice Walton was reported to have said to Mr.Leonard Hoffman, Q.C., acting for Burmah, "You are trying to push back the frontiers of the law in this case".

In the event the frontiers were not pushed back and Burmah lost its case on the grounds that "*pacta sunt servanda*": bargains were made to be kept.

I think the Burmah Oil case illustrates better than any the real importance to lending banks of covenants by the borrower to maintain financial ratios. Not only do they operate as an early-warning system, but they put the banks into a very strong negotiating position. They are much more effective from this point of view than that rather vague phrase which is so often seen in the events of default clause (which entitles the banks to make the loan immediately due and payable on the happening of certain events) to the effect an event of default shall occur if there has been "a material adverse change in the financial condition of the borrower". The Burmah Oil case also illustrates the importance of the wording of cross-default clauses in a loan agreement. The normal clause provides that the loan shall be capable of being declared immediately due and payable if any other loan of the borrower has been accelerated.

The more sophisticated cross default clause will provide in addition (if the borrower can be persuaded to agree) that the loan shall be capable of being declared immediately due and payable if any other loan of the borrower has become capable of being accelerated, so that the cross default operates irrespective of whether or not the other lenders choose to accelerate their loan.

This topic was the subject of an amusing article by Richard Youard in this year's July Edition of Euromoney which was written in response to an article in an earlier edition by Mr. J. Speed Carroll, a Member of the New York Bar, entitled "The Worst Clause in the Euromarkets".

8. Iran

The lessons from the Iranian crisis are still being learnt, but a number of issues can be identified as being likely to be the subject of more discussions than they were in the past:

(A) DECLARATION BY THE BORROWER THAT IT WILL NOT PAY ITS DEBTS

If a borrower makes a general declaration that it will not pay its debts, this could in certain circumstances be accepted as a repudiation of a loan agreement. It may not, however, be in the lenders' interest to claim that a borrower has repudiated a loan agreement since the banks would thereby lose all ancillary rights under the agreement such as, for example, rights to default interest. The syndicate would probably be in a better position if they were able to declare an event of default in these circumstances and it might be possible to expand the events of default clause to cover circumstances where a borrower declares that it will not pay its debts.

(B) PAYMENTS CLAUSE

A clause on the lines set out in Appendix D is often now included in syndicated loan agreements. This provides that if payment of dollars through New York does not continue to provide a satisfactory basis for the paying of monies between the borrower and any bank, the paying of monies between them thereafter may be made (after prior notification to the Agent) in such alternative currency and/or in such alternative manner as they may mutually agree in writing.

This clause is, of course, designed to enable payments to be made under the loan agreement in a currency other than dollars where payment in dollars through New York is illegal.

It is, of course, important that notification be given to the Agent because the Agent has to keep a record of all payments made between the banks and the borrower.

(c)   Individual enforcement by banks

A rather curious provision has recently been appearing in the clause which provides that if, when the borrower is in default, one bank receives more than its *pro rata* share of monies paid by the borrower, it must share the excess with the other banks. The new provision provides that if an individual bank sues the borrower on its own, the bank is entitled to retain for its own account all monies thereafter received from the borrower (whether as a result of such action or otherwise).

It seems to me that the taking of legal action by an individual bank against the borrower is against the basic philosophy of a syndicated loan, where major decisions, such as deciding whether to accelerate the loan or not, are taken by a majority vote. This means, of course, that an individual bank cannot accelerate its own part of the loan against the wishes of the majority of the banks. Consequently, unless the loan has been accelerated by a majority of vote of the syndicate, an individual bank can only sue for the monies which the borrower has failed to pay at the date of the suit.

The Iranian crisis incidentally illustrated the chaos that ensues where individual banks pursue remedies, such as attachment of assets and Mareva injunctions, on their own.

In my view individual action by banks should not be encouraged. One compromise might be to provide that such action may only be taken after the other banks have been given the opportunity of joining in the action and have refused to do so. It would also seem equitable to provide in the sharing round clause that an individual bank which takes action against the borrower on its own should only be entitled to retain for its own account the monies recovered as a result of that particular action.

I should add that the whole question of enforcement of an accelerated loan is very much an open one. Many would, I know, disagree with me and take the view that after acceleration each bank should be free to take its own individual enforcement action as it thinks fit on the footing that there is no reason why the banks should not agree at the time to centralise their efforts if this seems appropriate.

For example, French banks do not like to be put into a position where they can be forced to take legal action against their will.

Mr. Robert Thomas will be speaking to you this afternoon about other changes which the Iranian crisis introduced into the form of Eurocurrency loan agreements including:

(a) the exclusion of the Agent's right to accelerate the loan without consultation with the other banks when an event of default has occurred;

(b) increasing the majority required for the composition of an Instructing Group;

(c) provisions enabling the Agent to retire and for a successor to be appointed:

(d) [changes to] the sharing-round clause, which provides that where a bank receives more than its fair share of any payment to be made under the agreement by the borrower, it must share the excess among the other lending banks on a *pro rata* basis.

9. Chips

As from 1st October, 1981 international U.S. dollar transactions will be settled in immediately available funds instead of next day funds.

The effect of the new system will be that in the case of doubtful borrowers an Agent Bank will no longer have the opportunity of being certain before distributing repayments of principal or payments of interest to syndicate members that the relevant payment has been received from the borrower the day before.

The practice in the Eurobond market is to require payment from the borrower of sums payable to the bondholders one business day before the due date for payment, and a solution might be to introduce such a practice into the syndicated Eurocurrency lending market.

If such a practice is not adopted, it would seem prudent to ensure that in all future syndicated loan agreements there is an express provision enabling the Agent to claim back from the syndicate members monies paid to them by the Agent which the Agent has not received from the borrower, and to claim back from the borrower monies paid to it by the Agent which the Agent has not received from one or more syndicate members. The provision should also include an indemnity for any loss suffered by the Agent as a result of any such non-receipt, the amount payable to the Agent being calculated by reference to the cost to the Agent of funding the monies which should have been paid to it.

Appendix A

INCREASED COSTS

(A) If by reason of (a) any change in law or in its interpretation and/or (b) compliance with any request from or requirement of any central bank or other fiscal, monetary or other authority, (i) a Bank incurs a cost as a result of its having agreed to make advances hereunder, (ii) there is any increase in the cost to a Bank of making, funding or maintaining all or any of the advances comprised in a class of advances formed by or including the advances made or to be made by it hereunder or (iii) a Bank becomes liable to make any payment on or calculated by reference to the amount of advances made or to be made by it hereunder, then, the Borrower shall from time to time on demand of the Agent pay to the Agent for account of that Bank amounts sufficient to indemnify that Bank against, as the case may be. (i) such cost, (ii) such increased cost (or such portion of such increased cost as is in the opinion of that Bank attributable to its making, funding or maintaining advances hereunder) or (iii) such liability.

(B) A Bank intending to make a claim pursuant to this clause shall notify the Agent of the event by reason of which it is entitled to do so, whereupon the Agent shall notify the Borrower thereof.

(C) If a Bank claims indemnification from the Borrower under this Clause and within thirty days thereafter the Agent receives from the borrower at least fifteen days' prior notice of the Borrower's intention to prepay such Bank's share of the Loan, the Borrower shall on the last day of each of the then current Interest Periods repay such Bank's portion of the Advance to which such Interest Period relates.

(D) A Bank for whose account a repayment is to be made under this Clause shall not be obliged to make any advances hereunder or after the date upon which the Agent receives the Borrower's notice of its intention to prepay such Bank's share of the Loan, on which date such Bank's Available Commitment shall be reduced to zero. Any repayment made after the Termination Date pursuant to this Clause shall reduce rateably the remaining obligations of the Borrower under Clause 8.[1]

Appendix B

Taxes

(A) If the Borrower is required by law to make any deduction or withholding from any sum payable by the Borrower to any person hereunder, then the sum payable by the Borrower in respect of which such deduction or withholding is required to be made shall be increased to the extent necessary to ensure that, after the making of such deduction or withholding, such person receives and retains (free from any liability in respect of any such deduction or withholding) a net sum equal to the sum which it would have received and so retained had no such deduction or withholding been made or required to be made.

[1] The Repayment Clause

(B) If at any time the Borrower is required by law to make any deduction or withholding from any sum payable by it hereunder (or if thereafter there is any change in the rates at which or the manner in which such deductions or withholding are calculated) the Borrower shall promptly notify the Agent which shall promptly notify the Banks thereof.

(C) If the Borrower makes any payment hereunder in respect of which it is required by law to make any deduction or withholding it shall pay the full amount required to be deducted or withheld to the relevant taxation or other authorities within the time allowed for such payment under applicable law and shall deliver to the Agent within thirty days after it has made such payment to the applicable authority a receipt issued by such authority evidencing the deduction or withholding of all monies required to be deducted or withheld from such payment hereunder.

(D) Without prejudice to the foregoing provisions of this Clause, if a Bank is required by law to make any payment on account of tax or otherwise (other than tax on its overall net income) on or in relation to any sum received by such Bank hereunder or any liability in respect of any such payment is asserted, imposed, levied or assessed against such Bank, the Borrower will upon demand of such Bank and whether or not such payment or liability be correctly or legally imposed or asserted, indemnify such Bank against such payment or liability, together with any interest, penalties and expenses payable or incurred in connection therewith.

Appendix C

ALTERNATIVE INTEREST RATES

(A) If (a) the Agent determines that at 11.00 am London time on the Quotation Date for an Interest Period none of the Reference Banks was offering to prime banks in the London Interbank Market deposits in dollars in the required amount and for the required period or (b) before the close of business in London on the Quotation Date for an Interest Period the Agent has been notified by each of a group of Banks to whom in aggregate 35% or more of the Loan is (or, if an Advance were then made, would be) owed that the rate at which such deposits were being so offered does not accurately reflect the cost to it of obtaining such deposits, then, notwithstanding the provisions of Clauses 5 and 6. [1]

(i) the duration of the Interest Period shall be one month or, if less, such that it shall end on the next Repayment Date; and

(ii) during such Interest Period the rate of interest applicable to the Advance to which such Interest Period relates shall be the rate per annum which is the sum of the Applicable Margin and the rate per annum determined by the Agent to be the arithmetic mean (rounded upwards, if not already such a multiple, to the nearest whole multiple of one-eighth of one per cent ($\frac{1}{8}$%) of the rates notified by each Bank to the Agent before the last day of such Interest Period to be those which express as a percentage rate per annum the cost to each Bank of funding (whether in dollars or otherwise) from whatever sources it may select its portion of such Advance during such Interest Period.

(B) If (a) either of the events mentioned at (a) and (b) in sub-clause (A) occurs or (b) during any period of three business days none of the Reference Banks offers deposits in dollars to prime banks in London Interbank Market:

(i) the Agent shall notify the Borrower and the Banks of such event;

(ii) if the Agent so requires, within five days of such notification the Agent and the Borrower shall enter into negotiation with a view to agreeing a substitute basis (as for determining the rate of interest from time to time applicable to the Advances and/or (b) upon which the Advances may be maintained (whether in dollars or some other currency) thereafter; and

(iii) if the Agent has required the Borrower to enter into such negotiations, the Agent may declare (any such declaration to be binding on the Borrower) that each Advance shall become due and payable on the last day of its then current Interest Period unless by then a substitute basis has been agreed upon in relation thereto.

[1] The interest determination clauses.

Appendix D

If the Borrower and any Bank agree that payment in dollars in accordance with the provisions of this Clause does not continue to provide a satisfactory basis for the paying of monies between them hereunder then the payment of monies between them hereunder thereafter may be made (after prior notification thereof to the Agent) in such alternative currency and/or in such alternative manner (if any) as they may mutually agree in writing.

Index